POGO'S Will Be That Was

containing the complete volumes
of
POSITIVELY POGO
G.O. FIZZICKLE POGO

by

Walt Kelly

A FIRESIDE BOOK
PUBLISHED BY
SIMON AND SCHUSTER
NEW YORK

A Fireside Book
Published by Simon & Schuster, Inc.
Simon & Schuster Building
Rockefeller Center
1230 Avenue of the Americas
New York, New York 10020
FIRESIDE and colophon are registered trademarks
of Simon & Schuster, Inc.
Designed by Helen Barrow
Manufactured in the United States of America
7 8 9 10

Library of Congress Cataloging in Publication Data
Kelly, Walt.
Pogo's will be that was.
(A Fireside book)
CONTENTS: Positively Pogo.—G. O. Fizzickle Pogo.
[1. Animals—Caricatures and cartoons.
2. Cartoons and comics] I. Kelly, Walt.
G. O. Fizzickle Pogo. c. 1979 I. Title.
PN6728.P57K448 1979 741.5'973 78-31955
ISBN 0-671-24854-5

CONTENTS

POSITIVELY POGO

G.O. FIZZICKLE POGO

POSITIVELY POGO

A WORD TO THE FORE

The antics which have been drawn together in this book are huddled here for mutual protection like sheep. If they had half a wit apiece each would bound off in many directions to unsimplify the target.

These continue to be wondrous times when every man tries to find a formula for keeping the stranger's fingers from his throat. The simple expedient of holding hands will someday occur to a couple of people who will forever after be forgotten. We need to read and to think and to study the faces of our friends . . . a peaceful pursuit. But, in the light of our trial bombs bursting in air and the flash of the practice red rockets' glittering glare, the study of peace is a blinky business. This collection of strips reflects the skulking state of mind of one startled student.

W. K.

Here is a clutch of Odds and Ends,
Of Staggers, Leaps and Bobs and Bends,
Foolish, fretful, feeble, fancy,
For a Kelly, name of Nancy.

Preface

DID YOU EVER DREAM A DREAM WHAT HAD A JOKE IN IT, PORKY?
THAT'S WHERE I GET SOME OF MY BEST ONES.
I GUESS YOU COULD DREAM A GOOD ONE IF YOU PUT YOUR MIND TO IT.
IT DEPENDS ON WHO GITS INTO YO' DREAMS. SOME FOLKS GOT NO SENSE OF HUMOR!
I READ A BOOK ONCE WHAT SAID YOU KIN DO ANYTHING YOU WANTS IF YOU PUTS YO' MIND TO IT.
I DIN'T READ THE BOOK, BUT I IS DREAMED THE DREAM ... I ALLUS LIKES THE PART ABOUT THE COWBOYS.

CHAPTER 1

Merrily, Merrily,

YEP-P.T. AN' TAMANANNY IS GOIN' OUT OF SHOW BUSINESS INTO TEEVY.
THAT REMIND ME OF A OL' STORY- A FELLA SAY "IS A CARTOONIST A NEWS PAPER MAN?"

AN' HIS BOSS ANSWER... "IS A BARNACLE A SHIP?" HAW HAW HAW! OL' HARRY HERSHFIELD TOLE ME THAT'N HOO BOY!

A ROUSER! EVIDENTLY.
WOW!

FELLA SAYS "DOES A CARTOONIST WORK FOR A NEWSPAPER?" AND HIS BOSS SAYS "BARNACLES"-UH-MM-"BARNACLES" UH UM-WELL, HE TOLE HIM "BARNACLES TO YOU, JACK... BARNACLES!"
SERVED HIM RIGHT, TOO.
BOY OH BOY OH BOY OH BOY OH BOY!

HA! YOU DOG! HOLD ON THERE, VARLET, ERE I CARVE YOU STEM TO STERN.

OH, PLEASE SIR, SPARE ME, FOR I AM BUT A SIMPLE MAIDEN!
NAY... YOU ARE A SPY!

YES! I AM a spy. I'M HERE TO LEARN YOUR Washday SECRET!!
I USE LEOPARD OIL. IT CHASES SPOTS.
T.V REHEARSAL TODAY
YOUR DIRTY DUDS CAN SPARKLE ROYAL WITH JUST A DASH OF LEOPARD OIL! SWISHY-SWISHY ON A DISHY RUBBY DUBBY IN A TUBBY.
T.V

LISTEN TO THIS.. PROB'LY THE BEST SINGIN' COMMERCIAL EVER WROUGHT.
WHAT'VE I GOT TO LOSE BESIDE MY MIND?
YOUR GOOD NAME.. YOU COULD LOSE YOUR GOOD NAME..WHO STEALS YOUR MIND STEALS TRASH.
WHO STEALS MY PURSE STEALS TRASH.. NOT MY MIND.

LISTEN--HERE'S HOW IT GO-- WHAT PUTS THE GLAD IN GLADIOLA? OH, ASK ME, DAD.. KO KO MO KOLA
NOW WHAT DOES THAT LI'L MESSAGE IM-PEL YOU TO BUY?
A TICKET TO AUSTRALIA AND A KANGAROO TO TALK TO.

CHAPTER 2

O'er the Lea,

BLOOBLE BLOOB A BLUBBER WUBBA DUBBER BLUB
WHAT'S GOIN' ON?
HE'S ABUSING ME---ALL I TRIED TO DO WAS JAZZ UP HIS WELFARE!
WELFARE MY EYE! HE WAS DEMONSTRATIN' A TEEVY COMMERCIAL--ON ME! DUMPED STUFF ON ME--
HOW?
LARD

PUT LARD ON MY HEAD-- LIKE THIS--AN' SAYS: "DON'T DO THIS! IT SPOILS YOUR HAIR! DON'T PUT GUNK ON YOUR SCALP!"
THAT'S GOOD ADVICE.
SEEM TO ME HE WAS BEIN' HONEST-- RATHER'N ABUSE HIM, MEBBE YOU OUGHT TO THANK HIM.
MAYBE YOU'RE RIGHT-- THANKS, P.T., THANKS A LOT.

MEBBE IF P.T. AN' TAMANNANY GOES INTO TEEVY IT'LL BE MY OPERATOONITY TO WRITE THEM LI'L' JINGLES--
UM.

THE KIND WHAT ADVERTISES A PRODUCT--- LIKE KOKOMO KOLA.

"OH, KOKOMO KOLA
IS REALLY THE STUFF..
IT'S COOL, MAN, COOL
AN' NEVER ENOUGH!"
THERE, THAT'S GOT IT ALL!
EVER'THIN' 'CEPT A PRODUCT.

THERE'S NO SUCH THING AS KOKOMO KOLA.
WHAT!? AFTER ALL MY TROUBLE THEY RUN OUT ON ME? HOW ABOUT PENSACOLA? IS THAT DRIED UP, TOO?

SO YOU B'LEEVES YOU'LL GO INTO TEEVY, WRITIN' SINGIN' COMMERCIALS?
YEP.. HOW MUCH D'YOU S'POSE THEY'LL GIVE ME?

OH.. I DUNNO.. IT DEPENDS.. IF TURTLES GOT A STRONG UNION YOU MOUGHT GIT HUNNERDS AN' HUNNERDS.
WHAT?

THEN THE JOB IS OUT.. I CAN'T AFFORD TO TAKE IT.
CAN'T AFFORD IT! YOU AIN'T MAKIN' NOTHIN' DOIN' WHAT YOU'S DOIN' NOW!
I KNOW! AN' IF I LOSES THIS JOB.. WHAT'S I LOSE? NOTHIN'! BUT IF I EVER LOST A JOB MAKIN' HUNNERDS AN' HUNNERDS OF DOLLARS A WEEK IT WOULD BREAK ME. I COULDN'T AFFORD IT!
MEBBE I NEED NEW GLASSES.

FIRST THING TO DO IS TO PREPARE OUR TEEVY AGENDA
YES~PUT ME DOWN FOR THE LEAD IN YOUR FIRST OPUS.

LET'S HEAR YOU BARK!
BARK?.. YOU MEAN LIKE IN "BOW WOW" ?

EXACTLY -- FIRST WE WILL FEATURE A DOG FOOD COMMERCIAL ★ IT OPENS WITH A HAPPY DOG BARKING.
BOW WOW BOW WOW

You Don't SOUND VERY HAPPY!
HOW CAN I BE HAPPY..? I'M NOT A DOG.
VERY TRUE INDEED.

WHAT YOU NEED FOR THE JOB OF A HAPPY BARKIN' DOG ON YOUR TEEVY SHOW IS A REAL DOG!
WHAT!

I NEVER HEARD OF SUCH A UNHEARD OF THING -- -- A RANK AMATEUR DOIN' A REAL ACTOR OUT OF A JOB!

BUT I AIN'T A AMATEUR DOG! I'M A REAL DOG.. PERFECT FOR THE PART.
PERFECT..!? WHAT TALENT DOES THAT TAKE..? ANYBODY CAN BE THEMSELFS.. IT'S A INDICATION OF SHEER NOTHING!
HE'S RIGHT! YOU GOTTA SHOW US YOU CAN act IF YOU WANT THE JOB

MAYHAP, SIR, YOU CAN BECOME OUR TECHNICAL MAN?
YOU MEAN INASMUCH AS I IS A EXPERT DOG.. I COULD SHOW YOU HOW A DOG ACTS?
Well ~ IT OCCURS TO ME, YOU MIGHT KNOW SOMETHING ABOUT DOG FOOD!! IT'S OUR PRODUCT, YOU KNOW.. What's in it for EXAMPLE?

OOG. NEVER TOUCH IT, MYSELF- BUT IT SEEM TO ME IT'S MOSTLY HORSEMEAT.
HORSEMEAT?!
WE'RE GONNA NEED ANOTHER PARTNER!
AYE.. WHO DO WE KNOW WHO'S A HORSE?

CHAPTER 3

Verily, Verily,

DO YOU GOTTA LOOK LIKE THAT?
A MAN CAN'T HELP HIS OWN NATURAL BEAUTY, SON.

PERSON'LY I IS QUIETLY PROUD...
QUIETLY?

THAT BATHIN' SUIT IS SO LOUD IT SKEERS THE FISHES.
IT WAS LEFT ME BY MY PA.. A MAN OF EX-QUIZZLE TASTE.
GLAD TO HEAR IT.. I WAS THINKIN' IT LOOK LIKE THE TOP HALF OF YOU EX-CAPED FROM THE STATE BASTILLE.
COME TO THINK OF IT, PA DID SAY A GUMMINT BLOODHOUND WAS IN POSSESSION OF THE DRAWERS.

I JES' HAD A SHOCK!
SO IS I.
THAT SO? SAME ONE AS ME? IS YOU HEARD THAT NO DOGS IS ALLOWED TO PLAY THE PART OF A DOG ON THE TEEVY?
NO, BUT I CAUGHT A GLIMPSE OF YO' PANTS.

OH, THEM..? THEY'S MY DADDY'S BATHIN' DRAWERS.. HE WHUPPED 'EM OFFA A EX-CAPIN' OCCUPANT OF THE CALABAZOO WHEN HE WAS IN GUMMINT WORK.

A OUTLAW LIKE THAT OUGHT TO BE PURSOOT AN' CAUGHT JUST TO MAKE HIM TAKE BACK THEM BATHIN' TROUSERS.
BUT HOW COULD HE BE FOUND NOW?

HEIGHDY
FUNNY THING HOW I COME INTO THESE BATHIN' DRAWERS.. PA PULLED 'EM OFF A EX-CAPIN' CONVICK AN'-
HEIGHDY

TOODLE OO.

FUNNY THING HOW I COME INTO THIS BATHIN' SUIT --- PA LEFT IT TO ME CLAIMIN' IT WAS PART OF A SET AN'--

WHAT?!

IS YOU IMPLYIN' MY DADDY STOLE YO'PA'S BATHIN' DRAWERS?!
IS YOU CLAIM MY PA EX-CAPED FROM PRISON AN' YO'DADDY CAUGHT HIM BY THE TROUSERS?!
A DOGBONED INSULT!

AARGH! ROWF! YOWMF

BEHOLD, SON, HOW PUNY IN THE LEG BONES ALBERT IS GITTIN'... IT COME FROM THE MODDERIN AGE OF MOTOR CAR TRAVEL... WALKIN' IS A LOST ART.. THE HUMAN RACE IS BECOME SPINDLE SHANKED FREAKS AN' THERE'S THE PROOF!

NOW I KNOWS WHY FOLKS WEARS BATHIN' TROUSERS AN' SUCH... IT'S SO'S THEY KIN BE PICKED UP AN' RESCUED...
...WHEN THEY VENTURES FOOLISHLIKE OVER THEY OWN DEPTHS....
...LAY STILL NOW WHILST I ARTIOFFICIAL RES-PIRATES YOU...
LEMME UP! I AIN'T DROWNT.

THAT'S JES' IT--- YOU IS SORRY 'BOUT BEIN' NOTHIN'--I'M SORRY YOU IS SORRY BUT SORRIER THAT YOU AIN'T SORRY 'BOUT BEIN' SORRY TO BE SORRY 'BOUT THE OTHER SORRY THING YOU OUGHT TO BE SORRY OF---

I WANT TO COMMEND YOU ON THE FINE, MANLY WAY YOU ACTED DURIN' OUR RECENT DISPUTE.
AND I WANNA SAY YOU ACTED WITH UTMOST INTEGERTY.
NO-NO-MY DEAR FRIEND, IT WAS YOUR EXEMPLARY ACTION WHICH WAS LAUDABLE.
NO, IT WAS YOU WHAT WAS SO DADBLAMED DECENT IT LIKE TO MAKE A MAN BREAK INTO TEARS.

WHEN I SAY YOUR CONDUCT WAS IN THE FINEST NOBLESSE OBLIGE TRADITION, I DON'T WANT TO BE CONTRADICTED.
AN' IF I EXTENDS CREDIT TO WHOM IT IS BEHOOVED I DON'T WANT A LOT OF SICKENIN', SIMPERIN SELF EE-FACEMINTS.
AARGH!

SPLASH!

JES' IMAGINE YOURSELF PLAYIN' THE LEAD IN A DRAMA ENTITLED "FLOSSIE RETURNS"-YOU IS FLOSSIE THE SUPER-DOG BEE-LOVED BY CHILDRENS AN' BEAUTIFUL GALS...

MM

WHY COULDN'T I BE FLOSSIE, THE ALLIGATOR? BELOVED AN' ALL LIKE THAT ...ALLIGATORS IS LOVABLE.

THE PICTURE OF A FAITHFUL ALLIGATOR BOUNDIN' INTO DADDY'S LAP AIN'T ONE THE PUBLIC IS READY FOR.

CHAPTER 4

Blue.

YOU CAN TEACH ME TO BE A RED WHITE AN' BLUE BLOODED DOG OR NOTHIN'!
FAW.

VERY WELL FOR YOU TO SAY "FAW"-- BUT WHAT AM I GONE SAY WHEN I GOTTA BARK IN A FOREIGN LANGUAGE? YOU WANTS ME TO BE A KOMONDOR AND I DON'T KNOW A WORD OF FRENCH.
YOU WOON'T NEED IT.

WELL-- IN THAT CASE--IF I COULD BARK IN AMERICAN I MIGHT CONSIDER TRYIN' OUT--
THE KOMONDOROK (WHICH IS THE PLURAL OF YOU) IS DESCENT FROM THE AFTSCHARKA-- --YOU'D HAFTA BARK IN MAGYAR.
MAGYAR? WHERE WAS THIS DOG FOUND?
ON THE STEPPES.
OF WHOSE STOOP?

THIS BOOK ON "TRAINING THE NOBLE DOG" GOT A LOT IN IT ABOUT THE KOMONDOROK.
ATBLER

SEEM LIKE BEIN' THIS DOG IS JUST CUT OUT FOR YOU -- IT SAY HE GOT A FIERCE BUILD ON HIM --SQUARE SHOULDERS AN' A HANDSOME HEAD..

-UH--HANDSOME HEAD OF HAIR-- - MM-- HAIR-- WELL WELL-- HAIR! WODDYA KNOW? HAIR!
COULDN'T I BE A MEXICAN HAIRLESS KOMONDOR?
DOGS ETC.
WHAT? YOU!? A CHIHUAHUA? WHO! YOU? A CHIHUAHUA!
GESUNDHEIT!

MAKIN' A HUNGARIAN SHEEP DOG OUTEN YOU WOULD BE A CHALLENGE.
A CHALLENGE TO WHAT-- A DOG FIGHT?
HOLD IT ON ALL FOURS THERE WHILST I TRIES THIS MOP TO GIT THE BEAUTIFUL HEAD OF HAIR EFFECT WHICH THE DOG MANUAL DEMANDS...

NOW THIS OL' COLLEGE BOY FUR COAT ON YOU AND...

DON'T TELL ME That is MISS ERMENGARDE BEARCAT, my old GEOMETRY TEACHER....!?
A GOOD IDEA-- DON'T TELL HIM THAT!

MY word, BUT YOU ARE A DEADRINGER for my OLD GEOMETRY TEACHER!
AN' YOU IS A DEAD RINGER FOR A BONEHEAD.
GENTLEMEN, GENTLEMEN- PLEASE! ALBERT, HERE, IS LEARNING TO PLAY THE PART OF A DOG ... A FOREIGN TEEVY STAR.

MM- LET US HEAR A FOREIGN BARK, SIR.
CINCHONA! CINCHONA! CINCHONA! CINCHONA!
GREAT!! GREAT!! CARRY ON! IT'S A REAL AU NATUREL
CINCHONA IS A FOREIGN BARK?
CERT'LY... THEY MAKES QUININE OUTEN IT--ANY SWAMP CRITTUR KNOW THAT!

MEBBE MIZ MA'M'SELLE HEPZIBAH KNOWS HOW TO BARK IN MAGYAR --HOW'S THE KOMONDOROK GO, MIZ MA'M'SELLE?
THESE SONG I DO NOT KNOW --BUT THERE ARE A SWEET SMALL SONG ALL 'BOUT GIRL WHAT IS LOSE HER LIVER ON BANKS OF SEINE.
DON'T YOU MEAN HER LOVER!?

NON! SHE IS CAT FANCIER AN' TRAP CAT WITH LIVER -- POOF - ONE DAY SHE LOSE TWO POUNDS AN' HALF AN' SO SHE SING SAD SONG 'BOUT HIM LA LA LA LA LA LA LA ♫ ♫ LIKE SO...

THE KOMONDOROK AIN'T A SONG - IT'S A BREED OF DOG - FROM HUNGARY.
I'M GONE BE ONE.
DOES THE GOVERMENS AT BUDAPEST KNOW THESE NEWS?

'COURSE I WOONENT HAFTA BE ANY PARTICKLER FOREIGN DOG -- JES' SO'S I IS GLAMMERD UP SOME.
HOW WOULD A FRENCH DOG BARK, MA'M'SELLE?
I KNOW NICE DOG WHO IS CALL PAPILLONS.

AN' HE GO:
TUT TUT TUT TUT TUT TUT

HE PRONOUNCE THESE IN FRANCAIS, NATUREL, AN' HE ARE SMALL, TINY, LITTLE ANIMAL DOG USE FOR COTCH THE BOOSTERFLIES...

MAN! I'M GLAD SHE DIN'T IMITATE A BIG DOG!
SHE SURE GIVE ME A TURN, FRIEND...
MENS! FOOF!

CHAPTER 5

Raggedly, Baggedly,

CHANGE THE SONG, MY EYE! I'LL CHANGE THE PRODUCT -- COLLAR AN' DOLLAR RHYMES, DON'T IT?

A COLD KOKOMO KOLLAR?

BALDERDASH!--LISTEN TO THIS FAMOUS SINGIN' COMMERCIAL-
"COME, ALL YOU YOUNG SPORTS COME EAT UP YOUR WARTS FOR THAT IS THE WAY TO GROW!"
ACK! WARTS?
NOT REAL WARTS, STUPID-- WARTS SPELLED BACKWARDS IS "STRAW", THAT BONE BUILDING BELOVED CEREAL FAVORED BY YOUNG AND OLD-- ANYBODY KNOWS THAT-- 'CAUSE IT MAKES SENSE!
WHAT'S "UGH" SPELT BACK-WARDS?

I S'POSE YOU IS HEERD THE BIG NEWS? CHURCHY AN' ME IS GONNA MAKE A FORTUNE-- WE'LL SELL HIS SINGIN' COMMERCIALS TO THE TEEVY PEOPLE--
OH, I KNOW, HEH HEH-- YOU'RE GONNA SAY IF HE COUNTERBUTES THE SONGS-- WHAT'S I COUNTERBUTE? MY BRAINS, FRIENDS-- IT TAKES A HEAD TO GET AHEAD, HEH HEH?
GONNA USE YOUR HEAD, HUH?

WULL ··· MEBBE YOU GOT A POINT THERE, OWL--

AN' IF YOU COMBS YO' HAIR JES' RIGHT NOBODY'LL NOTICE.

CHAPTER 6

Through the True,

ALWAYS SOME LI'L' SLICK-TALKIN' DRUMMER LIKE YOU COMES IN TO MONKEY-WRENCH THE HONEST PURSUITS OF SOBER MEN.
YEAH!

WHY, OH, WHY DO THOSE OF US WHO EARNESTLY BEND OUR FRAIL BUT COURAGEOUS EFFORTS TO BENEFIT EVERYONE IN EVERY WALK OF LIFE CARING NOT FOR OUR SELFS ALONE BUT INWARDLY BLEEDING...

AND SUFFERING IN AN UNSTINTING AND SELF EFFACING NOBILITY OF GENEROSITY SET WITH THE DIAMONDS AND PEARLS OF LOVE, LOVE FOR OUR FELLOWS AND KNOWLEDGE OF OUR OWN UNBECOMING ....

UM-UH.. WHERE WAS I?
WHERE WAS YOU WHEN?
YOU TAXIED DOWN THE RUNWAY AND DUMPED YOUR GAS SO'S YOU COULD TAKE OFF!

WE WAS SEARCHIN' FOR "BOW-WOW" IN GERMAN WHEN YOU COME IN BE-LITTLIN' OUR SCHOLARLY QUEST.
WAU WAU

WHY DO YOU SAY "VOW VOW," FRIEND?
'CAUSE THAT'S THE WAY YOU BARKS IN GERMAN.

VOW-VOW? DOGS PRONOUNCE THEIR "V'S" IN GERMAN?
YEP.. I ONCE HAD A JOB AS A DOG IN A SMALL GERMAN BUTCHER SHOP.
WHAT? YOU WAS A DOG..? WHAT'D YOU CHASE, WEEVILS?
NOPE.. THIS WAS SUCH A SMALL SHOP IN GERMAN EAST AFRICA...NO ROOM FOR A DOG...SO, TO KEEP THE ELEPHANTS AWAY FROM THE COLD-CUTS I OFFERED MY SERVICES AND....

THIS PLACE WHERE I HAD THE JOB BEIN' THE DOG OF IN AFRICA TO KEEP THE ELEPHANTS OUTEN THE ICE-BOX WAS A HANGOUT FOR ALL KINDS WEIRD AN' EXOTIC TROPICAL CREATURES.

WHAT WITH THE BOER WAR BEIN' OVER WHICH I WON ON A SECRET MISSION EVERY BODY HAD NOTHIN' TO DO BUT HUNG AROUND THE STORE ALL DAY EATIN' CHEESE AN' PICKLES.

WHEN MEIN STADTHOLDER WHO WAS BOSS-MAN COMPLAINED ABOUT THE SALAMI BEIN' A TARGET TOO OFTEN, THESE HANGERS-ON WOULD BITE MR. STADTHOLDER UNTIL HE LOOKED LIKE A SWISS CHEESE HISSELF WHICH HE COULDN'T OF BEEN BECAUSE OF BEIN' GERMAN.

SO, FROM LIVERWURST AN' INK I CONCOCTED A SNAKE BITE CURE KNOWED AS RAWSON'S-OWN WHICH WAS POPULAR WITH ALL THE SNAKES AN' - WHAT?
I SAID WE'D LIKE SOME TALKIN' ROOM.

I WAS ABOUT TO TELL ABOUT MY FRIEND IN AFRICA WHAT WAS SUCH A BIG HERO..
WELL.. OUR LIVES IS SHORT AN' IF IT TAKES TOO LONG..
DID I HEAR SOME ONE PAGE ME?
A SNAKE!
SNAVELY!

SNAVELY! YOU'RE BACK.. BACK FROM YOUR TRIUMPHAL TOUR OF THE PROVINCES OR PERCHANCE STARTIN' OUT?
I'M IN SUMMER STOCK THIS SEASON.
SNAVELY AND HIS TRAINED WORMS. THEY GLIDE AND SLIDE, DIVE AND DANCE... SPELL, SING, ADD SUMS AND PROGNOSTICATE THE FUTURE.

IF YOU DON'T MIND, SIR, STEP OVER HERE INTO THE WANT ADS WITH ME.
HEY, WAIT.. SNAVELY WAS GONE ENTERTAIN WITH HIS APPRENTICE SERPENTS.

ENTERTAIN! HAUGH! WHAT A TAWDRY EXHIBIT THAT WAS YESTERDAY.. TALK..TALK..TALK CALL THAT FUNNY?

THEY BARGE IN··· WE WAS IN THE MIDST OF A HIGHLY AMUSING DISCUSSION AND I FOR ONE THOUGHT YOU WERE ESPECIALLY DROLL.
IS THAT GOOD?
EXCELLENT FOR OUR NOBLE PURPOSES, SIR·· AND WE CAN GO ELSEWHERE, GET INTO ANOTHER COMIC STRIP IF THIS ONE IS TO BE TAKEN OVER BY MICE, SERPENTS AND ANGLE WORMS.
COULD WE GIT JOBS GOIN' TO-SAY-MARS?

IMAGINE THAT! THEM TWO, ALBERT AND BEAUREGARD, WENT OFF WITH-OUT WAITIN' TO HEAR HOW MY ADVENTURES IN AFRICA COME OUT·· THEY DON'T EVEN KNOW IF I LIVED THRU 'EM OR NOT.
MEBBE THEY DON'T CARE.
HOW ABOUT THE THREE APPRENTICE COBRAS...? FIGGER THEY'D LIKE TO HEAR THE REST OF MY STORY?
FROM CRAWLIN' THEY IS DEVELOPED EXTREMELY STRONG STOMACHS SO··

MEBBE I OUGHT TO REMIND YOU THAT I WAS A SEMI-FINALIST IN THE JUDO TOURNAMENT AT RANGOON, NEWBRASKA IN 19 OUGHT 28.
AND I MIGHT REMIND YOU THAT IT WAS ME WHAT THROWED YOU.
WELL, YES BUT I HAD A SORE HAND.
WELL I DID IT NO HANDS.

IF THEY KIN JUST KEEP IN MIND NEVER TO BE TOOK BY SURPRISE.. THEY GOTTA LEARN THE WORLD IS FULL OF SNEAKY TYPES ALWAYS READY TO BE --

NO FAIR! NO FAIR! I WAS ATTACKED BY TWO OF 'EM.
YOU WAS NOT -- THE ONE WHAT THROWS YOU IS THE SAME ONE YOU'RE S'POSED TO BE TEACHIN'.
PHOO! WHAT'S THE DIFFERENCE BETWEEN 'EM? I CAN'T TELL 'EM APART.
NOTHIN' TO IT.. -- THESE OTHER TWO IS GIRLS.

HOWDY, GENTS! WE'S GONE HAVE A FRY AN' I'M LOOKIN' FOR VOLUNTEERS TO DIG A LITTLE BAIT.
MM -- WELL, WELL - YES INDEED. MM HM

I'D BE GLAD TO HELP BUT I HURT MY ARM SHOWIN' THE APPRENTICE COBRAS HOW TO DEE-FEND THEIRSELFS AGAINST SNEAKS, CUT PURSES AN' OTHER RIP JACKS.
ME TOO.

YOU HURT YOUR ARM, SNAVELY?
NO --- BUT WATCHIN' MOUSE HERE WAS A TRAUMATIC EXPERIENCE OF SUCH BOISTEROUS PROPORTIONS THAT I.. - UH - THE CHILDREN HERE MIGHT LIKE TO DIG A --
THEY'S RUN OFF! WHAT SOME PEOPLE WON'T DO TO AVOID WORK!
THEM WORMS KNOWS THE ANGLES.

CHAPTER 7

Haggardly, Haggardly,

NOW IN THIS SPOT, YOU, FLOSSIE THE NOBLE DOG, BURST INTO POLICE HQ WITH THE GENTLE JASMINIA IN YOUR MOUTH ··· THE CAPTAIN SAYS ···

"THIS GIRL HAS BEEN DRUGGED!" AND YOU SAY "I KNOW··
I DONE DRUG HER ALL THE WAY FROM PEACH TREE STREET!

OH THIS STUFF IS TOO RICH ··· TOO RICH·· TOO GOOD FOR TEEVY··· IT DESERVES A BETTER FATE!
TURN IT OVER TO FORT KNOX AND LET 'EM BURY IT FOR YOU.

WELL, THAT PROVES IT·· OUR HUMOR AIN'T APPRECIATED AROUND HERE·· THE WAY THEY RUNS THIS STRIP NOBODY LAUGHS AT NOTHIN' REAL FUNNY··· JUST AT CUTE STUFF.

PORKY DIN'T EVEN SMILE WHEN ME, FLOSSIE THE DOG, BRINGS THE GIRL INTO H.Q. AN' THE CAP'N SAYS "SHE BEEN DRUGGED!" AN' I SAYS "I KNOW·· I DRUG HER ALL THE WAY FROM CANAL STREET!"

URF! URF! URF!
YOU'S LAUGHIN' PORKY... YOU GITS THAT JOKE FROM YESTERDAY!
NO--BUT THE WITTY STORY OF LAST WEEK, "WHO WAS THE LADY EYE SORE WITH YOU LAST NIGHT?" NOW STRIKES ME AS EXTREMELY DROLL... ESPECIALLY IF THERE IS SOME SORT OF FUNNY REPLY.

THE KIND OF A DOG ALBERT OUGHT TO BE IS A BOXER.
I'M SURE HE'LL APPRECIATE THE SUGGESTION.

YOU SAY ALBERT OUGHT TO BE A BOXER? AN' BARK IN GUTTURAL REMARKS! THAT REE-MIND ME OF SOMETHIN' WE GONE USE ON THE "FLOSSIE, THE NOBLE DOG" SHOW!
MUMF!

FELLOW WINS TWO ELEPHANTS IN A RAFFLE AN' BRINGS 'EM HOME TELLIN' HIS WIFE THEY IS DOGS... "WHAT KIND DOGS IS THESE?" SHE ASKS.. "BOXERS," HE SAY, "CAN'T YOU SEE THEIR TRUNKS?"
WOW

HOW ABOUT A LITTLE COURTEOUS "HA-HA" ?
RIDICULOUS ON THE FACE OF IT...WHO WOULD RAFFLE OFF A PAIR OF ELEPHANTS?
WOW
WOW
ONE MEBBE, BUT TWO-?

SNAVELY AN' THE MOUSE TELLS ME YOU GOT A NEW JOKE 'BOUT BOXERS.

I COME OVER TO HEAR IT HOPIN' IT'S THE ONE ABOUT THE FELLOW SAYS HE'S A BOXER.. ON ACCOUNT HE JES' GOT A JOB CRATIN' MUSHMELONS.. I ALLUS LAUGHS AT THAT'N, SO SHOOT!

NO..THIS'N IS 'BOUT A FELLOW BRINGS HOME TWO ELEPHANTS AN' TELLS HIS WIFE THEY IS DOGS..BOXERS, HE SAY.. ON ACCOUNT OF LOOK AT THEIR TRUNKS..

NOPE.. I DUNNO THAT'N.. BUT THAT OTHER'S A FAVORITE OF MINE... I LAUGHS TWO OR THREE GOOD HEARTY LICKS AT IT IF'N I HEAR IT..

CHAPTER 8

Flee.

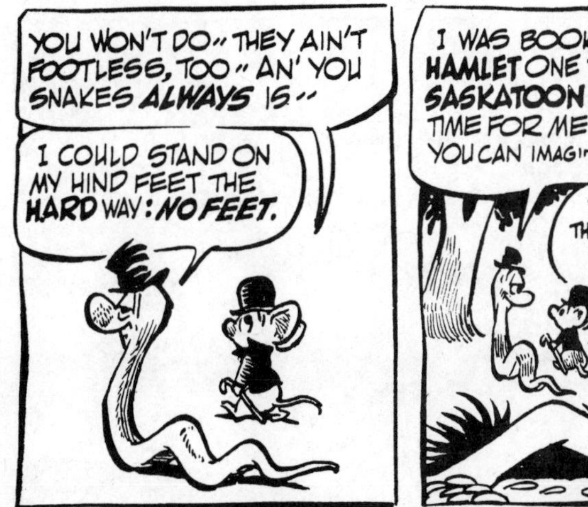

I JUST HAD A **GREAT IDEA!** ***PROB'LY*** THE FINEST TYPE IDEA OF THE **LOCAL SEASON**
GO EASY **GO** EASY.

WHY GO EASY? I GOT A **GREAT** IDEA FOR THE KIND OF **DOG ALBERT** OUGHT TO BE.. A IDEA WHAT SHOULD BE SHARED WITH THE **NATION**.. A IDEA TO BE GIVE OUT TO MEBBE A HUNNERD AND SIXTY MILLION SOULS AN'....

AN' MEBBE I'D MAKE A FEW **MILLION PESOS** OR POSSIBLY WIN A SPOT ON SOME **GUMMINT BODY**....
REMEMBER THE **LAST TIME** YOU TRIED THIS THE **BLUE COATS** TRIED TO PUT YOU IN THE **DEEP FREEZE** FOR **SIX MOONS**.
PHOOF.. I **STILL** SEE NOTHING WRONG WITH PRINTING ***EDIBLE*** MONEY.
BUT NOT ON THIN SLICES OF **CHEESE**.. ESPECIALLY WITH **HOLES** IN IT..

WHAT IS THIS **FOURTEEN KARAT STERLING** IDEA 'BOUT WHAT KIND OF A **DOG** ALBERT OUGHT TO BE?
NO- NO- YOU BELITTLED **MY** MONEY PLAN! CLAIMED BILLS PRINTED ON ANYTHING BUT PAPER WAS ***DE RIGUEUR MORTIS*** FOR WHOMSOEVER WAS CAUGHT.
BUT, DEAR BOY, THE **MONEY CONCESSION** IN THE GUMMINT IS GUARDED ***VERY JEALOUSLY.***
WHO ELSE EVER OFFERED TO PRINT IT ON **CHEESE?** ***NOBODY!*** NOT EVEN **HOLLAND!**

TALKIN' WITH YOU MAKES A MAN WISH HE HAD A ARM TO WAVE--- WHERE WOULD YOU GET THE CHEESE?
FIRST OF ALL WE'D EMPTY EVERY MUNICIPALLY HELD MOUSE TRAP IN THE LAND ---THEN WHEN THE BALL WAS ROLLIN'---

WE'D CALL IN THE COWS-- THINK OF THE EMPLOYMENT IT WOULD GIVE COWS.. TO SAY NOTHING OF GOATS..
OR CAMELS --YOU COULD BE HEAD OF THE DEPT. OF CURDS AN' WHEYS AN' MEANS.

HERE'S A IMPARTIAL OBSERVER, WE'LL ASK HIM WHAT HE THINKS OF EDIBLE MONEY..

S'POSE US GOT A JOB PRINTIN' MONEY ON CHEESE 'STEAD OF PAPER.. WOULD YOU TAKE OFF'N US 'STEAD OF THE GUMMINT CONCESSIONAIRES?
CHEESE? WHAT KIND?

OH, WHATEVER WE COULD SCARE UP--PORT SALUTE, LIEDERKRUNTCH, CAMEMBURKE, SWISS, JACK, STORE OR MOUSE TRAP---
YOU WOULDN'T TAKE CHEESE OUTEN TRAPS, SIR?
YOU'D BE ACCUSED OF STEALING FROM THE MICE OF OUR LAND--BAD PUBLIC RELATIONS--YOUR MONEY WOULD BE BOYCOTTED!
I GOT A SMACKER OF A POEM GOIN' HERE! WHAT RHYMES WITH LIVER-WURST?

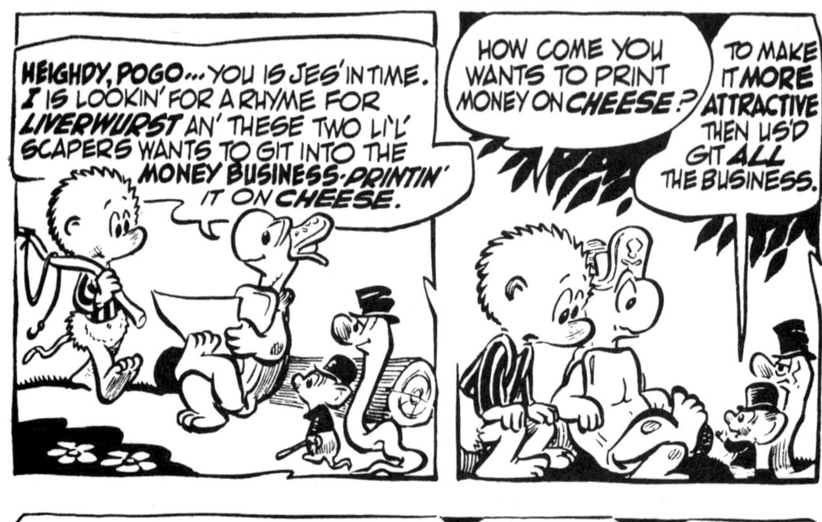
HEIGHDY, POGO... YOU IS JES' IN TIME. I IS LOOKIN' FOR A RHYME FOR LIVERWURST AN' THESE TWO LI'L' SCAPERS WANTS TO GIT INTO THE MONEY BUSINESS-PRINTIN' IT ON CHEESE.
HOW COME YOU WANTS TO PRINT MONEY ON CHEESE?
TO MAKE IT MORE ATTRACTIVE THEN US'D GIT ALL THE BUSINESS.

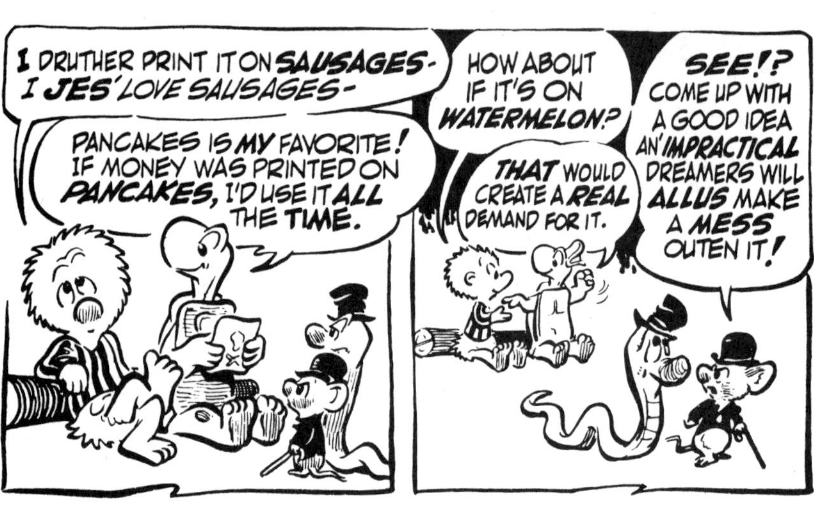
I DRUTHER PRINT IT ON SAUSAGES- I JES' LOVE SAUSAGES-
PANCAKES IS MY FAVORITE! IF MONEY WAS PRINTED ON PANCAKES, I'D USE IT ALL THE TIME.
HOW ABOUT IF IT'S ON WATERMELON?
THAT WOULD CREATE A REAL DEMAND FOR IT.
SEE!? COME UP WITH A GOOD IDEA AN' IMPRACTICAL DREAMERS WILL ALLUS MAKE A MESS OUTEN IT!

YOU STILL BUSY WORKIN' ON THEM TEEVY SINGIN' COMMERCIALS?
NOT AT THE MOMENT... RIGHT NOW I'M THINKIN': HERE IT IS AUGUST!

GOSH.. SO IT IS.
AN' HOW LUCKY WE IS THAT I THOUGHT OF IT...

LOTS OF PEOPLE IS THUNK OF AUGUST-- --OR JUNE--OR OF SEPTEMBER, EVEN...
NOT THE WAY I IS...I LOOKS AHEAD AN' SETS ALL OUR MINDS TO REST RIGHT OFF--NO NEED TO WORRY!
YOU ASKS ME HOW, FRIEND-- --I'LL TELL YOU--SEE THERE, DURIN' THE ENTIRE MONTH OF AUGUST, FRIDAY THE THIRTEENTH FALLS ON A SATURDAY-- THAT, SIR, IS A LUCKY PORTENT.

HOW KIN YOU HONESTLY CLAIM THAT FRIDAY THE THIRTEENTH FALLS ON A SATURDAY?
BEHOLE FOR YOU OWN SELF--THERE IT IS, IN BLACK AND WHITE-- NUMBER 13 ON A SATURDAY.
LOOK, JUST BECAUSE IT'S THE THIRTEENTH DAY DON'T MEAN IT'S FRIDAY THE THIRTEENTH...
FRIDAY THE 13 TH GOTTA FALL SOMEWHERE. IT DON'T HOVER IN THE AIR.

EVERY MONTH DON'T GOT A FRIDAY THE THIRTEENTH.
JES' CAUSE I SET YO' MIND TO REST EASY SHOWIN' YOU FRIDAY 13TH COME ON SATURDAY YOU IS FEELIN' MIGHTY PERKY, I MUST SAY.
IT JUS' GO TO SHOW I COULD GIT A REGULAR JOB ON THE TEEVY PREE-DICKIN' FAMOUS DAYS--LIKE FOURTH OF JOO-LY FOR A SAMPLE OR HAPPY NEW YEARS...THEY'S A DEE-MAND FOR THAT KINDA STUFF.

THE WORLD WOULD NEVER AGAIN HAFTA WORRY 'BOUT WHEN CHRISTMAS MIGHT COME.

WHAT MAKES YOU THINK PEOPLE'D WANT TO HEAR YOU PREDICT WHEN CHRISTMAS WAS DUE ON THE TEEVY?
IT'S THE RAGE -- I LOOKS UP CHRISTMAS -- SAY IT'S OCTOBER TWELFTH THIS YEAR -- THEN I-
BUT EVER'BODY KNOWS CHRISTMAS COMES ON DEC. 25 ...
DID YOU LOOK IT UP? NO! ONLY I IS -- ON THE CALENDAR -- SOON AS I FINDS THE DATE I RUSHES ON THE AIR.

GOOD EVENING MR. AND MRS. UNINETY STATES, I SAYS -- I GOT A HOT FLASH -- FRIDAY THE THIRTEENTH COMES ON A SATURDAY THIS MONTH -- REMEMBER HE WHO IS FOREWARNED IS FOREARMED!
FOUR ARMED?!

HE WHO IS FOUR ARMED GOTTA BE HALF A OCTOPUS -- WHO WANTS TO BE THAT?
HE GOT A POINT.

CHAPTER 9

Quickedly, Wickedly,

MEBBE THE MOUSE HAD A GOOD IDEA THERE... EDIBLE MONEY!
BUT EVER'BODY DON'T CARE FOR CHEESE.. MONEY PRINTED ON IT WOULD GO GOOD WITH MICE BUT HOW 'BOUT OTHER HUMANS?
OH YOU COULD PUT OUT A MENU ... GIVE FOLKS A CHOICE -- MONEY PRINTED ON TOAST, MONEY ON SLICED EGG-PLANT.
AN' ON OMELET.

OH, YES, WE COULD MAKE MONEY REAL POPULAR.
IMAGINE! MONEY PRINTED ON LICORICE - YUM!
WE COULD REVOLUTIONIZE THE FINANCIAL WORLD! CASH WOULD HAVE A TWO FOLD PURPOSE ... JUST THINK! FOLKS WITH MONEY WOULD NEVER HAVE TO STARVE!
GOSH!

JUST THINK! IF WE MADE MONEY OUT OF FOOD PEOPLE WOULD USE MORE OF IT--BUSINESS WOULD BOOM!
PENSACOLA · IT'S THE SPA

YOU FIGGER TO MAKE MONEY A HOUSEHOLD WORD?
PENSACOLA IT'S THE SPA

WULL ..

WHAT HOUSEHOLD WORD WOULD YOU MAKE IT? SPIGOT, CELLAR, FRYIN' PAN--CUPBOARD--JELLY JAR--DOG COLLAR-? ALL THEM IS USED... WHAT ELSE IS THERE?
BLUB

AIN'T YOU WORKIN' ON TEEVY COMMERCIALS?
NOPE--I'SE GONE OUTTA THAT LINE.. POGO'S IN CONFINEMENT-WE DIRTIED HIS LAST SHIRT.

HE'S YOUR NEW PARTNER?
NOT EGG-ZACKLY HE MORE OF A CON-SULTAN.

FIGGER ON MAKIN' MONEY WITH YO' NEW SCHEME, HUH? WHAT'S IT THIS TIME?
OH, WE GONNA MAKE MONEY.
I GUESSED THAT! DOIN' WHAT?
WE GONE MAKE MONEY.
I REPEATS: DOIN' WHAT?
I TOLE YOU AN' I TOLE YOU --
WHAT!?
MAKIN' MONEY.
IF YOU GONE STAND THERE AN' TELL ME YOU GONE MAKE MONEY, TELL ME HOW!
I'SE JES' PLAIN GONE MAKE MONEY!
I'M GONNA FIGHT YOU WITH TOOTH AN' CLAW! WITH FIST AN' FOIL - WITH CLUB AN' AXE.
I CHALLENGE YOU TO A DAGGER DUEL AT 100 PACES.
I'M GONNA SPLIT YOU WITH BOW AN' ARROW AN' RUN YOU THRU WITH MURDEROUS SPEARS.
I'M GONNA BLOW HOLES IN YOU WITH REE-VOLVERS AN' STUFF 'EM WITH DYNAMITE!
STOP! STOP!
WHO? US?

HOW 'BOUT THIS'N FOR OUR SHOW--? A MAN STRIPS THE BARK OFF'N THREE BIRCH TREES TO MAKE A CANOE- --OTHER FELLOW SAYS "THEM'S MINE! YOU IS BARKED UP THE WRONG THREE!"

GET IT?
I IS LEAVIN'... GONE JOIN P.T. AN' TAMMANANNY.

THAT LAST ONE WAS THE CAMEL WHAT BROKE MY BACK.

WAIT FOR ME! I 'GREES WITH YOU! DON'T LEAVE ME ALONE WITH THEM JOKES!

TAMANANNY AN' P.T. WILL BE OVER-JOYED TO SEE US ... INASMUCH AS THEY IS GOIN' INTO TEEVY THEY'LL NEED OUR HELP... AN' THEY LOVES US, SO.

MAYBE THEY'LL SAY THEY IS ALL FULL UP--OR WE AIN'T GOT NO EXPERIENCE...
BUT THEY AN' WE IS OLD FRIENDS! WOULD THEY ACT LIKE THAT?

PERHAPS-THEY MOUGHT FEEL WE'D ONLY HOLD 'EM BACK.
BUT THAT'S NOT OUR PURPOSE --WE ONLY WANT THEM TO BE A SUCCESS--USIN' OUR TALENTS.
THEY PROB'LY WON'T SEE IT OUR WAY--THEY'LL SAY: "NO!" AN' TURN THEIR BACKS!
WHY DO THEY HATE US SO!?

HOW TAMANANNY AN' P.T. COULD REFUSE OUR HELP I DUNNO! IT'S A INSULT! THEY IS JES' NO PLAIN GOOD!
I'VE ALWAYS DEE-SPISED AN' ABHORRED 'EM FIT TO KILL... I NEVER IS PULLED SUGAR MOUTH WITH THEM--I SPEAKS OUT ALLUS! YOU IS NO GOOD, I SAYS.
A NOTE.
FOR ALBERT AND HOUND DUG

THEY IS RASCALS AN' SCAPEGRACERS AN'... UH- WHAT'SITSAY?
IT'S FER US FROM THEM-- IT SAY "GOODBYE!"
P.T. BPT.
GOODBYE? JES' THAT? A CURSORY ADIEU TO DEAR FRIENDS SUCH AS WE... YOU MEAN THEY IS LEFT WITHOUT LEAVING A FAREWELL TOKEN OF ESTEEM?

WE BEEN DESERTED... LEFT IN THE LURCH.
AND RIGHT AT THE CHURCH.

WOE IS US, FRIEND... W-H-O-WOE.
WE WAS PERTY WOED-UP WHEN US GOT THE BAD NEWS.

NOBODY PAYS US NO MIND--- P.T. AND TAMANANNY IS RUN OFF AN' THE OTHERS JES' SCORN US...I TELL YOU, ALBERT, I'M GLAD I GOT ONE TRUE AN' NOBLE FRIEND.
AN'.. (TEE-HEE! TOO-HOO!) WHO WOULD THAT BE, PRAY TELL?

ME

DOES YOU IM-PLY THAT ONLY YOU IS FIT TO BE A FRIEND OF YOURN?

ALBERT, YOU GOTTA REMEMBER WHO IS MAN'S BEST FRIEND--THE NOBLE DOG IS, NATURAL, AN' WHO IS THE NOBLE DOG EVEN A FRIEND OF BETTER'N ANYBODY OF? THE NOBLE DOG, BUT OF COURSE..

LEMME GET THIS STRAIGHT-- YOU CLAIM YOU IS A BETTER FRIEND OF YOURN THAN I IS?
A REVERED FAMILY TRADITION OF IMMEMORIAL CONTINUITY.
OH YEAH! I'LL SHOW YOU WHICH OF US IS YOUR BEST FRIEND, YOU RUBBER-NOSED RAGABONES!

HOW CAN YOU SAY I'M NOT YOUR BEST FRIEND?!
WOWF!
DON'T YOU RECALL THE TIMES I IS COME TO YO' HELP--? AN' COMFORTED YOU?!
AAARGH!

EVERY THING I IS DOOD SINCE YOU WAS A PUP WAS FO' YO' BENEFINT--- CHILDHOOD'S GOLDEN DAYS WE SPENT PLAYIN' LIKE LAMBS LAUGHIN' THRU OUR TEARS!
DON'T MEM'RIES LIKE THEM CONVINCE YOU OF THE HIGH ESTEEM IN WHICH I IS ALWAYS HELD YO' REGARDS?

IT AIN'T **YOU** WHAT'S **MY** BEST FRIEND, IT'S **ME** WHAT IS **YOUR'N** IN THE **NOBLESSE OBLIGE** TRADITION OF THE **NOBLE DOG.**
IF I AIN'T **YOURN** YOU CAN'T BE **MINE.**
YOU INSULT A **HEREDITABLE** LIFE-LONG CHAIN OF NOBILITY
YOU IS A LEAKY BAG OF DOUGH-NUT HOLES.

A MAN'S BEST FRIEND IS HIS **MOTHER** AN' A KNOCK HEAD LIKE **YOU** COULDN'T NEVER BE **MY** MOTHER..
I COULD *TOO!*
DON'T TELL **ME** I AIN'T GOOD ENOUGH TO BE YOUR **MOTHER** ... I GOT A LOVIN' DISPOSITION ON ME WHAT COULD WIN A PRIZE IN **ANY** MOTHER'S DAY PARADE.

MOM! I DIN'T KNOW YOU CARED!

CHAPTER 10

Shy and Low,

WHY IS IT YOU TWO ALWAYS WINDS UP IN A STRUGGLE FOR SUPER-REMACY?
WE IS NOT!

DOES YOU MEAN TO TELL ME YOU AIN'T FIGHTIN'?
WE IS MERE--

HAVIN' A PREE-LIMINARY MEETIN' AN' DIS-CUSSION TO DECIDE ON THE MAIN POINTS OF COUNTER-VERSITY, WHICH...

-- WE'S GONNA FIGHT ABOUT LATER ON-

OWL DON'T FIGHT FAIR!
I DO, TOO.

SEE..?! HE BITES!
YOWP!
CRUNCH

SEEM LIKE HE ONLY BITES HISSELF.
BUT HE MEAN IT FOR ME.
MM M

ONE OF US IS GOTTA WASH HIS HANDS... THE WAY THINGS IS I CAN'T TELL WHO IS WHO FOR DIRT.. BESIDES IT'S UNSANITARY AN' ENDANGERS MY HEALTH.

TURTLE FIGGERS HE'S GOIN' INTO THE MONEY PRINTIN' BUSINESS.. GONNA PRINT IT ON FOOD TO MAKE IT POPULAR AN' OWL TRYIN' TO WORM OUT HIS SECRET.
I TOLE YOU MY SECRET.. I'M GONNA MAKE MONEY.
DOIN' WHAT?
MAKIN' MONEY.
AT WHAT?

HOW'S YOU GONE MAKE MONEY?
BY MAKIN' MONEY.
WHAT DOIN'?
GONNA MAKE IT.
WOWF!
THEY DON'T SEEM TO BE GITTIN' NOWHERES.

NOPE.. THEY IS OUTWITTIN' EACH OTHER.

SO CHURCHY IS GOIN' INTO THE MONEY BUSINESS? YOU SAY HE'S GONNA PRINT IT ON FOOD SO'S TO POPULARIZE IT?
YEP--- HE GONNA GIVE PEOPLE A TASTE FER IT--- FOR HISSELF, THO, HE GONE PRINT ALL HIS MONEY ON LIMBURGER CHEESE SO'S FOLKS WILL MORE OR LESS LEAVE IT ALONE AN' HE'LL HAVE IT TO HIS DYIN' DAY---
DETROIT NEWS
OL' PAUL AIRD

THAT STUFF GOT A MUSCLE ON IT, IN WARM WEATHER--- AN', BOY, THEY'S GONNA BE TROUBLE IF HE TRY TO TAKE IT WITH HIM---
OOM PAUL

MONEY AIN'T ALL BEER NOR SKITTLES, YOU KNOW.

CHAPTER 11

Higglety, Pigglety,

NOW IT'S TUESDAY AN' YOU STARTS FIGHTIN' AGAIN? WHAT'S YOU FIGHTIN' ABOUT?
WELL· UH··
UM···UH IT'S A··
WHAT'D YOU BRING THAT UP FOR?

WELL?

DON'T PRESS··· WE'LL THINK OF SOMETHIN'··

ONE THING I DOES REMEMBER AFORE ME AN' BEAUREGARD STARTED FIGHTIN'··· WE WAS GITTIN' UP A TEEVY SHOW·· WANNA HEAR ONE OF OUR STORIES? TELL ONE, HOUN'DOG.

SEEMS THESE TWO EX-CONVICTS BECOMED PEN PALS 'CAUSE THEY WAS IN THE SAME PEN TOGETHER.

THAT'S NICE.

WELL! THAT'S EE-NUFF FOR ME!
NOBODY LAUGHS AT OUR JOKES.

THAT PROVES YOU HATES US --- YOU LAUGHS AT EVERBODY ELSE'S JOKES --- EVEN ONES IN OTHER COMICAL STRIPS.

BUT I DIN'T KNOW WHAT YOU TOLE WAS A JOKE --- YOU NEVER TELLS ME THAT PART.
IT IS TRUE THAT HE SAID IT WAS NICE.

THAT'S ANOTHER INSULT --- POGO TAKE SO MUCH STING OFF'N EVER'THING HE SAY THAT A SIMPLE GOODNIGHT FROM HIM COULD BE ANOTHER MAN'S: DROP DEAD!
SO, BY "NICE," HE MEANS ---?

THE SHAMEFUL WAY WE BEEN TREATED IS SO SHAMEFUL IT'S ENOUGH TO MAKE A MAN COMMIT SUICIDE.
RIGHT! BUT WHICH MAN?
HON. MIKE LAPINE

IN FACT, FRIEND, IT'D SERVE THESE NUMP-HODS AROUND HERE RIGHT IF ONE OF US DID COMMIT SUICIDE! THEN THEY'D CHANGE THEIR TUNE.
TO WHAT?

TO A FUNERAL MARCH, I GUESS-- ONLY THING IS I'D MISS YOU SO WHEN I DOES IT.
I'LL MISS YOU, TOO-- JES' MAKE SURE YOU WRITES FROM WHERE-SO-EVER YOU GOES--PERVIDIN' IT'S COOL ENOUGH.

I AIN'T GOIN' ANYWHERES! YOU DIN'T THINK I WAS GONE START RIGHT OUT COMMITTIN' SUICIDE ON MY OWN LOVIN' SELF?
WELL, YOU AIN'T GONE WARM UP ON ME, SON.

WHY DOES WE ALLUS GIT ALL THE BUM BREAKS?
WELL, WE CAN'T HAVE EVERTHING, GOOD LOOKS, CHARM, BRAINS AN' PERFECT PITCH--.
RIGHT.
MISS MARIANNA

THE BEST BREAK ANYBODY EVER GETS IS IN BEIN' ALIVE IN THE FIRST PLACE.

GULP
GULP
MISSY CRONE

AN' YOU DON'T UNNERSTAN' WHAT A PERFECT DEAL IT IS UNTIL YOU REALIZES THAT YOU AIN'T GONE BE STUCK WITH IT FOREVER, EITHER.
MISS MA'IANNA

IT'S PERFECKLY ALL RIGHT FOR PORKYPINE TO SAY THE BEST BREAK YOU GITS IS FIRST BEIN' ALIVE AN' THEN IN NOT BEIN' STUCK WITH IT BUT--
HOLE THIS A MINUTE?

~HE FERGITS THAT WHEN A MAN GITS HANDED A LONG LIFE HE STANDS A GOOD CHANCE OF STARVIN' TO DEATH A-FORE IT'S OVER.
IT'S A FRIGHTENIN' THOUGHT.
HEY! DOES YOU TWO WANNA GIT THE RAW FISH COBBLES? THEM BRIM FISHES AIN'T MORE'N WARMED UP.

CHAPTER 12

Play.

MEBBE YOU KNOWS THAT FUNNY STORY 'BOUT THE FELLA WHAT WAS A BOXER 'CAUSE HE HAD A JOB BOXIN' MUSHMELONS.
UM

I CERT'LY WOULD AD-MIRE TO HEAR IT 'CAUSE IT ALLUS CHEERS ME UP ... IT'S MY FAVORITE JOKE -- GO AHEAD AN' TELL IT IF YOU KNOWS IT.
WELL

I KNOWS THE STORY 'BOUT THE FELLA WHAT TOLE EVERY-BODY HE WAS A BOXER 'CAUSE HE HAD A JOB BOXIN' BLUEBERRIES ... CARE TO HEAR THAT ONE?
.. OH .. MMM. NO

IT WOULDN'T BE THE SAME. I ONLY ENJOYS THE OTHER ONE ... IT ALLUS GIVE ME WHAT IS CALLED A BOFF.
TOO BAD .. YOU ALLUS LAUGH IN THE KEY OF F SHARP AN' I WANTED TO TUNE THIS THING.

HERE'S WHERE THEY TOLE ME OL' MOUSE LIVES AN' SURE 'NOUGH THERE'S HIS MAIL BOX.
MOUSE

MAILBOX, BUT NO HOUSE ... MEBBE HE JES' STOP BY FOR HIS MAIL.
MOUSE

I'LL JES' LEAVE A LI'L' NOTE AN'...
AGH! YOU PEEPERIN' TOM... A MAN GOT A RIGHT TO BATHE ALONE... BESIDES YOU IS BREATHIN' A DRAFT AT ME!
MOUSE
MOUSE

DIN'T KNOW YOU WAS TAKIN' A BATH IN HERE, MOUSE -- HERE LEMME SCRUB YO' BACK -- THERE WE ARE --
MOUSE

FLAG'S UP.. MUS' BE MOUSE GOT A PICKUP.
U.S. AND A. MAIL

ALL RIGHT... COME ON! COME ON! DON'T DEE-LAY THE UNINETY-STATES MAIL.. YOU'RE A AWFUL BIG PICK-UP... YOU'LL GOTTA GO PARSTEL POATS.
I AIN'T GOIN' NOWHERES... PARSTEL POATS OR NO OTHER WAYS ELSE!
DERN TOOTIN' YOU AIN'T! NOT WITH NO STAMPS ON.
MOUS
U.S AND A MAIL

I IS THRU WITH YOU...I IS SOCIALLY OSTRICH-SIZIN' YOU FROM MY LIST.
GO AHEAD! WE BEEN DID TO LIKE WHAT YOU SAY BY MORE FANCY PEOPLE THAN YOU IS!
MOUSE

PERSON'LY I COMED OVER TO FIND OUT WHAT SURE-FIRE PLAN IT WAS YOU GIVE CHURCHY FOR MAKIN' MONEY.
UM

LET'S SEE..COULD IT OF BEEN FOR TRADIN' DOUGHNUT HOLES TO THE BUTTON HOLE PEOPLE? ..OR-UM-SAY, I HAD A DANDY FOR THIS MOTORIZED AGE...
DON'T GIVE THIS AWAY, PAL.. BUT DRIVE-IN FUNERAL PARLORS COULD BECOME A LIVIN' RAGE...QUICK, EASY CURB SERVICE AN'...
MOUSE

LOOK ME IN THE EYE AN' TELL ME AGAIN YOU THINKS DRIVE-IN FUNERAL PARLORS WOULD BE A GOOD IDEA.
WHY SHOULD I? IF YOU DON'T KNOW A GOOD BUSINESS WHEN YOU HEARS IT?
MOUSE
NEXT YOU'LL BE TELLIN' ME THEY COULD BE SELF-SERVICE OPERATIONS.
WHY NOT?

YOU SURE YOU CAN'T REMEMBER ***NO*** OTHER SCHEME 'CEPT THE **DRIVE-IN FUNERAL PARLOR** AN' **SUBSTITUTE SICKNESS**?

MOUSE

WHAT'S THE ***MATTER*** WITH **DRIVE-IN** FUNERAL PARLORS WITH ***SELF-SERVICE***?

HOW CAN YOU ***EMBALM*** YOUR OWN SELF IF YOU'RE ***DEAD?***

'LONG AS A DRIVE-IN FUNERAL PARLOR IS OUT OF THE QUESTION, HOW ABOUT THAT SICK-SERVICE I DREAMED UP?
HOW'D IT GO?

LIKE THIS --LIE DOWN-- NOW I GOTTA PLAY TWO PARTS-- FIRST I IS SICK-- BUT YO' JOB IS TO TAKE MY PLACE-- TO SAVE ME THE TROUBLE OF HAVIN' A DOCTOR EXAMINE ME ---OKAY, NOW I IS THE DOCTOR--

WELL YOUNG MAN STICK OUT YO' TONGUE OOG IT LOOK LIKE LAS' WEEK'S FLYPAPER WELL HA HA NO USE GIVIN' UP HOPE IS THEY ANY UNSANITY IN YO' FAMBLY EITHER YOU AIN'T GOT NO PULSE OR MY WATCH IS STOPPED HO HO.

YOU AIN'T GOT NO WATCH! AN' ANYTHING I HATES IS A HA-HA TYPE OF MEDICAL MAN--YOU IS CHEERFUL ENOUGH TO BE A UNDERTAKER--
WHO'S SICK? ME! THAT'S WHO. I GITS ANY KIND DOCTOR I WANTS AN' BESIDES YOU GIVE ME FOUR DOLLARS FOR A HOME CALL!

ALL RIGHT, NOW WE REVERSE THE ROLES--YOU TAKE MY PLACE AS PATIENT AND I'LL BE THE DOCTOR.
I GUESS IT CAN'T BE HELPED THOUGH I FEEL SOUND AS A DOLLAR.
WHOOF! FIRST OF ALL TAKE YO' HAT OFF IN A SICKROOM--
SOME DOCTOR! YOU CRAWLS IN BED THE MINUTE YOU GITS HERE.

NOW, LET'S SEE..
HEY! HEY! HEY! HEY!
I'M SORRY, BUT ONE OF YOU WASN'T RUNNIN'.. I COULDN'T TELL IF IT WAS YOU OR THE CLOCK.
HIC! HIC I'M .. HIC.. RUNNIN' HIC NOW..

HOWDY THERE! HEIGHDY! HOW YOU BE! HULLO!
HOWDY CHURCHY!
I AIN'T SPEAKIN' TO HIM...
LOOK AT HIM HANGIN' AROUN' WAITIN' FER A WORD FROM ME.
WE BEEN TRYIN' TO THINK OF THE MILLION DOLLAR SCHEME I GIVE YOU.

I AIN'T SPEAKIN' TO HIM.
LESSEE.. IT KIND OF IS SLUPPED MY MIND TOO.
YEH.. THEY COME AN' GO.. A DIME A DOZEN.
I AIN'T SPEAKIN' TO YOU!
WELL... STOP NOT DOIN' IT SO LOUD!

CHAPTER

13

Happily, Flappily,

IS THIS BOAT GOIN' UP TO NEW YORK, POGO...? COULD YOU ROW ME UP?
HECK, NO! THERE'S NOTHIN' UP THERE BUT PEOPLE--
OL' JOH

AN' BASEBALL---THEY TELLS ME THE NEW BALL IS ACTUALLY A JACK RABBIT--- AN' I THUNK I'D GIT A JOB-

YOU COULDN'T GIT A JOB AS A BASEBALL.. THAT AIN'T WHAT THEY MEANS...EVEN IF ANYBODY COULD THROW YOU YOU'D NEVER LAST THRU BATTIN' PRACTICE.
I GUESS YOU'RE RIGHT--COUSIN COTTONSIDES WENT UP ONE YEAR AN' HAD TO TAKE A JOB AS A PIGEON IN BRYANT PARK- WHAT A COMEDOWN, HIM A EXPERT ON RABBITTIN' AN' ALL.
THE CITY'S FIERCE.
OL' JOHN DENSON

HERE COME OWL AN' MOUSE. PROB'LY JES' ACHIN' TO GIVE US A GAME OF BALL IN HONOR OF IT BEIN' WORLD SERIES TIME.

IT'S WORLD SERIES TIME.. US OUGHT TO BE GITTIN' INTO THE GAME.
GREAT... I'LL PITCH.
YOU?

CERT'LY ME! DIN'T I USETA TRAVEL WITH THE OL' SAINT LOOEY BROWNS? (UNBEKNOWNST TO THEM OF COURSE)... BUT IF THEY'D OF PLAYED ME I'D OF STOLT EVERY BASE IN THE LEAGUE.
PHOO
IN MY EXTREME YOUTH I TRIED OUT WITH A FELLA NAMED McGRAW BUT HE CLAIMED MY KEY PLAY, STEALIN' FIRST BASE, WAS ILLEGAL.
SOME FOLKS JES' DON'T LIKE MICE, I GUESS.

MEBBE US WILL COME AN' PLAY IN THE WORLD SERIES...
SURE, DON'T BE MAD NO MORE.. WE NEEDS YO' BAT.
GOT THE BAT RIGHT HERE WITH SOME LOOSE JAM AN' BIRDS EGGS I BEEN SAVIN'.
DID YOU HEAR OUR UMPIRE STORY, POGO?
NOPE
ALBERT

SEEMS THIS UMPIRE WAS A OL' ROOSTER AN' WHEN THE CHICKENS WANTED TO GIVE A DANCE HE SAID IT WOULDN'T BE A HIT BECAUSE IT WAS A FOWL BALL... ..HO HO?
HE WAS JES' MEAN.
HE WAS A SPOILSPORT.. PEOPLE LIKE THAT MAKES ME MAD.
WELL, AT LEAST IT GOT SOME REACTION OUTEN YOU.

WHERE'S EVER'BODY ELSE ? WE WAS GONE PLAY THE WORLD SERIES... OWL HAD A GLOVE -- RABBIT GOT A MASK -

I SUPPLIED THE BASES -- WE DUG UP A COUPLE OF BATS -- MOUSE DECIDED HE COULD BE UMPIRE - YOU GOT A CHEST PER-TECTOR -

WE EVEN GOT A COUPLE UNIFORMS -- TWO OR THREE SCORE CARDS - MAM'SELLE POPPED A PECK OF POPCORN - -- AN' WE WAS ALL SET TO PLAY BALL AN' - AN'
AN' SO THEY ALL WENT HOME.

S'MATTER THEN... ? NO INTER'ST?
NOPE -
NO BALL.

OH, WHAT A PITY WE NEVER PLAYED OUR WORLD SERIES -- I WAS SHARP AS A MOUTHFUL OF MUSTARD -- READY TO PLASTER THE BALL.

AN' I WAS EQUALLY READY TO BURN MY HARD HIGH ONE ACROSS THE PLATE AN' IN A DAZZLIN' MIXTURE OF BRAINY PITCHIN' I WOULD OF STRUCK OUT NINETEEN MEN.

NEXT, TO END THE GAME, I MOUGHT OF MADE A OVER-THE-HEAD-GOIN' AWAY CATCH OF A SURE HOMER.

IT'S A PITY WE DIN'T HAVE A SCOUT DOWN FROM THE BIG LEAGUES! WITH ME PLAYIN' LIKE THAT I'D OF BEEN NEXT YEAR'S BONUS BABY.

IF YOU REALLY WANTS TO GIT INTO A SPORTS JOB WHY NOT GO DOWN TO MIAMI AN' GIT A JOB AT A DOG TRACK?

YOU COULD BE THE FIRST NON-MECHANICAL RABBIT IN THE BUSINESS.
UM

THE DOGS SCARCELY EVER CATCHES THE RABBIT.
"SCARCELY" GOT A VERY UNPLEASANT RING OF FREQUENCY TO IT.
WULL, MAYBE YOU COULD GET THE DOGS CHANGED TO MECHANICAL DOGS 'CEPT IT WOULD PUT THE REAL DOGS OUTEN BUSINESS.
ANY OTHER ARRANGEMENT WOULD PUT ME OUTEN BUSINESS.

CHAPTER 14

Mock the May,

WHAT IN THE EVER LOVIN' BLUE-EYED WORLD IS THAT?
IT'S MY SELF-INVENTED PRINTIN' PRESS -- I'SE GOIN' INTO THE BUSINESS OF PRINTIN' MONEY ON FOOD -- GONNA CORNER THE MARKET.
RIGHT NOW I IS READY TO PRINT A TEN DOLLAR BILL ON A EGG --

--SAM' WICH

'COURSE MY MACHINE GOT A FEW WRINKLES TO BE IRONED OUT.

DON'T YOU FIGGER YOU KIN GIT A-RRESTED FOR PRINTIN' YO'OWN MONEY?
'COURSE NOT-- NOBODY EVER BOTHERS THE GUMMINT FER DOIN' IT.

BUT THE GUMMINT GOT THE CONCESSION -- EVER'BODY TAKES OFF'N IT -- IT BEEN PRINTIN' MONEY FOR YEARS.
ON PAPER!

MY MONEY GONNA BE TASTY! IT'LL BE ALL THE RAGE -- JES' IMAGINE, YOU GIVES A FELLA A DOLLAR PRINTED ON A PANCAKE -- HE GIVES YOU BACK A HALF A MUSHMELON IN CHANGE.

FOR SMALL CHANGE YOU COULD PRINT PENNIES ON CAVIAR.
NOPE! NOPE! NOTHIN' ILLEGAL ABOUT THIS... NO FOREIGN CURRENCIES.

YOU NOTICE HOW THINGS BEEN GOIN' 'ROUND HERE..? FIRST THEY DON'T LAUGH AT OUR JOKES..

NEXT THEY REE-FUSE TO PLAY THE WORLD SERIES, AS IS OUR WONT, ON ACCOUNT OF HAVIN' NO BALL -- AND YOU, BEIN' MY FRIEND, WILL ADMIT WHO WOULD OF BEEN THE STAR IN THAT...
SURE.

YOU'RE MY ONLY PAL -- MY ONLY ONLY ONLY PAL -- -- WILLIN' TO ADMIT WHO WOULD OF BEEN STAR..
AIN'T NO TWO WAYS ABOUT IT -- THE STAR WOULD OF BEEN--
---ME, YOUR ONLY PAL.
HOW'D YOU LIKE A PUNCH IN THE NOSE, ONLY PAL?

IF I HAD MY WAY THIS COMIC STRIP WOULD HAVE LESS DOGS IN IT.
BUT DOGS IS THE BACKBONE OF THE AMERICAN HOME--- WITHOUT DOGS THE COUNTRY WOULD BE IN RAGS.
WHAT'S DOGS GOT TO DO WITH IT?
PEOPLE GOT A DOG THEY THINKS TWICE 'BOUT GOIN' OUT AN' RAMPIN' AROUND---

IF THEY GOT A CHILE THEY HIRES A BABY SITTER-- BUT A DOG NEEDS A FRIENDLY HAND TO FEED AN' PAT HIM-- --A DOG WITH A GOOD PEDIGREE ON HIM COST TOO MUCH TO TRUST WITH STRANGERS.
SO DOGS KEEPS THE FAMBLY AT HOME YOU THINKS?
YEP-- IF A DOG PLAYS HIS CARDS RIGHT HE KIN BE 'BOUT AS MUCH TRIAL AN' GRIEF AS A SET AN' A HALF OF TRIPLETS.

BAZZ FAZZ!

IF NOBODY APPRECIATES US HERE WE'LL GO OFF AN' GO INTO BUSINESS FOR OURSELFS.
ALBERT

THIS HAT IS THE RAGE IN NEW YORK?
THEY'LL LOVE YOU IN IT -- IN 1917 IT SOLD FOR AS MUCH AS FIFTY CENTS.
ALBERT
A-PIECE?
WULL - NO-- THEY GUV YOU A BALL BAT WITH IT AN' A PICTURE OF THE HELL-GATE BRIDGE.

I HATE THE THOUGHT OF GOIN' UP THERE TO SELL OUR NEW COMIC STRIP.. WE COULD STAY HERE IF OUR JOKES GET ACROSS.. HOW'S THIS.. MAN SAYS TO BANKER "CAN YOU FLOAT A LOAN?" BANKER SAYS, "FLOAT ALONE? I CAN'T EVEN DOG PADDLE." HO-HO?
LET'S PACK.
ALBERT

I HEAR TELL YOU IS LEAVIN' FOR THE SHIMMERIN' GAYETY OF THE BIG CITY.
YOU MAY KISS MY HAND ADIEU.
IN THE EVENT YOU IS A HONEST MAN YOU WON'T MIND REE-TURNIN' A FEW BORRIES YOU IS MADE THE LOAN OF?
SUCH AS?

SUCH AS THEM REDINGOTES, YASHMAKS, BEAVERS, KILTS, STOMACHERS, FEDORAS, BURNOOSES, PANTALOONS, KNICKERBOCKERS AND OTHER IN-EXPRESSIBLES WITH WHICH YOU IS MACARONIED-UP.
IF WE GOES UP THERE NAKED-BORN WE'LL COTCH OUR DEATH!
`SIDES WE AIN'T HAD THE BORRY OF THEM MORE'N A YEAR.
MM

WELL I WILL BE HORSE-REDDISHED.. YOU'S RETURNIN' MY DUDS!
OOP

AIN'T MORE'N HALF OF THESE IS YOURNS. I JES' COMMANDEERED `EM BACK FROM ALBERT AN' HOUN'DOG WHICH BORRIED 'EM TWO WINTERS AGONE.
IT SO LONG SINCE YOU BORRIED THE LOAN OF 'EM MY BEAVER NEED TONSORIAL ATTENTION.

IF I'D OF BORRIED 'EM I'D OF REE-TURNED 'EM AFORE THIS.
EGG-ZACKLY WHAT I TOLE THEM TWO RASCAL BONES.
WELL -- I'LL BE HORSE-REDDISHED!

SAY NO MORE! SAY NO MORE! US PROBBLE BORRIED THEM FROM YOU TO WEAR TO MR. COOLIDGE'S INAUGURIAL BALL.
I WAS A DREAM IN THAT TARBOOSH.

WHAT'S THE MATTER WITH OL' OWL AN' CHURCHY ? THEY WALKS UP WITH A BUNCH OF SMELLY OL' CLOTHES AN' SAYS THEY'S MINE--- THEY NEVER BORRIED 'EM FROM ME!

YOO-HOO! COME BACK HERE!
THESE DUDS LOOKS GOOD -- COULD USE 'EM FOR COW-BOY CLO'ES.

WELL, I'LL JES' GETHER 'EM UP AN' TOSS 'EM IN A HOLE AN' THROW DIRT ON THE WHOLE SHOOTIN' MATCH.

YOU DO AN' YOU'S GONE BURY A MIGHTY FINE LI'L' BOY A-LIVE.

UNCLE POGO GIVE ME A OL' HAT TO PLAY A LI'L' SINGLE-HANDED COWBOY.. BANG
WELL, GO OVER AN' BANG 'ROUN' HIM--
YOU ALLUS IS REE-PRESSIN' MY TALENTS.
THE CHILE'S RIGHT--LET HIM BANG!

BY GEORGE Y. WELLS I IS LEAVIN'--- --I IS RUNNIN' A-WAY FROM HOME!
?
?

WAIT A MINUTE!
US'LL GO WITH YOU.

HOW KIN A MAN RUN AWAY FROM HOME IN ANY DECENT FASHION IF HIS WHOLE CRAWFISHIN' FAMBLY TRAIPSE ALONG TOO?
YOU IS SELFISH

THE WHOLE REASON FOR EX-CAPIN' IS TO GIT AWAY FROM YO' EVER-LASTIN' SLAB-A-JAB.
YOU WANNA DENY THE BOY THE ADVANTAGES OF BEIN' ON THE LAM?

A BOY NEEDS HIS DADDY'S STRONG HAND--'SPECIALLY IN MATTERS OF DISCIPLINE AN'
HEY HO!

S'CUSE ME! MA'M, WHYN'T YOU LET ME AN' PAP TALK THIS OUT MAN TO MAN.

CHAPTER

15

Rapidly, Vapidly,

WELL, OFF (LIGHT HEARTED) WE GOES.
RIGHT! OH, THIS CROWD HERE WILL BE SORRY WHEN WE'RE GONE.

THEY WILL NOT SOON FORGET THE HAPPY, SUNLIT DAYS WE SPENT TOGETHER... AH, THE TREASURES OF OUR OLD AGE ARE THE GOLDEN HOURS OF OUR YOUTH... THERE WILL BE MANY A TEAR-STAINED PILLOW WHEN THEY REALIZE THAT WE....

I'M GOIN' BACK.. I CAN'T GO ON.
WHAT IN THE BLUE-EYED WORLD FOR?

MY TEDDY BEAR MISSES ME.

HOW CAN YOU CHANGE PLANS NOW AND GO BACK? IT'S UNTHINKABLE.
IT IS NOT.. IT'S THINKABLE ENOUGH. I THUNK OF IT.. I'M GOIN' BACK TO MY TEDDY BEAR.
HOW CAN YOUR TEDDY BEAR MISS YOU? HE AIN'T HUMAN.
HE'S AS HUMAN AS YOU IS, FRIEND.

NEXT TO WOMEN AN' CHILLUN, DOGS IS THE MOST HUMAN OF ALL ANIMALS.
WELL, MY TEDDY BEAR BEEN IN MY EM-PLOYE LONGER'N YOU IS.
HE GOT SENIORITY AN' JUNIORITY RIGHTS GOIN' BACK TO 19-OUGHT-23.
YO' IS ALLUS BEIN' TURNT BY A PERTY FACE...

NOW LET'S SEE ... SOME WHERE HERE IS MY TEDDY BEAR... IF I TAKES HIM WITH US, HE WON'T BE LONESOME AN' GRIEF STRICK.
NOT MEANIN' NO HARM, ALBERT OL' FRIEN', BUT...
I NEVER THUNK YOU WAS THE TYPE TO BE SO SENTIMENTAL OVER A OL' TEDDY BEAR.
ALBERT

HEE-HEE.. I IS HEERD OF SOME GROWED BOY HERE A BOUTS GOT A NELLY BOO... A YALLER HAIRT, BLUE-EYE-BALLED DOLLY WHAT GO: "WA-WA."
THAT'S A BALL-FACE LIE.
SNF MY NELLY BOO SAY "DA DA"..... ..SO SWEET! "DA DA" IS HOW SHE GO..MSNFF.
ALBERT

HEE HEE! NEVER THUNK YOU'D HAVE A DOLLY WHAT GOES "DA DA."
WELL IT COULDN'T GO "MAMA"... NOT TO ME.
MMMF --WELL-- WHERE'S MY LI'L' OL' TEDDY BEAR--? AHA--HERE HE BE.
I MISSES NELLY BOO.
ALBERT

CUTE?
ALBERT

MAMA

YOU DON'T EGG-SPECK A MAN KIN LEAVE HIS OWN FLESHIN' BLOOD TO WITHER AN' WANE AWAY DOES YOU?
BUT THAT TEDDY BEAR AIN'T KIN!

THIS TEDDY BEAR BEEN MORE'N A DADDY TO ME --MORE'N A MOMMA-- MORE'N A HOT WATER BOTTLE--- IT BEEN MY CONSTANT COMPANION

HM-TUM-TUM
TA RA RA-TUM

BY NEDDIE DINGO THERE'S A CLUTCH OF 'EM NOW, SON--RUN AN' GIT THEIR AUTIOGRAFTS.

PA SAYS SIGN THIS AN' IF YOU IS FROM OTTER SPACE WHERE IS YO' FLY AN' SORCERS?
GOOD LAD.

WAW! THEY SAY THEY IS ONLY FROM DOWN THE ROAD AN' DON'T WRITE FER NOTHIN'.
IMPOSTORS! DEE-STROY A SON'S FAITH IN HIS FATHER WILL YOU--?! WHAT QUEASY QUACKERY!

THAT BEAR OUGHT TO OF BEEN ARRESTED FOR THE UGLIES IN 19-OUGHT-35.
PLEASE! NOT IN FRONT OF TEDDY.
I ADMIT HE'S KINDA RAGBAGGY LOOKIN' BUT IF YOU GOTTA SAY HE'S UGLY--SPELL IT OUT-- U-G-H-E-L-T-Y-E- THAT WAY YOU WON'T HURT HIS FEELIN'S--HE DON'T SPELL GOOD.

WE MUST BE MISSED PERTY BAD BY NOW.

OUR FRIENDS IS PROB'LY CRYIN' THEIR HEARTS OUT··· **SOBBIN'** AN' ***WEEPIN'*** -- ***YEARNIN'*** FOR OUR RETURN.
TWO SOLID WEEKS OF GRIEF WE IS GRATUITOUSLY GIVE 'EM.

THERE'S OL' PORKY-- ***LOOKIN'*** ***SAD!*** POOR PORKY.
PORKYPINE! DON'T ***MISS*** US SO-- **CHEER UP, WE'LL COME BACK!**

COME BACK? YOU BEEN AWAY?

CAN YOU IMAGINE ***THAT?*** **PORKYPINE** DIN'T EVEN KNOW WE WAS FIXIN' TO ***LEAVE***··· AN' **I** THUNK HE LOOKED **SAD** ON **ACCOUNT** WE WAS **GONE**.
HE'S A ***PROFESSIONAL*** **SAD-LOOKER**.
HE'S ***ALWAYS*** SAD-LOOKIN' WHETHER WE IS ***LEAVIN'*** OR **COMIN' BACK**--
I'VE **NEVER** SEED HIM **HAPPY**--TO GIVE HIM HIS DUE.

MATTER OF FACK HE LOOKED A TRACE LESS SAD THIS TIME-- HIS GRIMACE MOUGHT OF BEEN A SORTA CHEAP SMILE.
I WAS THINKIN' THAT TOO -- YOU FIGGER HE WAS AMUSED AT US?

US? THE BEST DRESSED MEN SOUTH OF WINNIPEGOSIS? WHAT IMPERTIMINTS OF HIM!
I GOT A GOOD MIND TO TELL HIM OFF -- MAKE HIM LAUGH ON T'OTHER SIDE OF HIS FACE.

NINE O'CLOCK AND ALL IS AS WELL AS CAN BE EXPECTED.
HERE I THOUGHT IF WE WENT TO A LOT OF TROUBLE TO LEAVE IT WOULD BE APPRECIATED AN'- WHAT'S THAT?

IT'S BIG BUN! IT CAN'T BE NINE O'CLOCK, BUN.
WHY CAN'T IT? WHO'S IN CHARGE OF THIS CLOCK?

THE HANDS SAY THREE O'CLOCK.
YOU GONNA BELIEVE A PIECE OF OL' McANNICKLE APP-ARATUMUS OR YOU GONNA BELIEVE ME, YOUR FRIEND?

LOOKIN' AT IT LIKE THIS, IT SAYS HALF PAST EIGHT.
AN' IT'D TAKE A HALF HOUR TO TURN THE CLOCK UPSIDE DOWN. BY THEN IT'S NINE ON THE NOSE -- WHAT MORE DO YOU WANT?

HOW'D YOU COME TO BE IN CHARGE OF A GRANDFATHER CLOCK, BUN?
I BOUGHT IT FROM A OL' PARTY WHAT NEVER RUN IT MUCH... HE ONLY LOOKED AT IT ON CHRISTMAS.
WAS HE A GRANDFATHER?
NATURALLY.. YOU GOTTA BE A BONA FRIED GRAN'PA TO DRIVE ONE OF THESE THINGS --STATE LAW YOU KNOW.

DOES YOU MEAN TO SAY YOU IS A GRAN'FATHER?
WULL -- WHEN HE TURNED OVER THE KEYS TO THE CLOCK HE GIVE ME HIS PEDIGREE, TOO.
TO BE A GRAN'PA YOU GOTTA HAVE GRAN'CHILLUN.. DID THIS FELLA TURN OVER HIS GRAN'CHILLUN AS WELL?
YEP--BUT THEY WAS A LAZY LOT.. HADN'T MOVED IN YEARS..WHEN HE TURNED 'EM OVER SPIDERS RUN OUT FROM UNDER SO WE LEFT 'EM BE.

WELL...YOU TOLE US WHAT HAPPENED TO THIS HERE GRAN'PA'S GRAN'CHILLUN BUT HOW 'BOUT GRAN'MA?
SHE EVIDENTLY RUN OFF WITH A ROCKIN' CHAIR SALESMAN, NAME OF LOUIE LOCHINVAR.
ALL WE HEARD AS THEY RODE OFF IN A TANDEM ROCKIN' CHAIR WAS THE PIERCIN' SOPRANO OF GRAN'MA SINGIN' "OL' LOCHINVAR GOT ME."
'TAIN'T NEW, FRIEND.

LOVE IS A OLD STORY! ANYWAYS THE GRAN'PA LIVED OUT IN THE CLOCK... IT WOULD GET MIGHTY COLD.. SO THE CHILLUN WOULD INVITE HIM IN FOR MEALS... ONE EVENIN' ONE SAYS, "LET'S HAVE COLD GRANDFATHER FOR DINNER."

"AIN'T YOU EVEN GONNA WARM HIM OVER?" I ASKED...SO THAT'S HOW I WON FAVOR AN' HE SOLD ME THE CLOCK WITH A NINETY-NINE YEAR GUARANTEE...
ON YOU OR THE CLOCK?
OORG.

IF THAT GRANDFATHER GIVE YOU A GUARANTEE ON THE CLOCK FOR 99 YEAR HOW COME HE DIDN'T MAKE IT A EVEN HUNDRED?
WELL--THEY'D GAVE THE CLOCK A TRIAL RUN AN' 99 WAS ALL SHE'D DO.. SO GRAN'PA SAYS, "IF SHE DON'T RUN 99 YEARS FOR YOU COME BACK AN'--"
OKEEFENOKEE
MR. WILL COX

DANG BLANG IT! IF YOU GONNA TELL SUCH STORIES WHYN'T YOU GO WHOLE HOG AND SAY A HUNDRED YEARS WHILES YOU'S AT IT?
AS OL' UNCLE WILL WOULD SAY, YOU WOULDN'T WANT ME TO LIE FOR JES' ONE MEASLY DOG-BONED YEAR, WOULD YOU?
THE HON. WILL COX
WAYCROSS

CHAPTER 16

Blow.

CHAPTER 17

Gimpily, Simpily,

ALL I WAS TRYIN' TO DO WAS MAKE **HAVIN' MONEY** A MORE TASTEFUL TYPE ACTIVITY.

WHAT COULD BE MORE PLEASANT THAN TO REACH INTO YO' **POCKLEBOOK** AN' PULL OUT A FIVE DOLLAR BILL PRINTED ON ***LIVERWISHT?*** BUT ***NO,*** THE GUMMINT AIN'T GONE LET ***NOBODY*** ELSE PRINT MONEY...

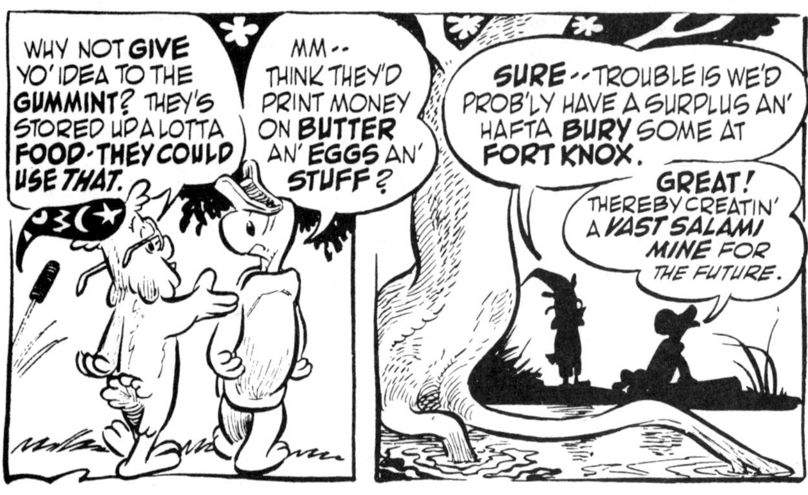
WHY NOT **GIVE** YO' IDEA TO THE **GUMMINT**? THEY'S STORED UP A LOTTA **FOOD**- **THEY COULD USE *THAT*.**
MM-- THINK THEY'D PRINT MONEY ON **BUTTER** AN' **EGGS** AN' **STUFF**?
SURE--TROUBLE IS WE'D PROB'LY HAVE A SURPLUS AN' HAFTA **BURY** SOME AT **FORT KNOX.**
GREAT! THEREBY CREATIN' A ***VAST SALAMI MINE*** FOR *THE FUTURE.*

IF THE GUMMINT ***DO*** PRINT MONEY ON SURPLUS FOOD MEBBE SOME OF IT'D GIT **ABROAD** AN' SOMEBODY'D GIT ***FED.***
PERFECKLY ALLRIGHT FOR ***THEM*** TO PRINT IT BUT IF **I** TRY IT I'LL GIT LOCKED IN THE **ROCK-HOCKEY HOUSE.**
FOR ***HUNDERDS*** OF YEARS AS OL' **MAILMAN DUCK** SAID--AN' THEN ***YOU*** SAYS I'D BE PRACTICAL **DEAD** WHEN **PENSIONED OFF**-
VIVE ST. CHA
LES

THERE'S NO FUTURE IN THAT.
YOU'D BE CONDEMNED! BUT THINK OF ALL THE HEALTHY BREAKFASTS THE CONDEMNED MAN... (NAMELY YOU) COULD EAT IN 200 YEARS.
THAT WOULD BE ROUGHLY 73,000 OF YOUR FAVORITE TYPE BREAKFASTS! FREE!
73,000 STACKS OF GRIDDLE CAKES AN' SAUSAGES? A AVERAGE OF SIX TO A STACK AN'-WHOO! I'D BE WORKIN' MY WAY THRU JAIL!
VIVE ST. CHARLES

H'LO THERE, UNCLE POGO, AN' H'LO THERE, GRUNDOON, I AIN'T SEEN YOU SINCE PA DECIDED HE COULDN'T AFFORD TO RUN AWAY FROM HOME 'CAUSE WE ALL WANTED TO GO WITH HIM, IS I?
GNX
NOPE
WHITE HOPES AND OTHER TIGERS
WELL.. HOW'S THINGS WITH YOU, GRUNDOON? KEEPIN' BUSY?
ZMNX KPSTVWN RQFSBD NP NP NP NP!
WHITE HOPES AND

NP!? GOSH, WODDYA THINK OF THAT, UNCLE POGO?
NOT MUCH.. AN' NEITHER DO YOU YOU KNOW OL' GRUNDOON'S TALK DON'T MAKE SENSE.
WHITE HOPES AND
WULL.. WHAT OF IT..? HE'S NO DIFFER'NT ANYBODY ELSE.. HE'S JES' INNERESTED IN TALKIN'... MAKIN' SENSE IS A ENTIRELY DIFFER'NT TALENT.

WHAT'S YOU USIN' FOR BAIT, UNCLE POGO?
THE USUAL, CAVIAR, BONBONS, CHAMPAGNE AND MINK.

BEST BAIT I IS FOUND FOR SURE KETCHIN' IS GRUNDOON.
GRUNDOON?

YEP, YOU GITS HIM BY THE PANTS AN' HANG HIM DOWN NEAR THE WATER--- HE MAKES A NOISE LIKE A FISH --- ONE SURFACES AN' SNAP!
GRS GRS

SNAP? MY SAKES! DO THE FISHES BITE HIM AN' YOU HAULS 'EM IN?
NOPE--HE BITES THE FISH AN' WE HAULS 'EM IN ---ONLY TROUBLE IS IT'S KINDA HARD MAKIN' HIM LET GO.
GRS

I SWEAR THAT TURTLE GITS BRAINLESSER AND BRAIN-LESSER EVERY DAY.
DON'T SWEAR 'N FRONT THE CHILDER.
RIGHT
GRS

I WASN'T SWEARIN'.. WHAT'S YOU DOIN'?
YOU WAS TOO.. YOU SAID SO.

I WAS NOT-- I TAKES MY OATH THAT I -
YOU AIN'T GONE USE NO OATH IN FRONT OF THESE INNOCEMENT EARS-- TEACHIN' BAD WORDS!
HOW 'BOUT MY EARS? I IS DELICATE.
HOW COULD I TEACH GRUNDOON BAD WORDS?--HE DON'T KNOW ANY GOOD ONES-- HE CAN'T TALK.
HE TALKS TO FISHES... YOU WANT THEM CURSIN' AN' CARRYIN' ON?
YEH... FISH GOT CHILLUN TOO.

HOW CAN YOU SAY GRUNDOON TALKS TO FISH?! HE CAN'T TALK A-TALL.
I TAKES THE WORD OF THE CHILE EXPERT HERE, RACKETY COON CHILE, ON ACCOUNT HE'S A EXPERT CHILE HISSELF.
RIGHT

ALL RIGHT, PROFESSOR, WHAT KINDA OF A NOISE DOES GRUNDOON THINK FISHES MAKES?
LISTEN
GRS

DO YOU TAKE ME FOR A NINCOMPOST? "GRS" HA! -- INDEED! IMAGINE A FISH RESPONDING TO GRS!

GRS!

I STILL DON'T BELIEVE THAT FISH SAY "GRS!" MAYBE OUT OF WATER--- BUT UNDERBENEATH OF IT? HA!
GRS
WHY DON'T YOU ROOM WITH A FISH NEXT SEMESTER AN' TAKE NOTES?
BY JING --- I'SE GONE FIND OUT RIGHT NOW!
BLOOB

YOU BETTER COME UP AFORE US HAFTA GIVE YOU ARTIE-OFFICIAL RESUSQUEHANNA.

DULLEST CONVERSATION I IS EVER LISTENED TO--"GRS--GRS--GRS GRS--WELL HELLO, GRS, HOW'S MRS. GRS AN' ALL THE LI'L' GRS'S?" PHOO ON FISH!
THEY ALLUS SPEAKS WELL OF YOU, GRS.

GOOD NEWS! THE PAPER SAY THEY IS GONNA DROP THE BOMB!
WHAT?
ON ARMISTICE DAY?
I MEANS THEY'S GONNA USE ATOMS FOR PEACE AN' STUFF LIKE THAT 'STEAD OF SO MUCH BOMBS AN' ALL..
YOU DIN'T SAY THAT--YOU GIVED US COLD COBBLES. YOU SAID THEY'S GONE DROP THE BOMB.
THE MUDFLAT MOAN

THEY IS? ON WHO?
ON NOBODY 'CORDIN' TO YOU.
I NEVER SAID NOTHIN'
YOU DID TOO! YOU SAID ...

TWO MINUTES OF SILENCE IS ARRIVED JES' IN TIME.

I WANT TO BE THE FIRST TO HAVE YOU CONGRATULATE ME!
WHAT HAVE I DONE TO DESERVE IT?

AS I PREE-DICTED, FRIDAY THE THIRTEENTH COME ON A SUNDAY THIS MONTH... NO BAD LUCK HARDLY A-TALL.
ONCE AGAIN I'M SPEECHLESS.
NOT ME.

I COULD SAY A FEW WORDS ABOUT WHAT YOU JUST SAID... BE GLAD TO SIR, ... I SAY, SIR-SIR?
BEHOLE, THERE GO THE CHURCH-MICE FAMBLY ... CELEBRATED THE DAY AT HOME NO DOUBT.
EVERYDAY IS SUNDAY AT OUR PLACE.
AN' IT'S MAKIN' ME OLD AFORE MY TIME ... 365 DAYS OF SUNDAY SCHOOL A YEAR ... 'NOUGH TO LAST THE AVERAGE SPRAT 'TIL HE'S A OL' MAN OF THIRTY OR MORE.
SIR?

CHAPTER 18

Crow the Cry,

HOME!! a masterpiece OF NAVIGATION ALL THE WAY TO THE SWEET SUWANNEE'S SOURCE FROM JERSEY CITY, LILY of the GARDEN STATE!!
WHAT WILL I DO WITH THE PUMPED-UP SEA HORSE, O MINE CRISTOBAL?
LEAVE IT BE!
LEAVE IT BE? IT'S GOT NINE HUNDERD CUBIC POUNDS OF MY PERSONAL BREATHIN' IN IT-- DON'T I EVEN GET MY BREATH BACK?

COME along.. COME A-LONG!
DRAGONS, MERMAINS, PIXLES, ELFS AND SEA SERPENTS ARE ALL NON-EXISTENT, JEROME, AS YOUR GRAMPA ALLUS SAID AN'...
YEH YEH YEP
AACK! YOU LEGENDARY LUNKHEAD! YOU'VE DESTROYED THE FAITH OF A SON IN BOTH OUR FATHERS!

HEY! HEY! HEY! DROP EVERYTHING! I GOT A SPECIAL DIS-PATCH FLASHED HERE FROM P.T. BRIDGEPORT AN' TAMMANANNY WHAT WENT UP TO RADIO CITY TO SEEK THEIR FORTUNES IN THE TEEVIES!
Z
ZZ
COME ON! DROP WHAT YOU IS DOIN'... THAT KIN KEEP.... THIS HERE'S A SPECIAL DEE-LIVERARY MESSAGE FROM TWO IM-PORTANT PEOPLE...
ZZZZ!

IS YOU IN CHARGE WHILST THEY IS BUSY? IF SO, MEBBE I KIN LEAVE THIS WITH YOU, SIR, AN' I KIN SIGN THE REE-CEET FOR YOU... WHAT'S THE NAME?
GNXBTQ
GNXB-WHAT?
PST! HOW DO YOU SPELL THE TAD'S NAME? I'M GONNA SIGN THIS FOR HIM SO'S TO NOT DISTURB YOU, MY DEAR SIR... HOW'S IT GO AGAIN...? GESUND-HOW?
ZNWZ!

A FINE THING.. HERE I RUSHES THIS SPECIAL DELIVERARY LETTER FROM P.T. AN' TIGER TO THEM AN' THEY'S TOO LAZY TO WAKE UP AN' SIGN FER IT...
OH, IT DON'T PAY... FOLKS WON'T SPEND THE EXTER FER AIRMAIL NEITHER. SO I NEVER GITS TO FLY... IT'S WALK WALK WALK WALK WALK
HA! THE MAIL-MAN...

CHAPTER 19

Dimpily, Limpily,

HERE; HOLE THE HAT WHILST I CRAWDADS AROUN' ON MY BACK... LEASTWISE YOU AIN'T A JABBY-WOCKER LIKE THAT RABBIT.... --HE MUST OF WAS BORNED ON THE TOP FLOOR OF A PHONO-GRAFT!

SMOOP

IS YOU FIGHTIN' OR KISSIN'?

YO' QUIET DEE-MEANOR DEMEANS OUR ACQUAINTANCESHIP..UNDER BENEATH YOU IS PLOTTIN' SOME KIND OF INSCRUTABOBBLE ORIENTAL LOW JINX.
YOU KIN SMILE AN' SMILE AN' YET BE A VILLAIN.

RUN OUT ON ME!
COMMUNIST! YOU PUT OUT MY SEE-GAR.

SPEAK TO ME! SPEAK TO ME! I DIN'T MEAN TO REALLY FLATTEN YOU... JUST WHEN WE WAS BEGINNIN' TO UNDERSTAND EACH OTHER, YOU UNEXPECTEDLY PASSES AWAY.

OH, THE GOOD FRIENDS WE COULD OF BEEN... WE WAS TWO OF A KIND... FULL OF ROBUST GOOD HUMOR.. THERE WE WAS, HAVIN' FUN FIGHTIN'.. (ME WINNIN' A LI'L) ...AN' YOU EXPIRES...

NO TIME FOR A FEW KIND LAST DYIN' WORDS--- YOU IS SEIZED SUDDEN BY A SEIZURE -- YOU TURNS TO ME, YOUR PAL, AN' "SSS!" YOU GOES--- "HISS-SSS," YOU HISSES AT ME!
SNIFF

YOU MISER'BLE DOG!

C'MON NOW-- STOP STALLIN'--- LEMME PICK YOU UP AN' ARRANGE A SUITABOBBLE BUNCH OF LAST RITES.

MMPH! SOMEHOW YOU IS PICKED UP CONSIDER'BLE WEIGHT.

DOGGONE! THE RIGORS OF YO' MORTIS IS THROWED A SNEAK PUNCH AFTER THE BELL..

ALBERT! YOU LOOKS PUZZLED.. MEBBE MY FRESH YOUNG BRAIN KIN HELP ON ACCOUNT I AIN'T USED IT TODAY.
I GOT A RIGOR MORTAL OVER THERE WHAT'S DEE-FYIN' HIS OWN FUNERAL.
MY WORD.. HE'S A FLAT ONE.. HOW'D HE GIT LIKE THAT?
WE WAS HAVIN' A LI'L' CONTEST OF SKILL AN' HE SUDDEN EXPIRED.

PHOOMPH.. YO' FRIEND AIN'T REAL ALIVE NO-HOW.
I KNOWS THAT.. HE PASSED ON UN-EXPECTED DURIN' THE FRACAS. BUT HE'S STILL PERTY TRICKY.
THIS HERE'S NOTHIN' BUT ONE OF THEM RUBBER BEACH HORSES!
BY JING, IT'S GITTIN' SO A MAN CAN'T EVEN DEPEND ON HIS ENEMIES.

CHAPTER 20

Do.

FUNNY THING, ME AN' ALBERT WAS THINKIN' OF GOIN' TO NEW YORK FOR NEARLY THREE WEEKS AN' NOT A SOUL MISSED US...

HERE I AN' P.T. IS OFF IN JERSEY CITY FOR MONTHS AN' NARY ONE "HELLO!". NOT A "WELCOME HOME." HAWGH!
TAMMANANNY! OL' TIGER!
HOUN'DOG! YOU OL' BEAUREGARD YOU!

BY NEDDIE DINGO! IT'S GOOD TO SEE YOU!
AND YOU! A SIGHT FOR SORE EYES!
I'M GLAD I'M BACK!
I'M GLAD I'M BACK!

YOU WAS AWAY?

IT SURE IS DISCOURAGIN' TO GO ABROAD AN' DON'T HAVE NOBODY DO NIP-UPS ON ONE'S RETURN.
I COULD OF SWORE YOU'D ALL BE OUT TO SHOUT, "WELL DONE!" WHEN WE RETURNED...

IT SEEMED TO ME THERE MIGHT BE A PARADE... LIKE WHEN HEROES RETURN TO LOWER BROADWAY THEY GITS A TICKER TAPE SHOWER!... BANDS PLAY... BEAUTIFUL GIRLS THROW ROSES... MAYORS GREET..

...NOT EVERYBODY GOES OFF TO SEEK HIS FORTUNE--NOT EVERYBODY HAS THE HEART--NOT EVERYBODY COMES BACK COVERED WITH GLORY, HONOR AND THE LOVE OF A GREAT PUBLIC--
IF WE'D ONLY KNOWED.

YES... LIKE I SAY, NOT EVERYBODY COMES BACK COVERED WITH GLORY, HONOR AND THE LOVE OF A GREAT PUBLIC ...BUT 'LEAST WE'RE BACK.
SOME DON'T GIT THAT FAR.

SOME PEOPLE GITS ALL THE BREAKS... YOU AN' P.T. GITS TO TRAVEL TO THE BIG TOWN AN' BECOMES INVOLVED IN SUCCESS.

SUCCESS..THE GILDED GODDESS WAS YOURS.. YOURS IN A EN-CHANTED LAND OF LOTUS AN' LACE.
SUCCESS?! ANYBODY CAN GET AS FAR AS JERSEY CITY WHICH WAS AS FAR AS WE WENT... NO ENCHANTMENT TO SPEAK OF.

WELL, AT LEAST YOU STRUCK OUT ON YOUR OWN.
WE STRUCK OUT ALLRIGHT-- WE DIN'T EVEN GIT A MAN ON FIRST BASE.

WHAT I MEANS YOU HAD THE GUMPTION AT LEAST TO BE ANYWAYS A FAILURE ...MOST OF US NEVER EVEN TRIES FER THAT.
DOGGONE! IF YOU WANNA BE A FAILURE, I CAN SHOW YOU HOW TO DO IT IN ONE EASY LESSON IN YO' SPARE TIME.

AS FER ME I FAIL TO SEE THE NECESSITY OF TRAVELIN' FAR AFIELD IN SEARCH OF OPPORTUNITY.
YOU MEAN YOU CAN GET THE CHANCE TO FLOP AT HOME AS WELL AS ABROAD?
IT'S ALL ACCORDIN' TO HOW YOU LOOK AT IT.. TAKE COUSIN EARS.. HE TOOK A JOB AS A HEARING AIDE ..SORT OF A VICE PRESIDENT TO A HARD OF HEARING GENERAL.

ONE DAY THE GENERAL CALLS IN EARS AN' SAYS: "SERGEANT, I'M WORRIED." AN' COUSIN EARS SHOUTS: "HOW CAN YOU BE? I NEVER TELL YOU ANYTHING THAT'LL WORRY YOU EVEN IF I HEAR IT."
"THAT'S WHAT WORRIES ME!" CRIED THE GENERAL, "HOW CAN I TELL IF THE ENEMY'S ON MY TRAIL?" "EASY" SCREAMED EARS. "YOU'LL SEE ME RUNNIN' AHEAD OF YOU WITHOUT WAITIN' FOR INSTRUCTIONS." STRANGELY, WE NEVER HEARD OF HIM AGAIN.

WHEN YOU AN' P.T. LEFT FOR THE BIG CITY WHAT LINE WAS YOU GOIN' INTO?
INTO TEEVY! WE DECIDED SHOW BUSINESS WAS DEAD AN' TO GIT INTO A EN-TIRELY DIFFERNT FIELD.
AH, YES.. THE LINE WHERE THEY ASKS YOU QUESTIONS AN' PAYS YOU BIG MONEY.
YEP.. I WAS ALL GROOMED FOR THE $63,999.99 QUESTION PROGRAM

$63,999.99 QUESTION PROGRAM? A ODD SUM.
YES... IT WAS A LOW BUDGET SHOW.. ...THEY KNOCKED A LITTLE OFF.

WELL, I ARRIVED AN' SAID, "I HAVE A $63,999.99 ANSWER FOR YOU!" "WHAT IS IT?" THEY INQUIRED. "THE ANSWER" I SAID CALMLY "IS NORTH DAKOTA IN THE YEAR 1822." "SPLENDID" SCREAMED A QUIET CHAP," BUT WE HAVE NO QUESTION FOR THAT ANSWER." WELL, I'D DONE MY PART SO I PHONED THE POLICE AND...

NOT MEANIN' TO BE NOSEY BUT WHAT KIND OF A QUESTION WOULD YOUR ANSWER "NORTH DAKOTA IN 1822" HAVE FITTED?
SHUCKS! THAT WASN'T MY JOB I WASN'T IN CHARGE OF THE TEEVY PROGRAM.
OL LOU CUWAN

BY GEORGE, IF THEY DIDN'T HAVE A QUESTION TO FIT THE ANSWER THAT WASN'T MY LOOKOUT.

I KNOWED A FELLOW OVER IN AUGUSTA WHAT GOT HOME TIRED IN THE AFTERNOON AN' SAT LOOKIN' OUT THE WINDOW FOR TWO HOURS FIGURIN' IT WAS A TELEVISION SET...
THE HON. MR. LOU C.

HIS WIFE LOOKED IN THE WINDOW TO SEE IF HE WAS HOME -- AN' WHEN SHE ENTERED, HE HOLLERED: "GERT, I SEEN YOU ON THE TEEVIES, BUT YOU COME IN UGLY." "AN' THAT'S THE WAY YOU'RE GOIN' OUT," SHE SAID, AN'.....
HO HUM

THE NEXT THING THIS FELLOW SAYS TO HIS WIFE WHEN HE'D BEEN LOOKIN' OUT THE WINDOW THINKIN' HE WAS WATCHIN' THE TEEVY WAS--"SAW THE BEST SHOW I EVER SAW-
OL' TIM WEEKS

"ALL ABOUT BIRDS--WALKIN' ON A LAWN JUST LIKE OURS." HIS WIFE SAYS: "YOU'RE A DOPE--- THE FINANCE COMPANY TOOK OUR SET THIS A.M.!---" (YOU FELLOWS PULL ANY FURTHER AWAY YOU'LL UPSET THE BOAT.)
WE KNOW.

"YOU," CONTINUES THE WIFE TO THE HUSBAND "HAVE JUST SPENT TWO HOURS LOOKIN' OUT THE WINDOW!" THE MAN WAS INSULTED.
OL' TIM

"YOU MEAN I BEEN WASTIN' MY TIME WATCHIN' REAL BIRDS?" HE HOLLERED--AN'.. HEY, FELLOWS, YOU'RE GETTIN' SO FAR AWAY YOU WON'T HEAR THE REST OF THE STORY...
WE KNOW.

CHAPTER 21

Hoppingly, Stoppingly,

HOW GOOD OF YOU TO TURN OUT TO WELCOME US BACK TO OUR NATIVE SOIL... WE, WHO DISCOVERED AMERICA...HUZZAH, MR. PRESIDENT.

BUT.. I ...UH. ...YOU..NOBODY HERE IS PRESIDENT ..UH... YOU MUST OF GOT OFF AT THE WRONG STOP.

HO HO! THANK YOU FOR THAT MODEST SPEECH OF WELCOME... IT IS GOOD TO SEE THAT THIS LAND WHICH WE DISCOVERED SO MANY YEARS AGO WAS LEFT IN SUCH GOOD HANDS.

YOUR STEWARDSHIP WAS WELL DISCHARGED! BOTH OF YOU MAY SIT DOWN... I'LL ISSUE YOU A PERMIT TO GO ON BREATHING IN THE MORNING.. HA HA TO ALL.
YOU SAID IT.

THE MINUTE I HEARD YOU WERE ELECTED PRESIDENT, MR. POSSUM, I SAID TO MY CRUSTY-CRESTED COCKADOO HERE, I SAID, "LET'S GO SEE HIM BEFORE HE INVITES US! HE'LL BE TICKLED TO DEATH."
POLLY WANT A CRACKER?
MY NAME AIN'T POLLY.

BUT I AIN'T PRESIDENT.. ALL'S WE HAD WAS NOMINATION CONVENTIONS.
YES...YES, YOUR SYSTEM HAS A FEW HOLES IN IT, BUT WE CAN FIX THAT.
YOU SAID IT.

EVEN SO, I WON'T BE ELECTED... I PROB'LY WON'T GIT MORE'N 25 PERCENT OF THE VOTE.
WHO WILL GET THE OTHER 99 AND 9/10 PERCENT...
WHAT!? ARE YOU CRAZY?
YOU SAID IT.
OF COURSE 99 9/10 PERCENT REMAINS FOR THE WINNER... IT REMINDS ME OF A PROVERB: "FIGURES DON'T LIE WHEN THERE'S ONLY ONE SET OF BOOKS...YOURS." WHY SHOULD THE WINNER HAVE LESS THAN A MAJORITY?
YOU GOT SOMETHIN'... MEBBE GLASSES WOULD HELP.

ME AND MY TRAINED COCKADOO HERE EXTENDS GREETINGS AND HA-HA WITH FLOWERS AND GARLANDS FOR YOU.
I DON'T WANT 'EM.

AND A GARLAND FOR YOU, SIR, WHICH YOU WILL WEAR WITH A HAPPY HEART SHOWING HOW GLAD YOU ARE THAT OUR VISIT TO YOU WILL LAST INDEFINITELY.

JES' A DOG BONED MINUTE! HOW KIN YOU PLAIN BARGE INTO OUR PERSONAL SWAMP AN' ALL OF A SUDDEN JES' TAKE OVER AN' TELL US WHAT TO DO?

WHY, IT'S INTRINSICALLY A FOREGONE AND WIDELY ACCEPTED PROVEN THEORY, AS EVERY ONE KNOWS; I, -- FRIEND, AM BIGGER'N YOU!
YOU SAID IT.

I BROUGHT A LITTLE TOKEN OF ESTEEM AND THANKS.. A GIFT... WROUGHT WITH LOVING CARE.
POLLY WANT A CRACKER? HA HA HA HA HA.
NO THANKS.
YOU SAID IT!
A HORSE... A WOODEN HORSE... INSIDE IT'S ALL HOLLOW... FIRST TIME IT'S EVER BEEN DONE! WE INVENTED HOLLOWNESS.
FOR HOLLOW WEEN?

NO.. NO.. FOR OUR BELOVED COUNTRY... WE WILL DEVELOP NEXT HOLLOW PEOPLE.
IN OUR COUNTRY WE FILL OUR HOLLOW HORSES FULL OF HORSE MEAT... IT'S A GOOD PLACE TO STORE IT UP.
FINE! FINE! JUST, HO HO, EVER SO FINE... I'LL ISSUE YOU BOTH A PERMIT TO INVENT THAT IDEA OR I CAN, HA HA, TAKE IT OFF YOUR HAND NOW.
YOU SAID IT.

YES, LITTLE COMPANIONS, YOU MIGHT LIKE TO KNOW THAT I HAVE JUST WRITTEN A BOOK, ALL ABOUT AMERICA... WRITTEN FROM A COMPLETELY UNPREJUDICED VIEW.

I DON'T KNOW A THING ABOUT IT AND SO HAVE HAD A FREE MIND... SEE, RIGHT THERE IN BLACK AND WHITE IT SAYS MY FATHER-IN-LAW DISCOVERED AMERICA IN 1906.
BUT THAT'S WRONG!

FUNNY CHILD! IT CAN'T BE WRONG, I WROTE IT! IT'S IN PRINT! DID YOU KNOW MY FATHER-IN-LAW? WERE YOU AROUND IN 1906? CHECK ONE: NO... OR NO....
SUPPOSE I SAID YES!
HA HO! A HUMORIST! MY QUESTION HAD NO "YES" FOR AN ANSWER... YOU ARE JOKING! AH, THIS IS GOOD! YOU HAVE KEPT LAUGHTER ALIVE IN MY FATHER-IN-LAW'S COUNTRY!
DO WE GOTTA GO ON BEIN' POUTE?

NOT MEANIN' ANY OFFENSE, 'CAUSE YOU IS A GUEST, BUT THO' YOU IS BIGGER'N ME, I GOT A FEW POINTS YOU AIN'T CONSIDERED.
YOU SAID IT.
A KINDLY WORD OF INSTRUCTION... I MAKE THE JOKES!
YOU SAID IT!

THIS ALL REMINDS ME OF AN OLD PROVERB: "A BIRD IN THE POT IS WORTH TWO IN THE MORNING." AMUSING, NO?
YOU SAID IT.
YOU SEE, LITTLE COMPANIONS, YOU CAN'T FIGHT IT... EVENTUALLY EVERYBODY LOVES ME.. AND I LOVE THEM TO PIECES... IT IS BECAUSE I AM SO JOLLY WITH ALL THE HA HA.
HA
HA

HAVIN' THIS HERE GUEST POSES A PROBLEM.. WE GOT ONE FISH... HOW WE GONNA DIVIDE IT?
THAT REMINDS ME OF A PROVERB.
"EVEN A MOUSE CAN HELP A LION BUT A LION HELPS HIMSELF."
HEY! HOW COME?

BECAUSE, AS IS GENERALLY WELL KNOWN, I AM BIGGER'N YOU! A LAW OF THE.... UM
YOU IS BIGGER'N WHO?

BUT, AS I WAS SAYING, BIG AS I AM, MY HEART HOLDS NOTHING BUT LOVE FOR EVERYBODY...'SPECIALLY FOR EVERYBODY WHAT'S BIGGER'N ME.

YOU GOT A NERVE COMIN' AROUND AN' ACTIN' LIKE A LANDLORD.
YOU BETTER MOVE ALONG A LITTLE.. THE ROAD AIN'T WIDE ENUF HERE FOR ALL YOU WHEELS.

BUT YOU DON'T UNDERSTAND... WE COME WITH OPEN HEARTS.
YOU SAID IT.
I AIN'T THE FRIENDLY TYPE.

AND I AIN'T GITTIN' ANY FRIENDLIER.. YOU BOTH LOOKS LIKE BUMS TO ME.
YOU SAID IT.

YOUR BIRD IS SMARTER NOR YOU ANYWAYS.
YOU SAID IT.
IF YOU'RE SO SMART, LEARN A NEW LINE.

I BEEN GLAD TO SEE YOU IN MY TIME, ALBERT, BUT I NEVER BEEN AS GLAD AS HOW GLAD I WAS THIS TIME.
I FEEL LIKE SMILIN' MYSELF.
WHY NATCH!
NOT ONLY WAS WE HAPPY TO HAVE MR. PIG RUN OFF BUT WE BEEN WAITIN' TO HEAR HOW THE CONVENTIONS COME OUT.

YOU MEAN YOU DON'T KNOW?! WHY, YOU IS IN LINE FOR CORN-GRATULATIONS, SON!
WHO CHOSE HIM FOR NOMINEE? DEMOCRATS OR REPUBLICANS?
WULL... NEITHER, EXACTLY...WE KINDA GOT LOST AN' WOUND UP FISHIN' OVER YONDER.. SO WE HELD OUR OWN CONVENTION AND NOMINATED AND ELECTED POGO PRESIDENT OF OUR NEW FISHIN' CLUB.
AW GOSH.

CHAPTER 22

Stow the Stew,

UNLESS I WEIGHS THIS LETTER AN' MEASURES HOW FAR I BRUNG IT, THE POSTAGE-DUE CAN'T BE PAID.
A EXCELLENT ARRANGEMENT.
THE GUMMINT GOT A NOBLE WAY ON 'EM.
AN' UNLESS YOU PAYS IT··· YOU DON'T GIT TO READ THE LETTER.
LIKE WE SAID, THE GUMMINT IS A PACK OF THIEVES.

ALSO, I FLEW A LITTLE ON THE WAY··· THERE'S AIR MAIL ADDED RIGHT THERE!
YOU WEREN'T UP IN THE AIR ALL THE WAY WERE YOU? THIS THING'S BEEN A LONG TIME ON THE WAY.
HOW ABOUT IF I READS IT TO YOU FOR A REDUCED RATE?
NOTHIN' DOIN'···· IT MAY BE VERY SECRET.
LET HIM GO AHEAD. IT'S PROB'LY NOT IN ENGLISH AN' HE WON'T UNDERSTAND A WORD OF IT.

IF YOU DON'T TELL ME WHERE THIS IS FROM SO'S I KIN GIVE YOU A RATE ON IT··· IT'S GONNA BE HARD TO READ THIS.
IF IT'S FROM WHERE I THINK, IT'S GONNA BE IMPOSSIBLE TO READ IT.
I GOTTA FIGURE HOW FAR I IS CARRIED THIS··· THEN, I READS IT AT SO MUCH PER WORD.
SOME OF THEM WORDS IN THERE IS BOUND TO BE PERTY CHEAP.

OTHERS IS BOUND TO BE PRETTY FLAT.. YOU GONNA GIVE US A FLAT RATE ?
OR A CHEAP RATE ?
IF YOU WAITS 'TIL THE OFF SEASON..
I KIN GIVE YOU THE WINTER RATE .... THAT RUNS YOU ABOUT HALF.
HALF WHAT ?
YOU ONLY WILL CHEAT HIM OUT OF HALF AS MUCH.

YOU IS IMPUNED MY IMPUNITY! YOU IS SUGGESTED THAT I DON'T PAY MY BILLS.
I NEVER SUGGESTED NO SUCH THING.

YOU TAKES IT BACK ? YOU SAYS YOU DIN'T SUGGEST I IS A NO-GOOD ?
I SAYS FLATLY YOU IS A NO-GOOD.

TO THINK THAT YOU IS TURNIN' ON ME, A FELLOW FIGHTER FOR THE DOWN-TRODS! AIN'T YOU GOT NO PRINCIPLES ?
YOU'RE RIGHT... WE SHOULD FIGHT THE COMMON ENEMY.

GOOD FOR YOU, GOOD OL' FELLOW FIGHTER FOR THE GOOD OL' GOOD OF ALL ... WHO D'YOU FIGGER IS THIS COMMON ENEMY ?
YOU.

HOW KIN YOU SAY I IS THE COMMON ENEMY? CAN'T YOU TALK NICER ABOUT A OLD COMRADE?
I COULD SAY YOU IS AN UNUSUALLY COMMON ENEMY.

WELL.. THAT'S BETTER... IT SHOWS YOU STILL CARES.
EVEN IF YOU IS OUR COMMON ENEMY, I IS STILL YOUR BEST FRIEND.

AN' THAT GOES FOR ME... THO' I IS YOUR ENEMY, WE IS BONDED BY THE BOUNDS OF FRIENDSHIP.
RIGHT! WE IS FELLOW BOUNDERS.

HEY! I BEEN HOLDIN' YO' LETTER EVERY-WINCH-WAY AN' IT STILL LOOKS UPSIDE-DOWN... IT'S THE ONLY LETTER I EVER SAW WHAT'S GOT TWO UPSIDE-DOWN SIDES.
IT'S FROM THE BOSS!

I'LL READ THIS LETTER THREE YEARS OVERDUE FROM THE BOSS.... YOU DECODE AS I GO, "DEAR CONFRERES: WELL, HERE IT IS MAY AND APRIL. WE ARE HAVING A BACKWARD SEASON.
CODES

"WE ARE THINKING OF SELLING MOTHER TO A CIRCUS AND DADDY SAYS THIS IS UNFAIR. HE MEANS UNFAIR TO THE CIRCUS...
SO FAR THE CODE SAYS... "DESTROY"!
CODES

"AUNT MOOBLE HAS RUN OFF WITH 400 POUNDS OF KNOCK-WURST AND THE MILKMAN." ...THERE...I'M HALFWAY THRU. WHAT'S IT SAY UP TO NOW?
IT SAYS: "DESTROY THIS BEFORE READING FURTHER."
CODES

I'M MAD! THEM COWBIRDS GOT A LETTER FULL OF CODE.
AIN'T THAT THEIR PRIVILEGE?

MOUGHT EVEN OF BEEN A FOREIGN CODE!
WELL... WHY NOT? IT WAS THEIR LETTER.

BUT SUPPOSE IT WAS SPY SECRETS AN' STUFF.... -- I WOULD BE RESPONSIBLE. ME, THE MAIL MAN.... I DELIVERED IT!
WHAT OF IT? YOU DIN'T KNOW WHAT WAS IN IT.

THAT'S WHAT BURNS MY TIME!

THEM COWBIRDS GITTIN' A SECRET CODIFIED LETTER IS SET ME TO THINKIN'.
UM.

I BEEN A-STUDYIN' AN' A-STUDYIN'... AN' I BELIEVE MY MIND IS 'BOUT MADE UP.
BULLY FOR YOU!

IF THEY GOT A SECRET CODE LETTER IT MUST OF BEEN SO'S NOBODY COULD READ IT.
WELL--- AIN'T THAT USUAL THE WAY?

TROUBLE WAS, NOT EVEN THEM COWBIRDS COULD READ IT.
REALLY SECRET, HUH?

IF THEM COWBIRDS COULD OF READ THEIR SECRET LETTER, THEY COULD OF TOLE ME ABOUT IT.
THEN IT WOULDN'T OF BEEN SECRET.

I WOULDN'T OF TOLE NOBODY EXCEPT MAYBE YOU.
SURE--WHAT GOOD'S A SECRET IF NOBODY KNOWS IT BUT YOU?

NO SECRET WHAT'S WORTH A HOOT OUGHT TO BE KEPT QUIET.
SECRETS IS USUALLY PERTY DOGGONE FASCINATIN'.
EGG-ZACKLY---- IT'S COMPLETELY ILLOGICAL TO KEEP A SECRET SECRET.
AN' UNFAIR.

I THINK I'LL GIT INTO SOME OTHER LINE OF COMMUNICATION---- IT AIN'T AS MUCH FUN BEIN' A MAILMAN AS IT USED.
HOW 'BOUT HOG CALLIN'?

NO---NO--- YOU CALL A HOG AN' WHERE'S IT GET YOU? EVEN IF HE ANSWERS ---WHAT'RE YOU GONNA TALK ABOUT?
IT'S ALL ACCORDIN' TO WHAT YOU CALL HIM.

IT AIN'T THAT I DON'T LIKE MAILMANNIN'---- BUT THE ZING GOES OUT OF IT WHEN EVER'BODY PUTS STUFF IN ENVELOPES. IT'S SNEAKY.
YOU PREFERS POST CARDS?

YOU'RE DERN TOOTLE! GIVE A MAN A DECK OF POST CARDS TO DELIVER AN' HE'S GOT A BUSY, HAPPY DAY AHEAD OF HIM, READIN' AN' CHUCKLIN'... BUT NOWADAYS PROSPERITY GOT EVER'-BODY MAILIN' STUFF THE EXPENSIVE WAY.
GOOD TIMES IS BAD?

WHAT HAPPENED TO MR. PIG AND HIS TALKY COCKADOODLE?
YOU INSULTED HIM AND HE UP AN' LEFT.
I NEVER--- I TOLE THE TRUTH---I CALLED HIM A BUM----
AN' YOU TALKED LIKE YOU WAS GONNA PUNCH HIM IN THE NOSE.

YOU FIGGER THAT MR. PIG IS IGNORIN' US?
BUT YOU CHASED HIM OFF.

I AND YOU WAS RIZ WITH THE CODE OF THE GENNLEMAN BURNED INTO OUR BABY BRAINS---- IT AIN'T POLITE TO NOT COME CALLIN' TO PAY YO' RESPECTS.
"GIT AWAY!" IS WHAT YOU TOLE HIM---

AN' GIT AWAY IS WHAT HE IS DOOD.
HE'S DEE-LIBERATE SNUBBIN' OF US.
BY JING -- HE BETTER NOT SHOW UP AROUN' HERE WITHOUT FIRST COMIN' BACK AN' PAYIN' HIS REE-SPECTS.

CHAPTER 23

Moppily, Sloppily,

IF ONLY WE'D OF NOT BURNED THAT LETTER AND READ IT INSTEAD.

BUT IT SAID TO DESTROY IT BEFORE WE READ IT--- WE READ THAT MUCH OF IT---

THEN WE BETTER KEEP IT QUIET--- IF WE WERE SUPPOSED TO DESTROY IT BEFORE WE READ IT---

-- WE SHOULDN'T HAVE READ ANY OF IT--- KEEP IT A SECRET OR WE'LL BE IN TROUBLE---
YEAH--- SHHH

WHAT WE'VE GOT TO DO IS KEEP QUIET ABOUT THE FACT WE READ AS MUCH OF THE LETTER AS WE DID.
RIGHT. KEEP QUIET.

I AM KEEPIN' QUIET--- I'M NOT TELLIN' ANYBODY---I'M QUIET!
IT MIGHT BE FATAL TO TELL 'EM THAT WE READ ANY PART.

YOU MEAN WHERE WE READ WHAT IT TOLD US TO DO ?
YES, WHERE IT TOLD US TO DESTROY THE LETTER BEFORE WE READ IT!
WELL, KEEP QUIET ABOUT IT YOUR OWN SELF.
I AM QUIET... WITH ME IT'S A SECRET THAT WE READ ANY PART OF IT!
IT'S NICE TO HAVE A SECRET AGAIN --- THE ONE ABOUT WHAT WE READ IN THE LETTER.
YEH.
YOU REMEMBER--- THE SECRET IS THAT WE---
SHHH! DON'T TELL IT--- NOT EVEN TO ME.
BUT YOU KNOW IT ALREADY--- WHY CAN'T I TELL YOU?
IT'S A SECRET! THEM'S ORDERS! YOU SHOULDN'T EXPOSE YOURSELF TO DANGER BY BEING CAUGHT TELLING IT.
AW--- WHAT'S THE FUN OF KNOWING IT THEN?
LET ME TELL IT TO YOU!

IF I CAN'T TELL YOU THE SECRET WE SHARES, I **AIN'T GONE LET YOU TELL ME!**
BUT I DON'T MIND EXPOSIN' **MYSELF** TO **DANGER** BY TELLIN' IT...
NONETHELESS I **AIN'T** GONNA LET YOU TELL ME IT.
OH, **YES**, YOU ARE!

OH, ***NO.*** I'M NOT! I'M **NOT** GONNA ***LET*** **YOU!**
YOU CAN'T ORDER **ME** AROUND! HERE I COME TO **TELL** YOU.
I WON'T ***LISTEN!***
OH, **YES**, YOU WILL... **HERE'S THE SECRET...THE LETTER SAID...**

I'LL REPEAT THE SECRET... YOU'LL HEAR IT!
NO I WON'T !
WHAT'S YOU TWO SHOUTIN' ABOUT?
PUL-LEASE! WOULD YOU HAVE US VIOLATE A CONFIDENCE?
YEAH... IT'S A SECRET!

COME BACK AN' LET ME TELL YOU OUR SECRET!
NO! NO! I WON'T LISTEN!

OHYESYOUWILL!
OHNOIWON'T --OOMP!

NOW! THE LETTER TOLD US TO NOT READ ANY FURTHER BEFORE WE...
NO! NO!

WELL, WELL...
YOU SAID IT.

IT'S A GOOD THING I PAID A VISIT TO THE COUNTRY WHICH I DISCOVERED.. --JUST TO CHECK UP ON WHAT YOU TWO ARE UP TO---
WE GOT YOUR LETTER AND DID LIKE YOU SAID.
YOU ALSO WERE TRYING TO TELL THE SECRET TO YOUR COMRADE.. ---A DANGEROUS PRACTICE!
YOU SAID IT.

YES, A VERY DANGEROUS THING TO DO--- SECRETS ARE NOT TO BE TOLD.
YOU SAID IT.
I WAS LOYAL! I DIDN'T LISTEN TO HIM.
AND THAT'S EVEN WORSE! SECRETS ARE NOT MEANT TO BE TOLD BUT THEY ARE MEANT TO BE LISTENED TO--- YOU BOTH HAVE FAILED IN YOUR DUTY.

THE INSTRUCTIONS IN THE LETTER WERE PRETTY PLAIN, I TRUST?
YOU SAID IT.
YOU SAID IT.
YOU SAID IT.

WHAT DID YOU THINK OF DIRECTIVE NO. 2 ?
WELL, MOSTLY IT WAS HARD TO READ.

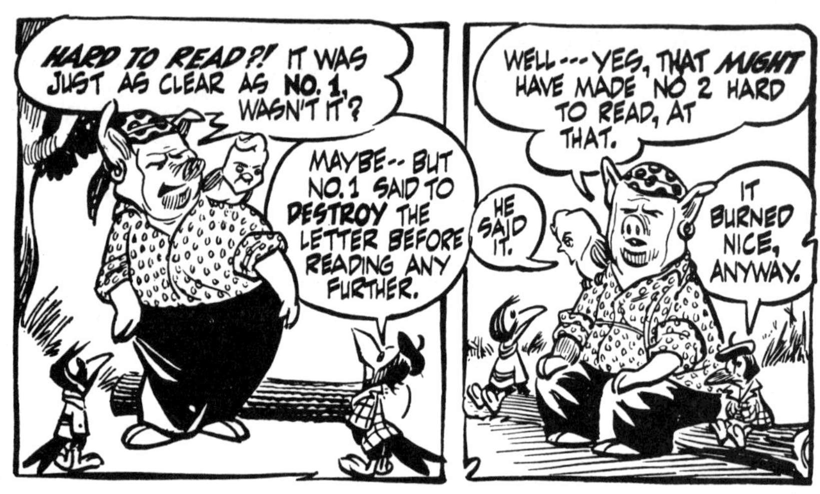
HARD TO READ?! IT WAS JUST AS CLEAR AS NO. 1, WASN'T IT?
MAYBE-- BUT NO. 1 SAID TO DESTROY THE LETTER BEFORE READING ANY FURTHER.
WELL--- YES, THAT MIGHT HAVE MADE NO 2 HARD TO READ, AT THAT.
HE SAID IT.
IT BURNED NICE, ANYWAY.

COME ON-- 'LONG AS YOU'RE VISITIN' US WE'LL TAKE YOU TO A GOOD PLACE TO EAT.
EXCELLENT! BUT I STILL CAN'T SEE WHY YOU DIDN'T READ MORE OF THAT LETTER.
BUT YOUR VERY FIRST INSTRUCTION TOLD US TO DESTROY THE LETTER---

--BEFORE READING ANY FURTHER.
BUT, BESIDES FOLLOWING OUT DIRECTIONS, YOUR DUTIES ALSO ARE TO PRY AND SNOOP.
YOU SAID IT.
MM, THE FOOD IS GOOD! WHAT LED YOU TO COME HERE?
POGO
WELL, THE DOOR WAS OPEN.

MMM! A DEE-LICIOUS AROMA FROM POGO'S KITCHEN--- I'LL JES' SNEAK IN AN' HAVE A LI'L' PLATEFUL IF POGO AIN'T HOME.
HELLO? POGO? ANYBODY HO----? HA-HM---

SO HA! IN HERE EATIN' POGO'S GRUB!

OH, WHAT A OUTRAGE! EATIN' ANOTHER FELLA'S VITTLES WITHOUT SO MUCH AS A SIMPLE "'SCUSE ME."

LOOK AT THAT! THAT PIG AN' THEM COWBIRDS JES' MOVED IN AN' SPREAD THEIR-SELVES A FEAST OUTEN POGO'S FOOD.

NEVER-- CHOMP---HEARD OF SUCH A HIGH--CHOMP HANDED THING IN ALL MY CHOMP-- BORN DAYS-- CHOMP--CHOMP!

IT'S A GOOD THING I COMED ALONG TO PROTECT POGO'S POOR DEFENSELESS VITTLES.

HEIGHDY, SON! I IS PROTECTIN' YO' FOOD FROM GITTIN' ATE BY OL' MR. PIG AN' THEM COWBIRDS WHAT WAS SETTIN' HERE EATIN'--- BUT YOU DON'T GOTTA THANK ME AN' ALL --'TWEREN'T NO TROUBLE.

IF YOU WAS IN HERE PROTECTIN' MY FOOD FROM THEM COWBIRDS AN' MR. PIG --- WHERE'S THE FOOD?
LIKE I SAY, I PROTECTED IT.

THESE PLATES LOOK SORTA EMPTY--- WHAT'D YOU DO WITH THE GRUB? SEND IT TO FORT KNOX?
YOU IS A QUIBBLER.

FACE UP TO IT-- IF I WAS TAKIN' CARE OF YO' GRUB--- KEEPIN' FOLKS FROM EATIN' IT--- I DESERVES SOMETHIN'--- SO I ET THE LUNCH--- KNOWIN' YO' BIG SOFT MUSHY HEART WOULD BLEED IF I DIN'T.
I GUESS YO' IS RIGHT.

HOWEVER, NEXT TIME, NO CARROTS IN THE CHICKEN FOOT STEW! I WASN'T BRUNG UP THAT WAY, SO WATCH IT!
I'LL WRITE A LETTER OF APOLOGY TO YOUR GOVERNESS.

CHAPTER 24

Fry.

WHAT'S THAT OL' MR. PIG WANT?
WULL, HE SAYS HE KIN CHANGE OUR ELECTION WAYS-- HE CLAIM WE IS OUTDATED.
OL' DAVE BRINKLEY

HE SAY OUR WINNIN' CANDIDATES DON'T GIT ENOUGH OF THE VOTE... SAYS HE KNOWS A WAY TO GIT 95% OF IT.
MARSE BRINKLEY

WULL... WHAT'S WRONG WITH THAT?
THE WAY HE DO IT... YOU JES' PUT UP ONE CANDIDATE... CONSEQUENTLY, MOST EVER'BODY'S FOR HIM... THEY'S NOBODY TO BE AGAINST.

OH, THAT'D NEVER WORK HERE... I USUAL VOTES 95% AGAINST SOMEBODY. HOW COULD I VOTE IF I DIN'T HAVE NOBODY TO BE AGAINST?
YOU COULD WRITE IN YO' OWN NAME.
UNCLE DAVE BRINKLEY

THE TROUBLE WITH YOU IS YOU GOT TOO MANY CAMPAIGN MANAGERS... I'M GONNA TAKE OVER AN' SETTLE THIS.

FER 'NINSTANCE, THERE'S OWL, AN' P.T. BRIDGEPORT AN' THE TURTLE AN' OL' HOUN'DOG AN' NOW THIS MR. PIG, WHO ADDS HIS TWO-CENTS WORTH.

FIRST PIECE OF ADVICE I GIVES YOU, AS YOUR CAMPAIGN MANAGER, IS GET RID OF ALL YOUR CAMPAIGN MANAGERS!
ALL OF 'EM?
GOOD ADVICE! IT'S TOO BAD TO HAFTA GET RID OF YOU SO SOON, BUT I VALUES YOUR HELP TOO MUCH TO GO COUNTER TO YO' ADVICE, SO GOODBYE.
SEEM LIKE I HANDLED THIS WRONG, SOMEHOW.

SOMETIMES I GOTTA ADMIT I DOESN'T UNDERSTAND YOU, POGO.
THAT MAKES US EVEN... I DON'T UNDERSTAND MYSELF SOMETIMES TOO.
THE AMERICAN HERITAGE
HMM... THAT'S QUEER... I ALLUS UNDERSTANDS MYSELF... 'CEPT WHEN I IS MAD AT MYSELF AN' ISN'T SPEAKIN' TO ME.

BUT YOU! I DON'T KNOW WHY YOU AIN'T OUT CAMPAIGNIN' AN' COUNTER-PAIGNIN'.
'CAUSE I'M GONE DO THE ONLY GOOD THING A POSSUM KIN DO... I'M GONNA VOTE.
THE AMERICAN HERITAGE
LEASTWISE YOU'LL VOTE FOR YO' OWN SELF...
I DUNNO... I'M GONE LOOK OVER ALL THE CANDIDATES AN' VOTE FOR WHO I THINKS IS BEST...
VOTE KIDS

YOU MEAN TO SAY YOU AIN'T GONNA DO NOTHIN' MORE 'BOUT THE EE-LECTION ?
SURE -- I'M GONNA DO THE MOST IMPORTANT THING A CANDIDATE KIN DO ---I'M GONNA VOTE.
YOU SEE ANY-BODY LOOKIN' FOR A BIRTHDAY ?
KATHRYN BARBARA

GOT A CAKE HERE I BAKED--- --FER FOUR WHOLE YEARS I BEEN LOOKIN' FOR THAT CHILD-- YOU KNOW WHERE SHE'S HIDIN' ?
NO, BUT EVIDENTLY SHE IS TASTED ONE OF YO' CAKES AT ONE TIME OR ANOTHER ---
NOW, ALBERT! THE MAN MEANS WELL.
MISS KATHRYN B.

DOES YOU MEAN YOU WOULD VOTE FOR SOMEBODY ELSE ASIDE FROM YO'SELF ?

I B'LEEVE SO--- AFTER ALL, ELECTIN' A PRESIDENT IS A SERIOUS MATTER AN' NOBODY OUGHT TO THROW AWAY HIS VOTE.

FIRST YOU STUMPS THE COUNTRY-- NEXT YOU STUMPS ME!
ANYWAY, IT WOULDN'T BE RIGHT FER ME TO VOTE FER MYSELF.
WHY NOT!? EVER'BODY ELSE DOES!
WELL--- WHEN I STOPS AN' THINKS OF IT--- I AIN'T OLD ENOUGH.

DID I HEAR YOU RIGHT? YOU AIN'T OLD ENOUGH TO VOTE?
POGO
YUP.

WHAT A BLOW! THAT MEANS YOU AIN'T OLD ENOUGH TO BE PRESIDENT, NEITHER.
RIGHT.

WELL! WELL! IT LOOKS LIKE I'LL GOTTA OFFER MY FAIR YOUNG BODY IN YOUR STEAD--- --I WILL RUN FOR PRESIDENT.
YOU!? YOU AIN'T ANY OLDER'N ME!

BUT I'M WILLING TO LIE FOR MY COUNTRY!

CHAPTER 25

Startedly, Heartedly,

IF WE MAKE A NEW ORIGINAL PLAN-- IT MEANS WE WON'T BE AS FRIENDLY THIS TIME. RIGHT?
MAYBE THEY'LL BE EXPECTING US TO SWITCH--- WE'LL HAVE TO OUTWIT THEM.
WE'LL BE MAD.

SO WE'LL NOT SWITCH. WE'LL BE FRIENDLY! WE'LL SMILE.
BUT THEY MIGHT FIGURE WE WON'T SWITCH-- THEY'RE PRETTY SHARP.

THEN WE'LL THINK PAST THEM--- WE'LL SWITCH BACK TO SWITCHING--- THAT'LL FOOL THEM.
NOT TOO FAST--- S'POSE THEY FIGURE WE'LL SWITCH BACK TO SWITCHING, SO WE'LL SWITCH BACK FROM SWITCHING TO NOT SWITCHING.
GOOD-- NOW DOES THAT LEAVE US BEING FRIENDLY OR UNFRIENDLY?
YOU SAID IT.

THE NEW ORIGINAL PLAN WILL BE FOR US TO BE FRIENDLY BUT FIRM--- WE WANT TO HELP THESE PEOPLE.
YOU SAID IT.

THE COMING ELECTION IN THIS COUNTRY IS BEING HELD IN A VERY OLD-FASHIONED WAY!--IMAGINE. TWO MAJOR CANDIDATES!
YOU SAID IT.

WE DO THINGS MUCH BETTER IN OUR COUNTRY-- JUST ONE CANDIDATE--- IT SIMPLIFIES THE ELECTION--- NOBODY IS IN DOUBT AS TO WHO TO VOTE FOR.
YOU SAID IT.
WHY NOT JUST APPOINT THE MAN--- AND DO AWAY WITH THE ELECTION?
WHAT? AND CRUDELY ABANDON THE SACRED PRINCIPLES OF TRUE DEMOCRACY?!
SHAME ON YOU.
YOU SAID IT.

IT'S OUR DUTY TO ADVISE THESE PEOPLE THAT TWO CANDIDATES ARE CONFUSING.
YOU SAID IT.
EVEN ONE CANDIDATE CAN BE CONFUSING.
NOW LET'S NOT BE SO FACETIOUS··· YOU NEED AT LEAST ONE CANDIDATE IN AN ELECTION··· BUT, WHY USE MORE? ONLY ONE MAN GETS ELECTED.
YOU SAID IT.

WHY USE TWO MEN TO RUN FOR OFFICE WHEN ONE WILL DO?··· IT'S A WASTE OF MANPOWER; IT SAPS THE COUNTRY'S STRENGTH.
YOU SAID IT.
SURE, WHY TIE UP TWO GOOD MEN?
TUT! ACROSS THE SEA IN OUR COUNTRY WE KNOW THERE IS JUST ONE GOOD MAN··· AND HE'S THE ONE WE RUN FOR OFFICE··· IN THAT WAY WE MAKE IT EASY FOR THE VOTERS··· THEY DON'T EVEN HAVE TO THINK.
YOU SAID IT.

FRIENDS, I'M GLAD YOU CAME ALONG AT THIS TIME... LET ME TELL YOU THAT YOU VOTE ALL WRONG IN THIS COUNTRY... IN MY LAND WE VOTE FOR JUST ONE CANDIDATE AND GIVE HIM 95% OF THE VOTE.
VOTE
VOTE
VOTE
VOTE
VOTE

THIS TAKES THE WORRY OUT OF VOTING... CHANGE YOUR WAYS, FRIENDS, DON'T LET ANYTHING HOLD YOU BACK!
YOU SAID IT.

VOTE
DON'T WORRY 'BOUT US... NOTHING IS HELD US BACK FER 180 YEARS... WE LIKES VOTIN' IN TWO OR THREE DIRECTIONS.
THEY'RE INCORRIGIBLE.

CHAPTER 26

See the Sea,

WAS THE LADY SURPRISED TO SEE MOUSE IN THE HOLLANDAISE SAUCE?
YES, SHE COMPLAINED THAT SHE'D WANTED THE EGGS WELL DONE AN' POINTED OUT THAT ONE WASN'T DONE AT ALL.
NOT ONLY THAT BUT SHE SAID I WAS MOVING! AN' I SPOKE UP AN' SAID I WASN'T EVEN A EGG!
MOUSE

AT THIS THE LADY SCREAMED AND SAID: "HE'S A MOUSE!" SOMETHING I HAD KNOWN ALL ALONG, AND DIDN'T THINK WAS SO SURPRISING... BUT YOU CAN'T PLEASE EVERYBODY AND...
YOU GOIN' SOMEWHERES?
YEP, TO THE OLYMPICS... I'M TRYIN' OUT IN THE FEATHERWEIGHT HATLIFT DIVISION.
MOU
P.A.A.

AS A MAN EXPERIENCED IN AIR TRAVEL HOW'D YOU LIKE TO PILOT MY SATELLITE?
NOTHIN' DOIN'... I'M GOIN' TO AUSTRALIA ON A GOOD SAFE AIRPLANE.
STEP OVER AN' SEE IT ANYWAYS. EVER'BODY AGREES THAT A MOUSE IS THE BEST LIVING THING TO SEND UP ON THE FIRST TEST FLIGHT.
EVERYBODY EXCEPT THE MOUSE.

THERE IT IS.... ALL SET TO BE SHOT INTO THE BLUE... A NEW TYPE OF MOON.
A GARBAGE CAN! IF THAT'S A NEW TYPE MOON, IT'LL NEVER BE POPULAR...HOW ROMANTIC CAN A GARBAGE CAN BE, SHININ' DOWN IN ITS FULL PHASE?

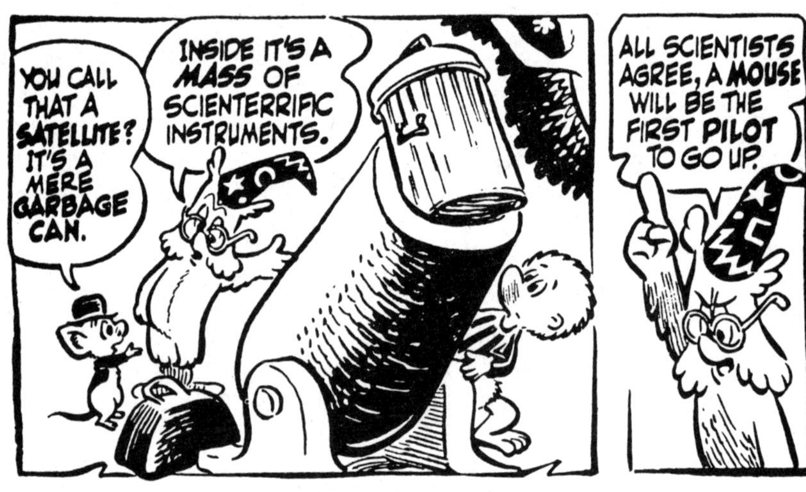
YOU CALL THAT A SATELLITE? IT'S A MERE GARBAGE CAN.
INSIDE IT'S A MASS OF SCIENTERRIFIC INSTRUMENTS.
ALL SCIENTISTS AGREE, A MOUSE WILL BE THE FIRST PILOT TO GO UP.

IF IT'S YOU, YOU'LL HAVE YOUR NAME IN NEWSPAPERS EVERYWHERE.
DON'T PUSH.. S'POSE SOMETHING GOES WRONG AN' AN'.. I DON'T COME BACK.
A MUCH BETTER STORY... YOU'LL REALLY MAKE PAGE ONE, THEN.

WHAT KIND OF SCIENTIFIC INSTRUMENTS ARE IN YO' SATELLITE?
ALL KINDS.. PENCILS, PAPER, STRING.
WHAT!?

A GLASS OF WATER FER WETTIN' THE THUMB TO GET WIND DRIFT, A POCKET MANUAL OF STARS, MOONS, BUTTERFLIES AN' OTHER HEAVENLY BODIES...

A TAPE MEASURE FOR MEASURIN' ALTITUDE--- A PAIR OF WATER WINGS IN CASE IT GOES DOWN AT SEA--- A ICE PICK IN CASE IT LANDS AT THE POLE--- GLASS BEADS FOR TRADE WITH NATIVES IN CASE IT HITS MARS---
AN' SAN'WICHES FOR ALL HANDS! NOW, HOW DOES ALL THAT MAKE YOU FEEL?
MIGHTY HALE AND FARE-WELL!

SET THERE, LIKE A GOOD FELLA, AN GUARD THE AMAZIN' APPARATUS--- I GOTTA DIG UP ANOTHER MOUSE TO BE A GUINEA PIG.
I GUESS GITTIN' A GUINEA PIG TO BE A GUINEA PIG WOULD BE A PERTY SLOPPY SCIENTIFIC APPROACH---
---WOZZAT!?

I HEARS SOMETHIN' IN THE SATELLITE... A SOMEBODY-IS-GITTIN'-AT-THE-SAN'WICHES TYPE OF NOISE... ANYBODY THERE?
NO.

IF I LOOKS IN... IT'S THE SAME THING AS CALLIN' HIM A LIAR... WHOEVER HE IS... THIS IS A VERY UNBARRASSIN' SPOT.

SPSSST!
WODDYA MEAN: SPSSST?

I MEAN COMERE! I SNUCK BACK TO PICK UP A SAM-WICH AN' LOOK AT EM! ALL KINDS!

BUT I'M S'POSED TO BE GUARDIN' THIS.
SO MUCH THE BETTER-- NOBODY'LL SUSPECT YOU.

A NEW TYPE OF GARBAGE INCINERATOR! WHAT MODERN MIRACLE WILL BE NEXT!?

A CLEVER WAY TO DISPOSE OF SLOPS! AN' THERE'S THE FUSE-- UM! WODDYA KNOW

EVEN IF OWL DID STEAL THESE SAM'WICHES FROM ME, I FEELS LIKE A BURGLAR, EATIN' 'EM.
WHAT!?
SPT

BURGLAR, I SAID.
NO TALKY GARBAGE CAN CALLS ME A BURGLAR.
SPUT
SPT

BAM!

STOP! DON'T DO THAT!
I NEVER KNOWS MY OWN MAGNIFICENT STRENGTH.

NOW YOU HAVE DID IT! YOU'VE BLOWED THE SATELLITE UP AN' AROUND THE WORLD.
I NEVER!
POGO WAS HERE-- WHERE'S HE NOW?
WULL-- I HEARD A VOICE INSIDE THE GARBAGE CAN.

THAT WAS HIM! NOW HE'S UP THERE CIRCLING THE EARTH EVERY NINETY MINUTES ON THE HOUR.
GOSH! WHAT'LL I DO NOW?
YOU MIGHT TAKE OFF YO' HAT AN' GIT READY TO WAVE... THE BOY'S ABOUT DUE BY...

CHAPTER 27

Markedly, Starkedly,

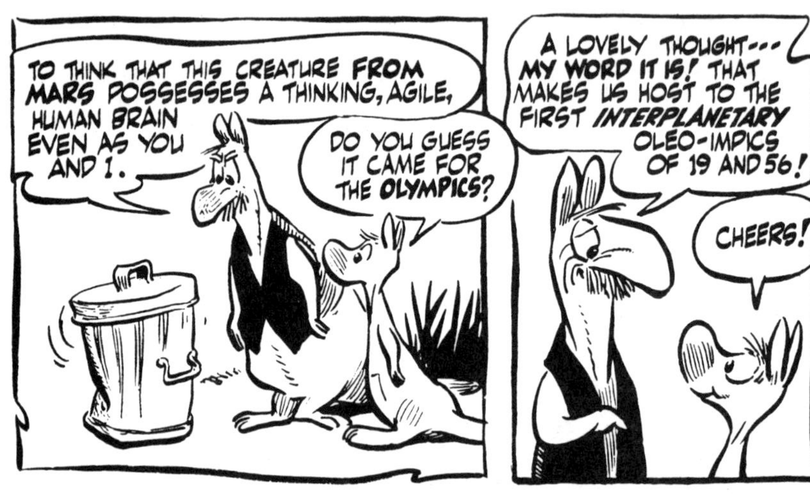
TO THINK THAT THIS CREATURE FROM MARS POSSESSES A THINKING, AGILE, HUMAN BRAIN EVEN AS YOU AND I.
DO YOU GUESS IT CAME FOR THE OLYMPICS?
A LOVELY THOUGHT--- MY WORD IT IS! THAT MAKES US HOST TO THE FIRST INTERPLANETARY OLEO-IMPICS OF 19 AND 56!
CHEERS!

HALLOO THERE! HALLOO THERE! HALLOO THERE--- I SAY, COBBER, THIS CHAP FROM MARS IS A BIT OF A WOWSER-- A STUFFY ONE.
MY WORD HE IS!

CUT OUT THE POUNDIN'!
A MARTIAN! AN UGLY PROOF THAT LIFE EXISTS ON OUR SISTER PLANET.
A COW!

WHAT'S HAPPENED TO THE SWAMP? --WHO ARE YOU FELLAS?

HE SOUNDS ALMOST HUMAN.
DINKY DIE HE DO!

WOTTO! HERE'S HIS FATHER!

I AIN'T NEITHER HIS FATHER.
HE'S ASHAMED OF HIM.
MAYBE HE'S HIS MOTHER.

WHY ARE YOU ASHAMED OF YOUR CHILD?
YOU DON'T UNDERSTAND.

TO THINK, YOU MUST GO WITHOUT A FATHER'S EVER-LOVING LOVE--WITHOUT A MOTHER'S FAITHFUL FAITH --POOR LITTLE COBBER--- WHY ARE YOU DESPICABLE?
COME TO THINK OF IT---WHY?

WHY DO YOU DENY ME A MOTHER'S TENDER CARE?
BECAUSE I'M NOT YOUR MOTHER, AND STOP BEING SILLY.
IF YOU DENY BEING HIS MOTHER, SIR, YOU ARE A CAD.
HE SHOULD SUE FOR BREACH OF PROMISE.

THINGS IS CRAZY HERE IN THE SWAMP EVER SINCE WE CLUMB BACK OUTEN THE SATELLITE.
YOU'RE NOT IN A SWAMP, MATE, YOU'RE IN AUSTRALIA.
WELCOME TO VICTORIA.
YOU MEAN TO SAY WE CAME ALL THE WAY AROUND THE WORLD IN THE SATELLITE AND LANDED IN AUSTRALIA?

RIGHTO, CHUM! ALL THE WAY FROM OUR SISTER RUDDY PLANET, MARS--- CONGRATULATIONS, MATE!
WE'RE FROM THE U.S.---NOT MARS!
WHAT, YOU? YOU'RE A YANK?
NOT A YANK! I'M FROM GEORGIA!
STONE THE CROWS! A FROTHING MADMAN!

THIS POOR CHAP FROM MARS THINKS HE'S A RUDDY AMERICAN!
HE'S NOT FIT, COBBER, TO TAKE CARE OF HIS BLOOMING OFF-SPRING.

SO I SUGGEST WE ADOPT THE NIPPER--- AND SEND HIM TO SCHOOL BACK IN BLIGHTY.

NOW THAT'S SETTLED HOW ABOUT A DISH OF TEA?
HEY! HEY! HEY!
LOVE A JUMPIN' DUCK, BUT YOU'RE A NOISY ONE.
RIGHTO! BE A BIT PATIENT, BUCKO, HERE'S YOURS NOW.
HOOPS! IT COULD STEEP A BIT, COBBER.
BLUB?
WACKO, COBBER! YOU DON'T LOOK LIKE A JUMPIN' JACKAROO TO ME! I'M A GRAFTER FROM THE WOOP WOOP, AND I SAY LET'S STAGE A DINKUM BEANO!
HUH?
DROP THE BUNDLE, JOEY.
LEMME OUT!
I'M SORRY, BUT I DON'T UNNERSTAND WHAT YOU AUSTRALIANS IS TALKIN' ABOUT.
GUESS THEY DON'T SPEAK THE KING'S-CROWNICAL-ENGLISH UP THERE ON BLINKIN' MARS --- WHAT I'M SAYIN' IS IF YOU'RE HERE FOR THE OLEO-IMPICS IT'S A GREAT DAY.
BUT I'M NOT FROM MARS!
NOW DON'T BE MODEST---WE'LL STAGE THE FIRST BLOOMIN' OLEO-DINGDONG-IMPICS BETWEEN PLANETS...... SHALL I PUT YOU DOWN FOR THE BROAD JUMP? YOU'LL UPHOLD THE HONOR OF MARS, OF COURSE COBBER?
OH WELL, WHAT'S MARS GOT TO LOSE?

CHAPTER 28

Bray.

I'M ALL SET TO TRY OUT IN THE 880-YARD DASH... AND THEN WE'LL HAVE OUR RACE.
DASH? THAT'S A SLEEPER JUMP.
BUT... PROCEED! I'LL WAIT.
MARS

WHAT? SIX SECONDS?

I ALLUS WAS PRETTY FAST ... I'M HOPIN' TO DO THE MILE IN TEN SECONDS.
LOOK, MATE -- HOW ABOUT YOU TOSSIN' THE SIXTEEN-POUND SHOT INSTEAD ?

NOW, AS REPRESENTATIVE OF EARTH IN OUR INTERPLANETARY OLEO-IMPICS AND AS THE HOST NATION, ALLOW ME TO INFORM YOU THE NEXT EVENT IS THE PENTATHLON.
WHAT?! WHAT HAPPENED TO THE HALF MILE RUN?
THE WAY YOU RAN THE HALF MILE WAS ILLEGAL -- BUT THERE'S PLENTY OF RUNNING IN THE PENTATHLON.
EARTH

I GUESS I RAN IT TOO SLOW... SIX SECONDS MUST BE OVER PAR.
RIGHT! NOW JUST WAIT AND I'LL GET THE EQUIPMENT FOR THE PENTATHLON.
EARTH
MARS
YOU HAVE TO RUN WITH THE JAVELIN, THE DISCUS AND THE SHOT-- ALSO THERE'S A CERTAIN AMOUNT OF LEAPING-- HOW DO YOU FEEL ABOUT LEAPING?
JUMPY.

YOU MEAN I'VE GOTTA RUN WITH THIS SPEAR?
RIGHTO--AND WITH THE DISCUS AND THE SHOT.
AND THE SHOT? RUN WITH IT? I CAN'T EVEN LIFT IT.
AW, NOW! TOO BAD, OLD BOY.
MARS

LOOK, COBBER, YOU LOAD YOURSELF WITH WHAT YOU CAN CARRY AND I'LL HANDLE THE BALANCE.
EARTH

NOW THEN! ON YOUR MARK! GET READY TO STREAK OUT THE TWO HUNDRED METERS.

HERE'S HOW I CAN TAKE EVERYTHING WHEN I RUN IN THE PENTATHLON... I'LL ROLL THE SHOT.
WELL, IT MIGHT NOT BE CRICKET BUT NIP TO IT, COVEY.
MIND! DON'T DROP THE DISCUS! EVERYTHING MUST BE FAIR DINKUM.
RIGHTO! I MEAN OKAY!

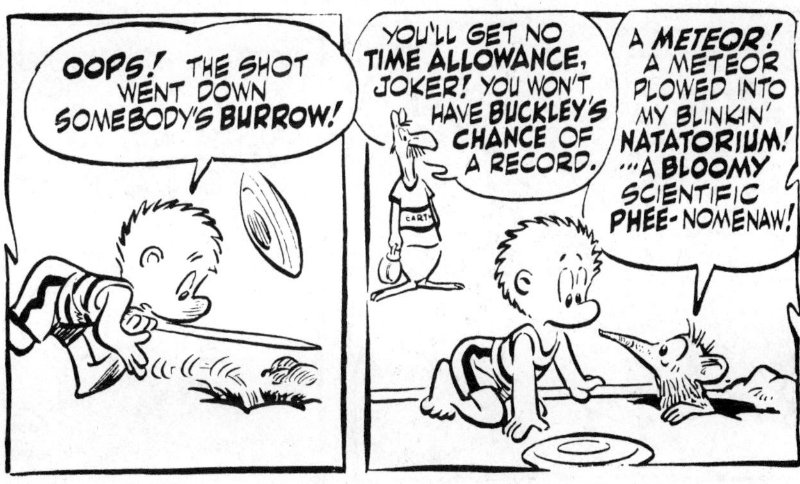
OOPS! THE SHOT WENT DOWN SOMEBODY'S BURROW!
YOU'LL GET NO TIME ALLOWANCE, JOKER! YOU WON'T HAVE BUCKLEY'S CHANCE OF A RECORD.
A METEOR! A METEOR PLOWED INTO MY BLINKIN' NATATORIUM! ...A BLOOMY SCIENTIFIC PHEE-NOMENAW!

WHY, YOU'RE A BANDICOOT!
TOO RIGHT YOU ARE! AND I'VE GOT A DING DONG LICENSE FOR THE JOB TOO, MATE! DID YOU HEAR ABOUT THE MIRACLE?
A MODERN-JUMPIN'-MIRACLE IT WAS, FRIENDS! I WAS SITTING THERE REVIEWING MY PAST, COUNTING MY MEDALS, WHEN "BLANG!"– IN CAME A SCIENTIFIC WONDER... A METEOR FROM OUTER-SPINNING-SPACE!

YOU ARE DELAYING THE INTERPLANETARY OLEO-IMPIC GAMES. MARS IS HAVING ITS INNINGS.
BUT YOU AIN'T HEARD THE HALF, COBBER.
JES' LIKE HOME.
EARTH
SO FAR YOUR OFFICIAL TIME FOR 200 METERS IS 24 HOURS AND 6 MINUTES AND THE END NOT YET ON THE HORIZON.
MARTHA... COME UP AN' TELL HOW YOU FELT.
EARTH

I'VE FAIR GOT THE JOES THINKING OF ALL THIS TIME GOING ONTO YOUR RECORD, COBBER.
BUT WE GOT TO GET THE SHOT BACK.
COME ON UP, MARTHA, AN' TELL ABOUT THE METEOR.
EARTH
MARS

MARTHA, MY HOUSEKEEPER, GENTS... SHE WAS THERE WHEN THIS METEOR PLUNKED INTO MY REFECTORY.. SHE'S A LIVING SURVIVOR AND EYE-WITNESS.. MY WORD, SHE IS!
OH, NOW, ALF.

LOOK HERE, OLD JOKER, THAT METEOR WAS A SHOT.. AND..
TOO RIGHT YOU ARE, MATE.. MARTHA LOSES HER VOICE IF EXCITED...SO EASY DOES IT... NOW GO AHEAD, MARTHA.
OH, ALF.
WELL, ALF AND I WAS SITTING THERE
WHEN ALL OF A SUDDEN "BLANG!"
WELL! SO

CHAPTER 29

Knitfully, Knackfully,

BE NICE TO THE LITTLE JOEY, MR. WOMBAT--- HE'S COME ALL THE WAY FROM MARS TO BE IN THE OLEO-IMPICS.
STONE THE CROWS!

WHAT'S YOUR SPECIALTY, COVE? JUMPIN' OVER JELLY BEANS?
NO-- I'M HERE TO TAKE THE SQUEAKIN' CHAMPEENSHIP.

SQUEAKING? HOW DO YOU--
SQUEAK!
THAT'S HOW.

AN' THAT'S HOW, TOO! YOU FAIR SQUEAKING COW YOU!
HEH HEH.

I DO WISH YOU'D STOP THE BICKERING WITH OUR FRIEND FROM MARS, MR. WOMBAT.
I HAVEN'T BICKERED A HA-PENNY'S WORTH.

WELL, PLEASE, DON'T EITHER OF YOU ARGUE THE TOSS.
HE'S THE ONE THAT'S FIGHTIN'.
OH, NO, I'M NOT!

OH YES YOU ARE! LISTEN AT YOU!
YOU'RE THE SKITIN' STAGER! I'M BEING FRIENDLY!
FRIENDLY! WHY YOU PUDDIN' NOSED DISC JOCKEY, YOU!
SPEAK ENGLISH, YOU BRUMBY BARRACKER! AND NONE OF YOUR CHIVVY!

ALL THIS ARGUING YOU TWO ARE DOING ABOUT WHO IS ARGUING IS A FAIR COW.
ON BEHALF OF MARS, I CHALLENGE HIM TO A INTERPLANETARY OLEO-IMPIC CONTEST.
ON BEHALF OF EARTH, I ACCEPT.
ON BEHALF OF ME, I CHOOSE THE WEAPONS.. BOOMERANGS AT TWENTY PACES... A CHAIN APART.

CAN YOU TOSS A BOOMERANG, LITTLE JOEY?
NO, BUT DON'T LET IT MAKE YOU NERVOUS.
THE DINKUM OIL IS THAT I AM A REAL BONZER EXPERT.
WELL THAT NARKS THE SHOW, JOEY... EVERYBODY OUT!
I HAVE A SET OF MATCHED AND LOADED BOOMERANGS IN MY QUARTERS.

I'LL GET COZY OVER HERE BEHIND THE TREE AND OUT OF YOUR WAY.
HERE'S THE WEEPIN' BOOMERANGS.
YOU SAY THEM THINGS IS LOADED?
THAT'S RIGHT, MATE, LOADED!
WELL, I AIN'T GONE PLAY WITH NO LOADED BOOMERANGS.

THERE'S NOTHING TO IT... A FAIR SNAP... YOU TAKE IT LIKE SO... THEN-
LIKE SO, AND THEN..?

AND THEN.. WOW! I SAY! LET GO!
NOW, HE TELLS ME.

YOU'RE BREAKIN' ALL RECORDS ON HOW LONG IT TAKES YOU TO GET THRU THE PENTATHLON.
SHHH! YER DISTURBIN' MARTHA!
EARTH
MAR
OH MY!
NOW SHE'LL HAVE TO START ALL OVER.... I TOLD YOU SHE LOSES HER VOICE WHEN EXCITED... --START OVER WITH YOUR LIVING EYEWITNESS OF THE METEOR, MARTHA.
OH ALF!

WELL! I AN' ALF WAS SETTIN' THERE WHEN WHIST! THERE'S ANOTHER!
BOOM
RANG
A

NOW YOU HAVE DID IT--! MARTHA WILL HAVE TO BE REVIVED AND START OVER.
I'M NOT STARTIN' OVER, JACK.
MARS

IT'S AMAZIN'! FAIR DINKUM AMAZIN', COBBER! YOU'RE BREAKIN' ALL RECORDS.
MARTHA'S COMING OUT OF IT NOW, MATE... NOTHING LIKE A SPOT OF TEA.
LET ME SEE...COO! YOU STARTED A WEEK AGO ON THE PENTATH-LON....IT'S TAKEN YOU 168 HOURS SO FAR AND YOU'RE NOT FINISHED!
MARS
EARTH

WOW!
MARS
EARTH

THE NEW CHAMP! THE NEW BLINKIN' CHAMP!
HEY! YOU BARRACKER! YOU'VE STONKERED POOR OLD MARTHA AGAIN!
EARTH

YOU'VE DONE YOURSELF PROUD, COBBER ... THE EARTH IS PROUD, MARS WILL BE PROUD ... I'M PROUD.
POGO'S THE CHAMP... HE TOOK LONGER'N ANYBODY TO DO THE PEN-TATHLON...AND DIN'T EVEN FINISH.
AT THAT RATE, I SHOULD BE CHAMPION... I DIDN'T SO MUCH AS MAKE A BLOOMIN' START.
EARTH
MARS

HERE'S YOUR DOGGONE BOOMERANG BACK... I THOUGHT THESE THINGS WAS SUPPOSED TO RETURN OF THEIR OWN ACCORD?

THE DINKUM OIL IS, COBBER, THAT YOU OFTEN MUST GO OUT AND PERSUADE THE JOKERS A BIT.
HERE'S TO RUDDY OL' MARS, OUR SISTER BLINKIN' PLANET!

CHAPTER 30

Know the Nay,

YOU SAY YOU CAME DOWN TO AUSTRALIA ON A ELK'S CONVENTION, UNCLE ANTLER?
YEP, BUT ALL I FOUND WAS A BUNCH OF GUYS RUNNIN' AROUND IN THEIR UNDERWEARS.

THEY SAID IT WAS THE OLYMPIC GAMES, BUT I THINK THEY WAS LOONEY BIN BAIT.

SO I GOT A JOB AS A NIGHT WATCHMAN AT A DAIRY FARM, BUT THERE WASN'T MUCH TO WATCH.

AND I DIDN'T MIND WHEN ONE FELLOW CALLED ME A COW, BUT WHEN ANOTHER COME AT ME WITH A MILK PAIL I DECIDED TO CLIMB THE FENCE AND HEAD FOR HOME.

IF YOU WANT TO GO BACK HOME, COME ALONG WITH ME.
SURE, HOW YOU GOIN'?

WELL, A FELLOW IN A RED SUIT, WEARIN' A WHITE BEARD, IS IN TOWN WITH A REINDEER GROUP.
THAT SOUNDS LIKE...

SAID HE CAME DOWN HERE TO GET A LITTLE WORK DONE HERE BEFORE CHRISTMAS... FOUND HIMSELF SHORT-HANDED AND HIRED ME TO HELP PULL THE SLEIGH... HIGH OVER ROOF TOP AND STEEPLE..
WE LEAVE TONIGHT FOR THE STATES.
HOW CAN YOU, A MOOSE, DO THAT?
WELL... I SUPPOSE IT IS A LITTLE DISHONEST... I TOLD HIM I WAS A REINDEER.

WELL, ANYWAY... LET'S GET GOIN'.. I'VE GOT TO BE BACK IN TIME FOR THE CHRISTMAS PAGEANT.
SURE, LET'S GO OVER TO THE SLEIGH.
THIS PART I GOT IN THE PAGEANT IS A BIG IMPORTANT ROLE
--THE STORY IS CALLED "THE NIGHT BEFORE CHRISTMAS."

I PLAY THE PART OF "NOT-EVEN."
"NOT EVEN?"
SURE, YOU KNOW WHERE IT SAYS "NOT A CREATURE WAS STIRRIN', NOT-EVEN: A MOUSE." WELL, I'M THE "NOT-A-CREATURE" WHO IS STIRRIN'... "NOT-EVEN," THE MOUSE.

REMEMBER NOW, SNEAK INTO HARNESS RIGHT BEHIND ME ... AND DON'T FORGET, IT'S TEAMWORK THAT COUNTS.

YESSIR, TEAMWORK!

YOU CAN'T GREET POGO WITH A CAROL WHEN HE GETS BACK UN-LESS YOU PRACTICES -- NOW FOLLY ME.
I IS SHEER FOLLYIN'.
READY.. ONE - TWO ..
DECK US ALL WITH BOSTON CHARLIE, WALLA WALLA, WASH., AND KALAMAZOO!
HEY!

I THOUGHT I TOLD EVERYBODY TO FOLLOW ME...OH.. IT'S YOU!
NORA'S FREEZIN' ON THE TROLLEY, SWALLER DOLLAR CAULIFLOWER ALLEY-GAROO!
AW..GO BACK.. WE'RE NOT READY TO WELCOME YOU YET.
HEY!!

DECK US ALL WITH BOSTON CHARLIE, WALLA WALLA, WASH., AND KALAMAZOO... NORA'S FREEZIN' ON THE TROLLEY, SWALLER DOLLAR CAULIFLOWER ALLEY GAROO!
MR. OHO
DON'T WE KNOW ARCHAIC BARREL LULLABY LILLA BOY, LOUISVILLE LOU! TROLLEY MOLLY DON'T LOVE HAROLD, BOOLA BOOLA PENSACOOLA HULLA-BALOO!

DON'T DESPAIR! YOUR SCREAMS FOR HELP HAVE AROUSED THE NOBLE DOG AND HE STANDS READY TO SACRIFICE HIMSELF TO SAVE YOU ALL! 25¢ A PIECE AND A SPECIAL RATE FOR THE BOAT.
LIFE GUAR
WE AIN'T SCREAMIN' FOR HELP .. WE'RE SINGIN'.
CHEAP SKATES.

CHAPTER 31

Pitifully, Wittifully,

ALL RIGHT NOW-- THIS YEAR WE GONNA BE LETTER PERFECK ON CAROLS.
AIN'T GONE BE WITH THIS BOOK.
I TOLE YOU AN' I TOLE YOU-- TURN IT RIGHT SIDE UP.
CAROLS
THERE I DID IT-- AN' IT AIN'T NO HELP.
ON THE FIRST DAY OF CHRISTMAS WHAT DID MY TRUE LOVE SEND TO ME?

A PARSNIP IN A PAN-TRY -- ON THE SECOND DAY SHE SEND OVER TWO PIGEONS AN' ANOTHER PARSNIP.
THEM'S PARTRIDGES NOT PARSNIPS.
THAT GAL WAS BIRD HAPPY -- SHE SEND OVER GEESE, SWANS, PARTRIDGES FRENCH HENS, CALLIN' BIRDS AN' PIGEONS.
WHOOSH! WHAT A SQUAWKY CHRISTMAS THAT MUS' OF BEEN-- TWELVE DAYS OF IT, TOO.

BEFORE US GOES ANY FURTHER LET'S FIND OUT WHAT THIS 12 DAYS OF CHRISTMAS CAROL IS ABOUT.
LET'S PRACTICE.
IT'S ABOUT ALL THEM BIRDS.
CAROLS
WHY WOULD THIS FELLA'S TRUE LOVE SEND OVER ALL THEM PARTRIDGES? AN' IN PEAR TREES, TOO-- AN' PIGEONS--SIX GEESE-- FRENCH HENS.. CALLING BIRDS--AN' SWANS SWIMMIN'.. SEVEN OF 'EM.
SHE LOVED HIM.
CAROLS

YOU CALL THAT LOVE? SENDIN' OVER ALL THOSE POULTRY? CLACKIN' AN' QUACKIN' AN' GOOFIN' AROUND LIKE BIRDS USUAL DOES-- SHE MUST OF HATED HIM.
SHE SENT RINGS TOO.
LET'S PRACTICE.
CAROLS
CAROLS
YEAH, BUT LOOK AT THIS-- SOMETHIN' QUITE ELSE! SHE SENT EIGHT MAIDS A-MILKIN'--- THEY MUST OF BEEN MILKIN' SOMETHIN'-- --GOATS, COWS, CAMELS, BUFFALO-- WHAT A RACKET-- YOU CALL THAT LOVE?
MEBBE HE WAS HUNGRY.
PRACTICE?
CAROLS
NOW S'POSE YOU WAS MY TRUE LOVE AN' YOU SENT ME OVER THIS SET OF POULTRY PLUS MILK MAIDS MILKIN' GOODNESS KNOWS WHAT--- AN' SWANS SWIMMIN' IN SOMETHIN'.
IT'S A HARD S'POSE BUT I'LL DO IT.
THESE GOIN'S ON IS TOOK OVER A WEEK-- SUDDENLY ON THE NINTH DAY OF CHRISTMAS YOU SENDS OVER NINE LADIES DANCIN'-- NEXT DAY IT'S TEN LORDS LEAPIN'.
BOY!
TEN LEAPIN' LORDS! WHAT KIND OF DOIN'S IS THAT! NINETEEN PEOPLE FRACASIN' UP THE PLACE BESIDES ALL THEM MILKMAIDS MILKIN' HAND OVER FIST.
ALL ACCOUNT OF LOVE.
AN' NOT ONLY THAT! BUT YOU SENDS CONSTANT EVERY DAY ANOTHER DOGBONE PARTRIDGE IN A PEAR TREE! WHAT'S YOU DOIN'? CLEANIN' OUT YO' ATTIC?
I JES' WANTS YOU TO ALLUS REMEMBER ME.

IF YOU WAS MY TRUE LOVE AN' SENT OVER ALL THAT STUFF FER TEN DAYS TO GIMME SOMETHIN' TO REE-MEMBER YOU BY I'D HAFTA HAVE TOTAL REE-CALL JUST FOR THE LIVESTOCK ALONE.
TEN DAYS?
CAROLS
WAY I REMEMBERS THAT CAROL IT'S CALLED THE 12 DAYS OF CHRISTMAS-- AS YO' TRUE LOVE I KEPT SENDIN' STUFF...
WHOO! YOU IS RIGHT --ON THE EE-LEVENTH DAY YOU SENDS EELEVEN PIPERS PIPIN'-- .... PLAIN PLUMBERS!
CAROLS

NEXT YOU SENDS TWELVE DRUMMERS...SO THAT WAS YO' GAME ALL ALONG! ALL THIS OTHER FOOFARAW WAS JUS' ADVERTISIN'-- ADVANCE MEN FOR THESE SALESMEN-- THESE DRUMMERS.. BRUSH SELLERS!
FILLIN' MY HOUSE WITH PEOPLE JUMPIN' AROUND IN MILK AN' PARTRIDGES JES' TO SELL ME INDOOR PLUMBIN' AN' BOOKS, BRUSHES AN' WOTNOT--YOU AN' ME IS THRU.
I COULDN'T OF MARRIED YOU ANYWAY.. WITHOUT THE QUEEN'S CONSENT.
BOOP?

EVERYS YEARS AN' EVERYS YEARS CHURCHY AN' YOU, M'SIEUR, CONDUCT THESE CAROL WRONG..SO WE LADIES HAVE BRING OVER RIGHT MUSIC!
MMPH
HEH
DECK THE HALLS WITH BOUGHS OF HOLLY

LONG AS THEY'S NO WAY OUT, MIS' MA'M'SELLE AN' MIZ BEAVER, I BE GLAD TO MAKE INSTANT USE OF IT...
C'MERE GRUNDOON.

OOPS! GRUNDOON IS CLAMPED HIS JAW BONES ONTO PAGE 22 AN' I CAN'T TURN TO SEE WHAT'S THE REST OF THE CAROL.

WHAT A PITIES! --QUICK! OTHERELSE YOU MUST SING WITH ONLY HALF THESE CAROL.
NO DANGER OF THAT! GRUNDOON IS ET THE ENTIRE BOOK··· TOO BAD! WE'LL JES' HAFTA DO IT THE OLD WAY.

WELL, WELL! EVERYBODY READY WITH THE NEW CAROL?
ALBERT SAY IT DON'T MAKE SENSE.
SO WE GONNA SING LAS' YEAR'S ALL OVER AGAIN.
READY!
DECK US ALL WITH BOSTON CHARLIE WALLA WALLA WASH AN' KALAMAZOO! NORA'S FREEZIN' ON THE TROLLEY SWALLER DOLLAR CAULIFLOWER, ALLEY-GA-ROO!

DON'T WE KNOW ARCHAIC BARREL? LULLABY LILLA BOY, LOUISVILLE LOU! TROLLEY MOLLY DON'T LOVE HAROLD BOOLA BOOLA PENSACOOLA HULLA-BALLOO!
NOW HOW 'BOUT "GOOD KING SAUERKRAUT, LOOK OUT! ON YO' FEETS UNEVEN WHILE THE SNOO LAY 'ROUND ABOUT-"! UH-WHAT'S SNOO?
NOT MUCH, AS YOU KIN SEE.
THESE MAKES MORE SENSE?

CHAPTER 32

Plea.

G.O. FIZZICKLE POGO

THE ABOMINABLE SNOWMAN

In these days when most of our heads seem rising to a peak and summit conferences wax and wane in the manner of everybody's moon it might be a good idea to remember the two frogs. You will recall that each started from his home country, traveled along a road, each heading toward the other, both intent upon seeing what sort of land lay beyond the mountain on the middle border.

They met at the summit and each stood erect for a quick preview of the place he'd like to see. Naturally, with their eyes on the tops of their heads, like respectable frogs everywhere, each frog's gaze projected backward along the route that he had taken. So, with a certain amount of grumbling and complaint they decided to return home. "For," as one said to the other, "everything in your country is exactly as it is in mine."

Of course, each had again looked at his own land, and the miracle of the story lies not in the fact that both were fooled, but that from such a vantage point neither had seen anything strange, wonderful or new about his home country. Presumably, neither had seen his country from the top of a hill before. Both frogs, for their entire lives, had been having a frog's-eye view of their homelands, a view that leaves something to be desired by those of us who are not professional frogs.

There is at the summit of any international or world-wide effort to bring about understanding, the Abominable Snowman of Ignorance, who is but dimly seen. He is there determined to crowd out even the frogs who, their mouths full of stones, might scale any slippery modern Acropolis with the intention of exchanging views of their home towns, pictures of the baby, and rearrangements of their prejudices.

Perhaps those of us who meet (with a certain amount of grim surprise) the stranger at the summit should come prepared to learn that his home is very much like our own, and our own very much different than we think. There is not room enough on the horn of Mount

Dilemma for us, the frogs, and him, the Abominable Snowman, the glacial child of our coldhearted war.

The eighteen months of the G. O. Fizzickle Year, wherein we have plumbed our depths and flung moons into the stars, could be followed by a Year of Man, a never-ending year devoted to the study of inner space. For, as has been said before, how can we understand the outsider if we do not know the stranger who is in our skin?

A WORD TO THE FORE

Chapter 1

Uncle Sam, You Made the Months Too Long

In which a doughty band decides to take a dim view of the planetary pulse thru the keyhole of science~~~

IT'S AS PLAIN AS THE NOSE ON YOUR FACE... THE INNERNATIONAL G-O-FIZZICKLE YEAR IS EIGHTEEN MONTHS LONG.. THAT'S THE LAW! ENDORSED BY CONGRESS AN' EMINENT MEDICAL AUTHORITIES.

AN' THAT MAKES EVERYTHING ELSE HALF AGAIN AS LONG-- --TAKE FOR INSTANCE A BANANA --HALF AGAIN--UM--EQUALS EIGHTEEN TO THE DOZEN.

NOTHIN'S AS PLAIN AS THE NOSE ON MY FACE -- I JUST NOTICED, I AIN'T GOT NO NOSE.

DON'T COME COMPLAININ' TO US THAT YOU AIN'T GOT NO NOSE-- WE'RE BUSY MEN-- BUSY MEN!

BUT YOU SAID THE G-O-FIZZICKLE YEAR BEIN' EIGHTEEN MONTHS LONG WAS PLAIN AS THE NOSE ON MY FACE, AN' IF I AIN'T GOT NONE, HOW PLAIN KIN IT BE?
ASK HIM HOW DO HE SMELL.

LEMME ASK YOU JUS' ONE SIMPLE QUESTION-- IF THE G-O-FIZZICKLE YEAR IS 18 MONTHS LONG, HOW LONG IS OCTOBER?
LESSEE, THIRTY DAYS HATH SEPTEMBER APRILJUNE ANNOVEM BER --UM THIRTY ONE!
THIRTY-ONE!? MAN, EITHER THEM MONTHS GOTTA HAVE EXTRA DAYS OR THE YEAR GOTTA HAVE EXTRA MONTHS.
HMM

AND ANOTHER THING.. WHAT IS FRIDAY-THE-13th (WHICH FELL ON SUNDAY THIS TIME) GONNA BE CALLED, FRIDAY-THE-NINETEENTH-AN'-A-HALF?
LEMME FIGGER.
COURSE IT WOULD BE NICE TO THINK UP NAMES FOR SIX NEW MONTHS ... UM .. AN' WHERE WILL WE PUT 'EM ... INTO WINTER OR SUMMER?
DIVIDE 13 BY TWO.. CARRY THE SIX AND MULTIPLY THE..

THE G.O. FIZZICKLE YEAR KIN HAVE EXTRA MONTHS NAMED AFTER FLAVORS ... SEPTEMBERRY, OCTOBERRY NOVEMBERRY, DECEMBERRY ... YUM!
LET'S NOT MAKE A FARCE OUTEN THIS.

JUST A MINUTE ... DID YOU SAY THIS IS THE G.O. FIZZICKLE YEAR?
YEP..A BIG ONE..EIGHTEEN MONTHS LONG.. US G.O. FIZZISTS IS GONNA MEASURE THE WORLD.
WHAT'S G.O. STAND FOR?

IT STANDS FOR "GRAND OLD".. US GRAND OLD FIZZISTS IS GONNA FIND WHAT SHAPE THE WORLD IS IN.

A GOOD IDEA ....I IS ALWAYS WONDERED HOW SQUARE CAN A ROUND WORLD BE.
OR HOW LUMPY.

THE FACT YOU G.O.FIZZISTS IS GONNA MEASURE THE WORLD REMIND ME OF A STORY 'BOUT UNCLE MERVIN WHAT THE ONLY TIME HE GOT MEASURED WAS FOR A FUNERAL... HIS..
KAPPIE OPPER

IT SEEM UNCLE MERV EX-PLODED ONE DAY AN' WHEN THEY MEASURE HIM FOR HIS GOIN' AWAY SUIT THEY FIND HE IS TEN SIZES BIGGER'N THE CLOTHES HE USETA WEAR...

"NOW I KNOW THE CAUSE OF DEATH," SAYS AUNTIE WOGGET, "OL' MERV JUS' GOT TOO BIG FOR HIS BRITCHES AN'--"
WHAT'S THAT GOT TO DO WITH MEASURIN' THE EARTH? WE'S S'POSED TO BE DOIN' IT FOR THE FIRST TIME --NOT THE LAST!
MIZ FRITZ

Chapter 2

AROUND THE MAST IN EIGHTY DAYS

Wherein our heroes take life in teeth and set sail with the rockets red glare bursting bums in the air~~~

TURN BACK! WE CAN'T START! FRIDAY-THE-THIRTEENTH FALLS ON WEDNESDAY THIS MONTH.
BALDER DASH!
THIS BEIN' THE G.O. FIZZICKLE YEAR, IT'S EIGHTEEN MONTHS LONG.. ..AN' SO NOVEMBER IS A HALF MONTH LONGER.... TODAY WOULD ACTUALLY BE DECEMBER TWENTY-EIGHTH!
WE MISSED CHRISTMAS.
OL' DAVE PARSONS

IF THE G.O. FIZZICKLE YEAR MAKES EVERYTHING ONE AN' A HALF TIMES AS LONG, THEN TODAY MUST BE DEC. 29 ... ON ACCOUNT NOVEMBER FOURTEEN WOULD BE FORTY-FIVE DAYS FROM NOW AND CHRISTMAS IS BACK THERE.
AND NO LUNCH YET.
BREAK OUT THE CHOW! THE CREW IS STARVIN'!
CHOW?

GOOD-BYE CHRISTMAS, GOOD-BYE CHRISTMAS.
CHOW! I'M THE CAPTAIN! NOT THE COOK.
I'M QUITTIN'! I WANT MY FULL PAY OF TIME AN' A HALF.
THE GENERAL MUDGE
TIME AN' HALF FOR ORNERY TIME?
YEP, WAIT'LL ALL US UNION MEN FINDS OUT THIS IS THE BIG TIME AN' A HALF YEAR.

THE LOOKOUT IS ON STRIKE SO CLIMB THE MIZZENMAST AN' KEEP YOUR EYES ABAFT FOR A LANDFALL.
HUH?
LOS ANGELES
OL' CAP'N ED

WHAT DO YOU MEAN "HUH"? WHERE'S YOUR SEA SCOUT TRAININ'? ALOFT WITH YOU.
AYE, AYE, SIR! ALOFT IT IS, SIR.

PARM ME, SIR, BUT I IS S'POSE TO CLIMB THE MAST---AND YOU GOT A MASTY LOOK ABOUT YOU.
I AIN'T SPEAKIN' TO THE CREW.

I IS MAINTAININ' A ALOOF, NOBLE, DIGNIFIED, KINDLY, COURTEOUS, WOUNDED AN' SECRET SILENCE AS A GENTLE REPROOF TO THE MANAGEMENT WHICH IS A GOGGLE-EYED, KNOCK-KNEED BURGLAR AN' BUM.
OOP
ED
REAP

OOP
GANGWAY! I'M MI-GRATIN' WITH A DUCK TEAM.

YOU, A BAT, MIGRATIN' WITH A MESS OF MALLARDS?
THEY WAS A LI'L SHORT-HANDED.. CARE TO JOIN?

IF YOU WANTED TO JOIN THIS DUCK GROUP FLYIN' SOUTH I THINK I COULD GET YOU A JOB.
NO.. I AIN'T MUCH FOR FLYIN'.
HUP TWO THREE FOUR! HUP TWO..
LUCKY JACK

TURTLES AIN'T SO MUCH BIRDS LIKE BATS IS.
OH, WE AIN'T REALLY BIRDS.

BUT YOU FLIES AROUND.. FLAPPIN' YO' WINGS LIKE UNTO A EAGLE.
WELL SHUCKS, FAR AS THAT GOES, TURTLES LAYS EGGS.

OH SOME SHOW-OFF TYPES DOES, BUT I ALWAYS FARMS THAT KIND OF WORK OUT TO THE EASTER BUNNY.
HUP TWO THREE FOUR HUP T....
HANDSOME J. LARKIN

IT'S A GOOD THING I TOOK OVER THE DUTIES OF THE MILITARY.. ... WATCH ME CHANGE THE GUARD NOW IN ONE OF OUR COLORFUL CEREMONIES.
THE MACDOUGAL ROCKET

PREE-SENT ARMS! SHOULDER THE REVEILLE!

ABOUT FACE....
..PARADE!
HUP TWO
KLANK!

WHY IS GUNS ALWAYS LOADED?
WHO AIN'T?
M.R. WERNER

THIS GUN IS A TRICKY, SNEAKY, BACKBITIN', MALFEASIN', LOWLIVIN' PIECE OF TURNCOATIN' MACHINERY.
H.M.S. CALLAHAN

AND NO DAGNAB GUN IS GONNA TAKE ME UNAWARES! YOU HEAR!? Y'HEAR! YOU.. YOU..

YOU..
BLAM

THIS IS MORE INTERESTIN' THAN DUCK WORK.
BULL'S-EYE!
I'M NOT SPEAKIN' TO THE CREW.

HOLD IT!
HEY, WHERE YOU GOIN'?
I AIN'T NO COWARD. AS CAPTAIN OF MY SUNK SHIP, I IS RETURNIN' TO WHAT'S LEFT OF THE SUNKEN WRECK.
WHAT?
YOU ABANDONED SHIP! US SURVIVORS IS IN CHARGE. MARITIME LAW SAY WE GOT SALVAGE RIGHTS OF THIS HULK.
MUTINY!
YEAH!
GRR.
JUST A DOG-BONE MINUTE!
YOU IS PART OF THE SHIP.. QUIET!
YEAH, YOU IS ROCKIN' THE BOAT.
YOU JUMPED SHIP ON THE HIGH SEAS..SO I IS CAPTAIN.
THIS HULK IS MINE.
I AIN'T NO HULK!
BESIDES, YOU BLEW UP THE SHIP.
I RISKED MY LIFE TRYIN' TO AVERT A EXPLOSION.

HAW! YOU SAW! HE DELIBERATE PULLED THE TRIGGER.
ALL I DID IS GO LIKE THIS..
WHEN.. OOP
BAM!
YOU IS ALL WHAT'S LEFT OF THE BOAT, ALBERT.
AN' I IS THROUGH!
BUT YOU CAN'T BE ... YOU WAS THE MAINMAST.. WE GOTTA BUILD A WHOLE NEW BOAT AROUND YOU..OR THE PATAGONIANS WILL MEASURE THE WORLD AFORE US.. IT'S A PATRIOTIC DUTY.
ALL I CAN DO IS GIVE YOU A HAND.
YOU HEARD HIM.. OUR RIVALRY TO SEE WHO IS IN CHARGE GOES ON UNDYIN'.
I IS FOR NOT DYIN'.
HE SAYS HE'LL GIVE A HAND... I CHALLENGES YOU TO A DUEL, 'TIL DEATH DO US PART, FOR ALBERT'S HAND.

Chapter 3

A DUAL DUEL TO A PARLIAMENTAL DEFICIENCY

Here it is demonstrated that after the vote was cast they destroyed the mould---

I'M GLAD YOU THUNK OF VOTIN' FOR CAPTAIN, 'STEAD OF FIGHTIN'..
IT WOULD SAVE WEAR AN' TEAR AN' BLOODSHED.
AN' WHEN YOU SAYS I COULD CAST THE DECIDIN' VOTE IF TURTLE VOTES FOR HIM AN' YOU VOTES FOR YOU.. I APPRECIATES THE HONOR...
GOOD!
--I COULD CAST A DECIDIN' VOTE FOR ME.
HUT TUT-- IT HASTA BE A MAJORITY VOTE..YOUR WAY WOULD MAKE IT ONE APIECE.
EVERYTHING BEIN' EQUAL..YES! BUT I'M BIGGER'N YOU TWO...I'M TWICE AS EQUAL.
SORRY.. I GOT THE LAW ON MY SIDE AN' BESIDES I'M COUNTIN' THE VOTES.
LOOK, FACE IT...I GOT THE PERSONALITY, BRAINS, GOOD LOOKS AN' CLOTHES FOR THE JOB OF CAPTAIN.
A SNAP JUDGMENT.
YEH, BUT I IS HAD THAT SNAP JUDGMENT FOR YEARS..IT IS STOOD THE TEST OF TIME...NOW, ON THIS VOTE, LET'S MAKE A DEAL.
FAIR AN' SQUARE.

S'POSE ONE OF US WAS PERSUADED TO VOTE FOR ANOTHER?
CHURCHY! HE'S STUPID ENOUGH TO VOTE FOR ME.
YOU STOLE MY IDEA! YOU IS S'POSED TO BE STUPID ENOUGH TO VOTE FOR ME...
YOU FIGGERS WRONG... TURTLE IS EVEN STUPIDER.

WE'LL GO SEE TURTLE AN' STRAIGHTEN THIS OUT ONCET AN' FOR ALL...
WE'LL WALK OVER QUIETLY AND ASK HIM WHO'LL HE VOTE FOR..
HO! HE'S NOT STUPID ENOUGH TO VOTE FOR YOU.. HE'S STUPID ENOUGH TO VOTE FOR ME.
HE'S EVEN STUPIDER... HE'LL VOTE FOR ME.

WE'LL WALK OVER QUIETLY AND ASK HIM ...WE'LL SEE HOW STUPID HE IS.
YOU AIN'T THE JUDGE OF STUPIDNESS LIKE I IS... I'M A EXPERT.
HEY! WE'RE S'POSED TO WALK QUIETLY.
I'M QUIET.

HUMPH HUMPH HUMPH HUMPH
WHAT'S YOU SO HUMPHY ABOUT?

OWL AND ME IS ENGAGED.
WHAT?

..ENGAGED IN ANOTHER LIFE-LONG DUEL TO THE DEATH.
WHO'S AHEAD?
OH, ME.. I WON THE LAST TWO DUELS AN' HE AIN'T WON ANY.
PO

WHEN'S THIS BIG DUEL 'TWEEN YOU AND OWL GONNA START?
SOON AS WE'RE ALL TOOLED UP.
TOOLED UP? YOU GOING TO USE REAL WEAPONS THIS TIME?
YEP, DAGGERS, ROCKS, FISTS, STICKS AND MEBBE A COUPLE JET FIGHTERS FROM A FOREIGN POWER.

AIN'T THAT GONNA BE A LI'L' DANGEREST?
YES.. IT UPSETS ME TO THINK OF WHAT IF I WINS...

I'LL LOSE ONE OF THE BEST FRIENDS A BOY EVER HAD.

IT WORRIES ME TO THINK THAT I MIGHT WIN THIS DUEL WITH OL' HOWLAND ...I'D MISS HIM SOMETHIN' FIERCE.

JUS' DON'T THINK OF IT THAT WAY.. MAYBE YOU WON'T WIN.
YEH.. THAT'S RIGHT.

WHAT!?

Chapter 4

Visions of Sugar Bums

In which Christmas is won if not too and the Christmas tree is forth---

ON FURTHER THOUGHT, MAYBE I BETTER NOT JUST WALK IN ON OWL ··· HE MAY BE STILL SORE ··· MAY BE ARMED AN' SORE.

AFTER ALL, FRIDAY-THE-THIRTEENTH IS COMED ON A FRIDAY THIS MONTH··· HE COULD SHOOT ME DOWN IN MY OWN DEAR LOVIN' COLD BLOOD.

THERE HE IS NOW, THE GOOD OLD PAL -- WHAT A CHUM! WAIT 'TIL HE TELLS YOU HE'LL VOTE FOR ME!
MY BUDDY! HE'S ALL FOR ME.
TWO OF 'EM!

I'LL NEVER BE TAKEN ALIVE ··· OR DEAD.

BOOM
BOOM
BOOM
SHOOTIN' AT ME FROM THE FRONT!

PAL! CHUM! OLD DEAR FRIEND!
COMPANION OF MY CRADLE! DEAR OLD BUDDY BOY.
IF YOU'VE COME TO JOIN THE CAROL PRACTICE, KEEP A LI'L' QUIET WHILST WE GOES THRU THE BASS DRUM SOLO.

OL' PAL, OL' CHUM.. OWL SAYS YOU'RE STUPID ENOUGH TO VOTE FOR HIM..
WHAT?
ALBERT SAYS YOU'RE STUPID ENOUGH TO VOTE FOR HIM.. TELL HIM HAHA OL' BUDDY.
BOOM
BLAM!
BOOM

WE DECIDED YOU TWO WOULDN'T HAVE NO DUEL, BUT WE'D VOTE TO SEE WHO'S GONE BE CAPTAIN ..SO I EXPECTS YOU'LL VOTE FER ME... HAVE A PUFF ON MY SEE-GAR?
ON ACCOUNT YOU'RE MY BEST FRIEND, VOTE FOR ME FIRST.
HEY! HOW ABOUT A LITTLE QUIET SO'S WE CAN PRACTICE OUR CHRISTMAS CAROLS?

WE IS MERE DISCUSSIN' WHO'S GONNA BE ELECTED CAPTAIN...
BUT CHRISTMAS IS PRACTICAL AT HAND AN' WE AIN'T REE-HEARSED.. HOW 'BOUT A SHORT BURST OF "DECK US ALL"?
THE GLEE AND PERLOO SOCIETY

DECK US ALL WITH BOSTON CHARLIE, WALLA WALLA, WASH., AN' KALAMAZOO! NORA'S FREEZIN' ON THE TROLLEY, SWALLER DOLLAR CAULIFLOWER ALLEY-GA-ROO!
LIKE YOU SAY, CECIL, I KNOW IT AIN'T A AIR RAID, BUT THEY IS A-NOTHER VERSE TO COME..

DON'T WE KNOW ARCHAIC BARREL? LULLABY LILLA BOY, LOUISVILLE LOU! TROLLEY MOLLY DON'T LOVE HAROLD, BOOLA BOOLA PENSACOOLA HULLA-BALOO!
BOY! JUST THE SPOT FOR MY BASS.
BUM BUM BUM BUM BUM

HEY! HEY! YOU PUT TOO MANY "BUMS" INTO THE REHEARSAL.
BUM BUM BU B- HUH?

YOU ASK ME, I'D SAY NATURE BEAT ME TO IT.

I DON'T MEAN TO CARP, BUT THAT ONE WE SING AIN'T THE McCOY.
"DECK US ALL WITH BOSTON CHARLIE?"
NO... I MEAN YES.. THE ORIGINAL, A TONE POEM OF CELESTIAL QUALITY, IS CALLED "BARK US ALL BOW-WOWS OF FOLLY."
WHAT?
BOOM

"BARK US ALL BOW-WOWS OF FOLLY?"
SORRY.. DRUM'S GETTIN' AWAY.
BOOM
BOOM

DON'T LEAVE ME ALONE WITH A TITLE LIKE THAT!
BOOM
BOOM
BOOM
BOOM

HUH?
I SAID WHY DOES EVERY SPOT YOU PICK FOR A PICNIC HAVE TO BE IN THUNDERSTORM COUNTRY?
BOOM
BOOM
BOOM
BOOM
I DON'T SEE NO CLOUDS..ALL I SEE IS A DRUM.

HEIGHDY, BEAUREGARD. BUSY DAY?
HEIGHDY, BUNCE! DRUM GOT AWAY.. HEH HEH.
LAND!
I WISH YOU'D STOP HANGING AROUND THE FIREHOUSE--THAT FRIEND OF YOURS MADE OFF WITH OUR TEAPOT.
BOOM
BOOM
BOOM
DON'T LIKE TEA NOHOW.

ANOTHER JET PILOT! WHAT'S ALL THE TRAFFIC?
HOWDY, MIZ RABBIT AN' HOWDY, BUNCE... DID YOU SEE A DRUM, A UNFINISHED POME AN' A HOUN'DOG GO BY, IN THAT ORDER?
DAG NAB, THEM SINGLE FELLOWS HAS ALL THE FUN.

I ALMOST DROWNT GETTIN' THE DRUM BACK, BUT I HEROICALLY HELD ON.
IT'S DRIVIN' ME CRAZY ... I GOTTA KNOW WHAT'S THE REST OF "BARK US ALL BOW-WOWS OF FOLLY."
SPLOCK!
HOW DO YOU SPELL THAT "SPLOCK"?

YOUR CAROL ENDED WITH A "SPLOCK" .. KIND OF ABRUPT, AIN'T IT?
PHAWSH! I FELL OVERBOARD.

IT GOES .. "BARK US ALL BOW-WOWS OF FOLLY, POLLY WOLLY CRACKER AN' TOOD ALOO! HUNKY DORY'S POP IS LOLLY GAGGIN' IN THE WAGON WILLY FOLLY-GO-THROUGH ..

HEY! THERE'S MORE ..
NEXT YEAR ..! C'MON! THE OTHERS IS WAITIN' FOR US TO GO SING THE REALLER McCOY.
HURRY UP ..! ASK HOUN'DOG HOW HE SPECTS TO CARRY A TUNE ON A WET DRUM?

Chapter 5

MANY HAPPY RETURNS OF THE GIFT

Chapter 6

Crazy as a Bug in a Rug

Here we scratch a flea and find a bite of gold~~~

I DON'T BELIEVE YOUR COUSIN'S PLAN TO SHOOT PEOPLE INTO OUTER SPACE WILL BE POPULAR.
IT'LL BE POPULAR WITH MICE.

YOU MEAN MICE ARE TIRED OF BEIN' EXPERIMENTED ON?
FAFG! YES! WHEN I THINK OF THE HUNDREDS OF CIGARETS, CIGARS AND SALAMIS THAT I'VE TESTED IN MY TIME.

WHAT'S THE ORDINARY MOUSE GOT TO LOOK FORWARD TO? IF HE'S GOT A JOB IN A GOOD FAMILY HE GETS TO SWEAR AT THE CAT.. BUT S'POSE YOU WANT YOUR BOY TO GO TO COLLEGE.. TO ESCAPE A MENIAL POSITION.
BING! RIGHT AWAY HE HAS TO GO IN FOR LABORATORY WORK... BY THE TIME HE'S ALL GEARED UP WITH TEST TUBES HE LOOKS LIKE A DRUG STORE.. BY JING, I'M NOT RAISIN' MY BOY TO BE NO GUINEA PIG.

WHAT'S YOU GOT AGAINST GUINEA PIGS?
US MICE JUS' DON'T WANT TO BE USED AS GUINEA PIGS, THAT'S ALL.

SOME OF THEM EXPERIMENTS WHAT SCIENCE MAKES WITH US IN COLLEGE IS FRIGHTENIN'.

BY JING, HUMAN PEOPLE DON'T TREAT ANIMALS RIGHT.
HUH?

A FLEA BUG! I SAID PEOPLE DON'T TREAT US ANIMALS RIGHT.
I AGREES --THEY IS TROUBLE-MAKERS.

MY COUSIN FROM RUSSIA WROTE SAYIN' THE MICE OF SIBERIA HAVE PERFECTED SATELLITES AN' THEY'RE MANNIN' THEM WITH MEN.
REVOLUTIONARY.

TURNABOUT IS FAIR PLAY... THEY BEEN MICIN' ROCKETS WITH MICE FOR YEARS... LOOKIN' INTO OUR STOMACHS THRU LITTLE WINDOWS ...TRYIN' TO PERFECT THE BETTER MOUSE TRAP... DISGUSTING!
I'D OF GIVE A PERTY TO OF BEEN IN THAT SPUTWURST NO. 2.

YOU, A FLEA, MAY BELIEVE THAT DOGS IS MAN'S BEST FRIEND.. BUT I, A MOUSE, KNOW THAT MICE IS.
DOGS IS MAN'S BEST FRIEND IF THAT MAN IS A FLEA..

NO MAN, NO SELF RESPECTIN' MAN IS A FLEA... HE MIGHT BE A DOG, HE MIGHT EVEN BE A MOUSE, BUT MIGHTY FEW IS FLEAS.
THEY AIN'T BUILT FOR IT... THAT'S ALL! ..IT'S A HARD LIFE.

WHAT!? HARD LIFE? I COULD BE A BUG WITH ONE ARM TIED AHIND OF MY BACK... BUGS HAVE IT EASY.. YOU EVER HEAR THE MAXIM "COZY AS A BUG IN A RUG"?
THAT'S COZY?

HOW'D YOU LIKE TO BE WORKIN' IN A RUG? NOBODY TO TALK TO BUT THEM BRAINLESS MOTHS AND A FEW CIGARET ASHES.. ..DID YOU EVER TRY TO PUT THE BITE ON A CARPET?
FOOMPH FOOMPH FOOMPH

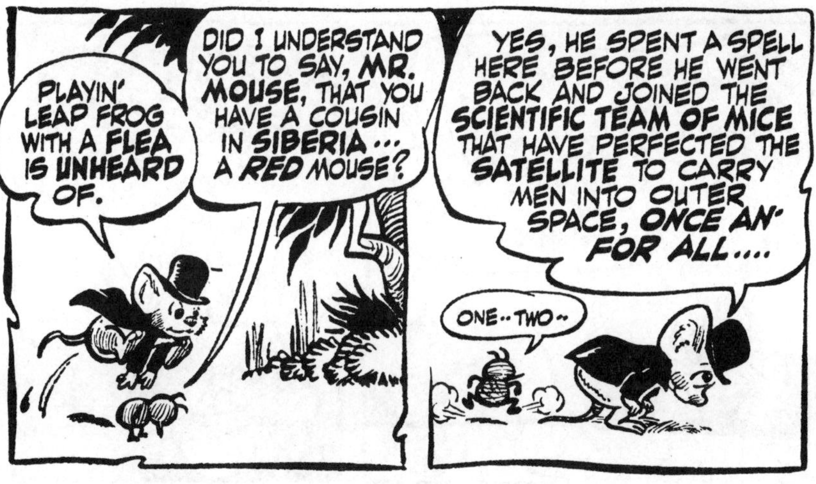
PLAYIN' LEAP FROG WITH A FLEA IS UNHEARD OF.
DID I UNDERSTAND YOU TO SAY, MR. MOUSE, THAT YOU HAVE A COUSIN IN SIBERIA... A RED MOUSE?
YES, HE SPENT A SPELL HERE BEFORE HE WENT BACK AND JOINED THE SCIENTIFIC TEAM OF MICE THAT HAVE PERFECTED THE SATELLITE TO CARRY MEN INTO OUTER SPACE, ONCE AN' FOR ALL....
ONE.. TWO..

THR..
I AND HIM HAD A JOB IN A OL' LADIES HOME...IT WAS OUR DUTY TO SQUEAK UNDERBENEATH OF THE BEDS TO CAUSE A LITTLE EXCITEMENT. BUT WHENEVER ONE FOUND IVAN SHE'D HOLLER "THERE'S A MOUSE UNDER MY BED AN' BESIDES HE'S A COMMUNIST!" WELL, THAT KIND OF POLITICAL TALK JUST SICKENED IVAN AN' HE WENT BACK TO THE REINDEER FARM AND......
HELLO?
EE!

Chapter 7

THE SONG OF THE FLEA

In which the flea cries the blues and we scale a summit for the key to the economy~~~

WHEN I WAS A YOUNG'N EVERYBODY CLAIMED DOGS WAS MAN'S BEST FRIEND, EXCEPT SOME SAID CATS AND PIGS.
PIGS!?

SURE! PIGS PROVIDES SUITCASES, PIGS FEETS, HAM AN' EGGS, BACON AN' TOMATO SAN'WICHES AND FOOTBALLS.
BUT PIGS AIN'T CHUMMY.

I STILL SAY DOGS IS MAN'S BEST FRIEND IF YOU IS A FLEA WHICH I AM AND PROUD OF IT.
WHAT KIND OF A DOG YOU GOT IN MIND?

OH, CHOCOLATE, STRAWBERRY, VANILLA, OR ANYTHING WHAT'S HANDY-- PERSONALLY, I PREFERS COLLIES-- THEY TASTES LIKE SAUERKRAUT AN' SPARE RIBS.
ME, I GOT A SWEET TOOTH FOR GORGONZOLA.

THIS FLEA NUMBSKULL KEEPS TALKIN' ABOUT DOGS... IT'S UN-AMERICAN TO CLAIM DOGS ARE MAN'S BEST FRIEND... DOGS ARE BEST FRIENDS OF RUSSIANS!
LOOK AT THE SPUTWURST-- WHO GOT A RIDE? A MOUSE? NO, A DOG!
BUT RUSSIANS ARE MEN-- EVEN AS YOU AND ME... --AND WHY SHOULDN'T DOGS GET A RIDE ON THE SPUT-NITCH? THEY'RE FREE, WIDE, AND TWENTY-THREE SKIDDOO.
I HATE ANIMALS!

BUT YOU'RE A ANIMAL YOUR-SELF--ALL US HUMANS IS ANIMALS---EVERYTHING WHAT MOVES, BREATHES, GROANS, JUMPS, SLIDES, SWIMS, WHISTLES, FLIES, BURROWS, CRAWLS OR JIGGLES IS A ANIMAL...
NOT ME..I DON'T DO NONE OF THEM..
YOU BREATHES, DON'T YOU?
NOT OF MY OWN FREE WILL I DON'T..

ONE THING IS SURE! IF DOGS ARE MAN'S BEST FRIEND, HE BETTER KEEP 'EM.. ..IT'S BETTER'N NOTHING.
YOU'RE JEALOUS.
JUST BECAUSE MAN DON'T WANT A CLOUD OF MICE BURSTING OUT THE DOOR TO GREET HIM AT NIGHT, LEAPING INTO HIS LAP CARRYIN' SLIPPERS, DON'T MEAN DOGS AIN'T WANTED...
DOGS ARE FRAUDS.

HOW ABOUT CATS?
CATS AND DOGS ARE ALL THE SAME.. ..FRUSTRATED MICE! ..LOUNGIN' AROUND THE HOUSE, MAKIN' OUT LIKE THEY GOT A HONEST JOB..HA!
WHO KEEPS 'EM EMPLOYED? US MICE! THE CATS CHASE US; THE DOG CHASES THE CAT; THE LADY OF THE HOUSE CHASES THE DOG...THE KIDS CHASE THE MOTHER...IT'S WORK FOR EVERYBODY..WHO PLANS IT ALL?..MICE! THE KEY TO THE ECONOMY!

OH, BAZZ FAZZ

WHEN I SAID "MICE IS THE KEY TO THE ECONOMY," I MEANT WE KEEPS THINGS STIRRED UP..
I WAS IN STIR ONCE WITH THE WARDEN'S WATCH DOG.

YOU WAS ROOMIES ?
FOR SIX SEMESTERS.. HE FINALLY GOT SPRUNG ON A WRIT OF HABEAS CORPUS DELICTI.

A LEGAL MANEUVER?
NO, A FELLA NAME OF HABEAS C. DELICTI WRIT TO HIM.

WHAT'D HE SAY ?
HE SAID "YOU GOT A FLEA.." MEANING, AT LEAST, ME.. HE SAYS "IT SAYS I GOTTA FLEE, IT SAYS," HE SAYS SO, HE HOPPED A RATTLER, THE SNAKE, AND I TOOK IT ON THE LAM..NEVER TRUST A SHEEP DOG.

IMPORTANT WORK LIKE SITTIN' AROUND FISHIN' REMAINS TO BE DONE.

YOU TWO STILL QUARRELIN'?
WE AIN'T QUARRELIN' -- WE'RE HAVIN' A DYNAMIC INTELLECTUAL EXERCISE.
YOU BEEN TO THE BRINK OF FIGHTIN' ?
NO, THAT WOULD BE A FATEFUL CATACLYSM.. .... WE BEEN HAVIN' A PRELIMINARY MEETING OF MINDS.
SO'S YOU CAN HAVE A SUMMIT SESSION.
YEH -- UP TO NOW WE JUST BEEN HORSIN' AROUND FIGGERIN' ON WHAT WE'LL FIGHT ABOUT LATER.
HOW'S IT LOOK..? THINK YOU'LL GET ANYTHING SETTLED?
WHAT! AN' DO OURSELVES OUT OF A JOB?
SURE... IT'S BETTER TO BE WORKIN' EVEN IF YOU'RE NOT DOIN' ANYTHING...
RIGHT!
Z

Chapter 8

THE BRANCH AND BARK OF A DOG

Wherein a dog's eye view of a flea is found to be myopic if at all~~~

HOW CAN A FLEA CLAIM TO BE A FRIEND OF ME?
HE GOT A SWEET TOOTH FOR YOU.
BUT FLEAS IS ALWAYS TOOK ADVANTAGE OF US DOGS.. HOOKIN' RIDES, LUNCHIN', GETTIN' A ROOF OVER THEIR HEADS WITHOUT PAYIN' ANY RENT....

ALL FLEAS IS NO GOOD FREELOADERS... NOT ONLY THAT BUT THEY IS TWO PARTS BURGLARS AND THREE PARTS CANNIBALS.
YOU TAKE A DOG WHAT GOT A SKIN FULL OF FLEAS AN' I'LL SHOW YOU A DOG WHAT AIN'T GOT NO PRIVACY... --HE'S NEVER REALLY ALONE.

HOW CAN YOU DENOUNCE A POOR INNOCENT FLEA AFORE YOU EVEN KNOWS HIM?
I DON'T WANT TO KNOW HIM.

BUT MAYBE TO KNOW HIM IS TO LOVE HIM.. --HE MAY BE INTERESTING, GAY, A WIT, A BON VIVANT, A BRILLIANT CONVERSATIONALIST.

A GREAT JUDGE OF WINES, A DISCRIMINATIN' CRITIC OF LITERATURE, ONE OF THE FEW WHO CAN ROLL A CIGARET NO HANDS.. A FINE VIOLINIST.

A GOURMET.
SEE!? HE'S A BUM RIGHT THERE.

YOU CAN'T BLAGGARD A MAN JES' 'CAUSE HE'S A GOURMET.
I CAN IF HE'S ALSO A FLEA.
I SHOULD THINK IT'D BE A HONOR TO YOU FOR SOMEBODY TO PREFER THE COMPANY OF DOGS.
IT WOULD BE IF HE DIN'T COME AT ME WITH A KNIFE AND FORK.

BUT HE CLAIMS YOU MEAN A LOT TO HIM.
TO HIM I'M JUST A BIG PILE OF POTATO SALAD WITH COLD CUTS ON THE SIDE.
'S FUNNY... I NEVER LOOKED AT YOU QUITE THAT WAY.
I DO SOUND DELICIOUS, DON'T I? IT MAKES A MAN SORTA QUIETLY PROUD.

Chapter 9

Hark, Hark, The Lark Doth Bark!

In this episode marriage and eternal love raise their ugly heads to outstare each other~~~

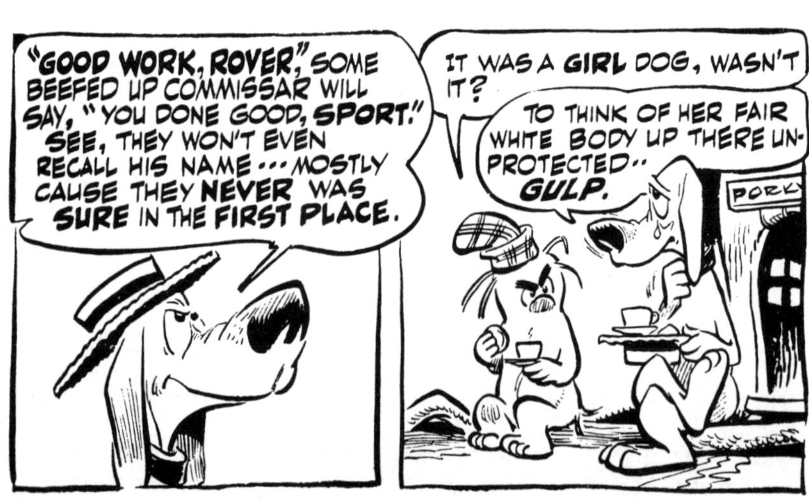

ANONYMOUS? I THOUGHT SHE HAD MORE NAMES THAN A MEXICAN NOBLE --**LINDA, KUDRYAVKA, KOZYAVKLA, LIMONCHIK, MALYSHKA, DAMKA**...

THEM WAS JUST **NEWSPAPER** TALK; EVEN IN RUSSIA WHEN THEY CALLS A DOG THEY DON'T HOLLER, "**COMERE LINDA, KUDRYAVKA**, COME GIRL, HERE **KOZYAVKLA**.. HOO HOO, **MALYSHKA!**

NO NORMAL DOG'LL PUT UP WITH TALK LIKE THAT--- HE'D JUST **LAUGH!** DOGS **REE-**SPONDS IF YOU SCREAMS: "**HERE, SPOT, YOU BLACK-HEARTED NO-GOOD FREE-LOADIN' SPOT!**" THEN YOU **YANK** ON THEIR CHAIN.

SO... **SPOTNIK**, EH?

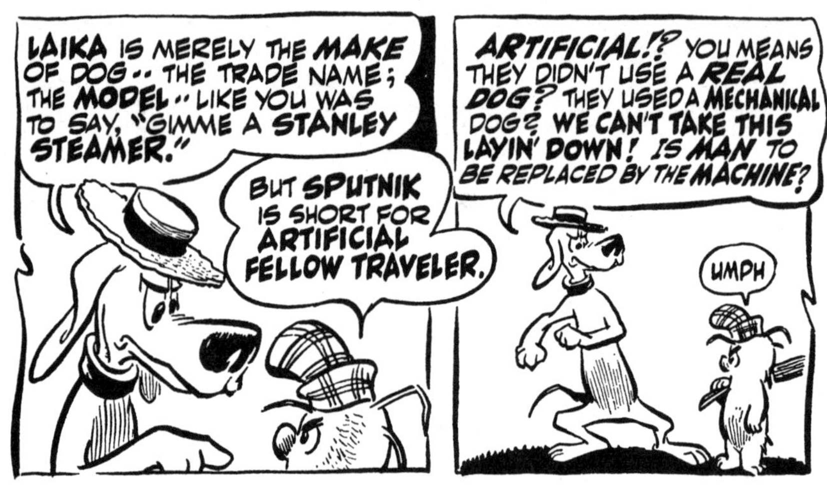
LAIKA IS MERELY THE MAKE OF DOG.. THE TRADE NAME; THE MODEL.. LIKE YOU WAS TO SAY, "GIMME A STANLEY STEAMER."
BUT SPUTNIK IS SHORT FOR ARTIFICIAL FELLOW TRAVELER.
ARTIFICIAL!? YOU MEANS THEY DIDN'T USE A REAL DOG? THEY USED A MECHANICAL DOG? WE CAN'T TAKE THIS LAYIN' DOWN! IS MAN TO BE REPLACED BY THE MACHINE?
UMPH

MOUSE, DO YOU REALIZE THE SPUTNIKS SENT UP A ARTIFICIAL DOG? WHAT'S WE COMIN' TO?
PROB'LY NO LIVE DOG HAD THE SPUNK TO VOLUNTEER.
THAT GOT ALL THE EARMARKS OF A INSULT... D'YOU KNOW US SCIENTIFIC EXPERIMENTALITIES IS BEIN' DONE OUT OF JOBS BY MACHINES?

HAS MAN EVER BEEN ABLE TO BUILD THE BETTER MOUSE TRAP? NO! AN' WHY NOT? BECAUSE SCIENCE BEEN WORKIN' WITH REAL MICE.. SO THEY'LL USE MECHANICAL MICE WHAT'S BUILT FOR THE JOB... THEN YOU'LL BE OUT OF BUSINESS.
HOWDY, I'M A FLEA AND I'D JUST LIKE TO SAY: YUM!

I WAS RAISED ON A COLLIE... BUT I THINK IT'S YOU FOR ME. WHY NOT GET HITCHED, SWEETHEART ?
I'M NO COLLIE... AN' I COULDN'T SUPPORT YOU IN THE STYLE TO WHICH YOU ARE A CUSTOMER.

TWO CAN LIVE AS CHEAP AS ONE, HONEY!
NOT ON ME THEY CAN'T.

WHY DO YOU FLEAS ALWAYS PICK ON DOGS ?
I'M NOT PICKIN' ON YOU·· I JUST WANT TO MARRY YOU.

WHY DON'T YOU MARRY SOME HUMAN? THEY'RE THE ONES WITH THE MONEY.
HUMANS ARE TOO CHANCY··SOME ARE NICE, BUT SOME AIN'T··SOME GOES TO ONE CHURCH SOME ANOTHER... SOME ARE DEMOCRATS SOME REPUBLICANS SOME IS EVEN COMMUNISTS.

YOU DON'T HAVE TO JOIN 'EM·· ALL YOU WANT TO DO IS MARRY ONE.
I DUNNO 'BOUT THAT·· LET ME ASK THE MAN IN THE STREET·· MIZ WEEVIL, HOW'D YOU LIKE YOUR DAUGHTER TO MARRY A COMMUNIST?

I WOULDN'T WANT MY DAUGHTER TO MARRY ANY KIND OF A HUMAN BEAN.
AW, NOW, MA!

Chapter 10

THE FUTURE FIDGETS AND GROANS

Wherein we discover that the tourist's main problem in space will be to avoid tourists ~~~

FOR EXAMPLE, EVERY-BODY'S YACKIN' ABOUT A TRIP TO THE MOON--- PEOPLE WHAT NEVER EVEN BEEN TO LITTLE ROCK SUDDENLY WANT TO HIT BLUE SKY...
MEBBE THEY KNOWS MORE FOLKS ON THE MOON.
YOU IS BEIN' FACETIOUST.. EVERYBODY KNOWS THEY AIN'T NO PEOPLE ON THE MOON.
THE HON. HARRY ASHMORE

OL' HARRY

THAT MIGHT BE WHY THEY WANTS TO GO THERE.
THE S.S. ASHMORE
THE GAZETTE

WHY DON'T I GET TO SAY ANYTHING FUNNY ONCE IN A WHILE?

IF YOU FEELS SO STRONG ABOUT THE MOON WHY NOT DO SOMETHIN'?
I IS CURRENTLY PUTTIN' THE RESOURCES OF MY POWERFUL BRAIN TO WORK ON THE SUBJECT.

YOU THINKS THE MOON IS GETTIN' SHORT SHRIFT, SO, WHY NOT START A ORGANIZATION TO DEFEND THE MOON?
EXACTLY WHAT I WAS THINKIN'.

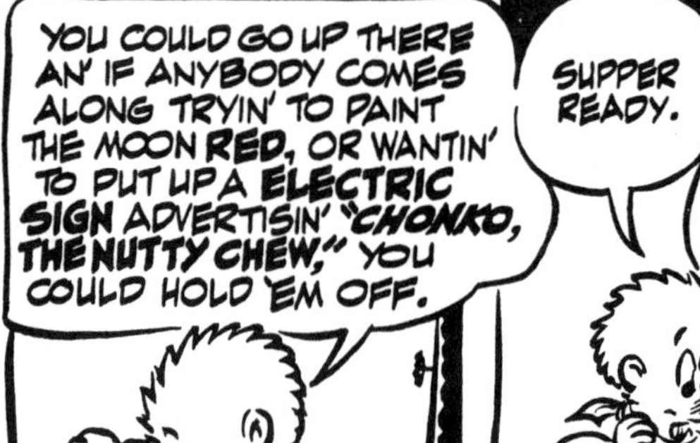
YOU COULD GO UP THERE AN' IF ANYBODY COMES ALONG TRYIN' TO PAINT THE MOON RED, OR WANTIN' TO PUT UP A ELECTRIC SIGN ADVERTISIN' "CHONKO, THE NUTTY CHEW," YOU COULD HOLD 'EM OFF.
SUPPER READY.

WAIT'LL I GET THIS PIPE OFF'N MY FINGER -- I TELL YOU, POGO, I WAS THINKIN' THEM THINGS... YOU HANG 'ROUN' ME AN' YOU'LL HAVE GOOD IDEAS, TOO.

THE OTHER THING YOU COULD DO BESIDES DEFEND THE MOON DURIN' THIS G.O.FIZZICKLE YEAR IS DO SOMETHIN' TO PROTECT PEOPLE.
I'M THINKIN' OF THAT TOO.

FOR A SAMPLE, ANIMALS FROM ALL OVER CAN HOLD A INTERNATIONAL MEETING TO FIND SOME FORMULA TO PREVENT PEOPLE FROM BEIN' CRUEL TO PEOPLE.
MY OWN THOUGHT TO A "T."

YOU'D CALL IT THE ANIMAL SOCIETY TO PREVENT CRUELTY TO PEOPLE ... IT MIGHT BE THE HIGHSPOT OF THE G.O. FIZZICKLE YEAR.
I HAVE GIVEN IT ALL CONSID'RABLE THOUGHT.
DOGGONE, ALBERT, I'M GIVIN' OUT IDEAS AN' YOU CLAIMS THEY'S YOURS! DON'T YOU THINK OF NOTHIN' ALONE EVER ?
I THINKS OF NOTHIN' ALONE CONSTANTLY, FRIEND.

'COURSE THEM FOLKS GAVE UP A WHOLE EIGHTEEN MONTHS TO A G.O. FIZZICKLE YEAR..
RIGHT! I THUNK OF THAT...
SO, IF WE FORMS A CLUB FOR THE PREVENTION OF CRUELTY TO PEOPLE, WE OUGHT TO TAKE AT LEAST A YEAR TO STUDY PEOPLE
UGH, BUT MY OWN IDEA.

EIGHTEEN MONTHS TO STUDY FIZZICKLE PROPERTIES AN' A YEAR FOR PEOPLE... ACTUALLY IT'D TAKE A LIFETIME; BUT WHO CAN COUNT ON ONE THESE DAYS?
I GAVE THAT THOUGHT, TOO.
DOGGONE AGAIN, ALBERT! YOU KEEP SAYIN' YOU THINKS OF EVERYTHING FIRST!
IF IT WASN'T FOR ME, YOU WOULD STARVE TO DEATH! WHO THUNK OF COMIN' TO YOUR PLACE FOR SUPPER ?

Chapter 11

A FLEA BETRAYED

Here a heart is broken and a bug is found in our spacemanship~~~

GO! FIND THE FLEA! MANKIND A-WAITS!

ONCE MORE MANKIND WAITS FER MOUSEKIND TO DO THE WORK.

WHOOP
WHOOP
YAHOO
WHERE YOU BEEN, FLEA? OL' HOWLAND OWL BEEN LOOKIN' ALL OVER FOR YOU.
I BEEN ST. PATRICK'S DAY PARADIN'.

PARADIN' FOR THREE DAYS? MAN', THAT MUST OF BEEN A LONG PARADE! HUNDERDS OF THOUSANDS!?
NOPE, JUS' ME, THE DOG, AND JOE COSTELLO.. ..NOT SO LONG AS LOUD.

HOW CAN JES' THREE OF YOU MARCH FOR THREE DAYS? WHERE DID YOU GO?
IT AIN'T SO MUCH WHERE YOU GO AS HOW--WE DID A LOT OF IT ON OUR HANDS AN' KNEES.

I TELL YOU, FLEA, SIR, A BUSY EXECUTIVE SCIENTIST MUST FIRST OF ALL FIND WHAT HE'S TALKIN' ABOUT; AND I WAS TALKIN' ABOUT YOU. BUT YOU COULDN'T BE FOUND.. GET IT?

SO I, OF COURSE, SENT OUT A TEAM OF EXPERTS, NAMELY THE MOUSE, HERE, AND SO, WE'VE FOUND YOU.... WELL, WELL.... LOOKS LIKE EVERYTHING'S SHIPSHAPE... BENEFICIARY IS YOUR ESTATE, WIFE OR ASSIGNS; YES, YES

'SMATTER? DON'T YOU GOT NO RESPECT FOR SECURITY?
I LOVE IT.. AND HAD PLENTY 'TIL YOU STARTED SENDIN' ME TO THE MOON.

ONE THING MORE OUTTA YOU AND YOU DON'T GO.
NAME IT! NAME IT! TELL ME WHAT MUST I DO!

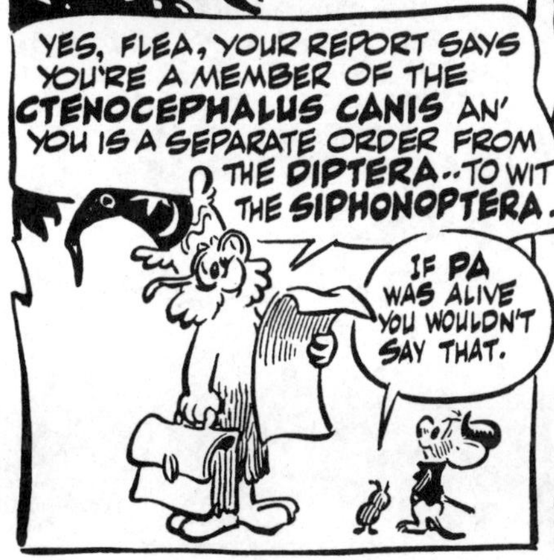
YES, FLEA, YOUR REPORT SAYS YOU'RE A MEMBER OF THE CTENOCEPHALUS CANIS AN' YOU IS A SEPARATE ORDER FROM THE DIPTERA.. TO WIT THE SIPHONOPTERA.
IF PA WAS ALIVE YOU WOULDN'T SAY THAT.
THERE, THERE, THESE ARE ALL PERFECTLY PATRIOTIC SOCIETIES... OUR FYI FILES SHOW YOU HAVE A HARD LATERALLY COMPRESSED BODY.. JUST RIGHT FOR OUR PURPOSES.
AND JUST RIGHT FOR MINE, TOO.

HOW CAN I GO TO THE MOON LEAVIN' MY NEW HUSBAND NAMELY, THE DOG?
NAMELY, THE DOG?

DO YOU KNOW A DOG NAMED NAMELY?
THE FLEA MEANS BEAUREGARD. OL' FLEA BEEN WANTIN' TO MARRY THE HOUN'DOG.

OH, YES, THAT SLIPPED MY MIND... UH, DON'T YOU THINK BEAUREGARD IS A LITTLE TOO OLD FOR YOU? HE'S NO CHICKEN YOU KNOW.
IF HE WAS A CHICKEN I WOULDN'T LOOK AT HIM TWICE.

WELL, YOU CAN'T TAKE HIM TO THE MOON.
WHO WANTS TO GO ON A HONEYMOON ALONE?
BLACK WIDOW SPIDERS ALWAYS DOES... SMACKIN' THEIR LIPS, TOO.

THERE HE IS NOW, FLYIN' BUTTERFLIES AS USUAL.
AN' IDLIN' AWAY PRECIOUS TIME.

A FINE THING! HERE YOU IS FRITTERIN' AWAY VALUABLE MINUTES.. WHEN EVERY SECOND COUNTS.. US IN A RACE WITH RUSSIA AND YOU IS FLYIN' BUTTERFLIES.
NATCH

IF WE IS EVER ATTACKED BY SQUADRONS OF BUTTERFLIES, WHO WILL BE PREPARED? ME! ONLY ME.
HEAD ME SOUTH, DOC.

WHY DOES THIS FLEA HAVE TO BE SO BRAINLESS AS TO WANT TO MARRY A DOG?
OL' FLEA MAYBE IS A SOCIAL CLIMBER.
AFTER HIM!

HOLD ON A MINUTE ··· YOU BETTER TAKE A LOOK AT THE MARRIAGE LICENSE.
A MARRIAGE LICENSE! OURS! OH JOY.

YOU GOT MY NAME SPELLED WRONG ··· UH, NO! THIS IS YOUR OLD MARRIAGE LICENSE! ·· YOU MARRIED A GAL NAME OF JULEP IN 1883! HOW COULD YOU OF?
I WAS YOUNG.

I BEEN BETRAYED! JILTED! LEFT COLD AT THE CHURCH DOOR! I'LL NEVER LIVE IT DOWN ··· LIFE DON'T HOLD NO CANDLE FOR ME NO MORE.
THAT MARRIAGE LICENSE SHOWS YOU WAS TRYIN' TO LEAD ME INTO A LIFE OF BIGAMY...
HOW COME THE MARRIAGE LICENSE GOT YOU DOWN FOR BEIN' BORN IN 1858? YOU AIN'T A HUNDERD YEARS OLD!
WODDY-YOU CARE? I AIN'T MARRYIN' YOU.

THERE'S ONLY ONE WAY OUT·· SUICIDE!
A GREAT IDEA! WHY NOT COMMIT SUICIDE UNDER OUR AUSPICES?
NOW YOU CAN GO TO THE MOON·· GO OUT IN A BURST OF GLORY! SEE THE MOON EN ROUTE TO ETERNITY.
I'D ALLUS HOPED TO LIVE A GOOD CLEAN LIFE AN' GO TO CALIFORNIA AT THE END.

Chapter 12

THE DEFENSE OF UTTER SPACE

Our heroes form an organization of heroes to protect the moon from other heroes~~~

ONE TROUBLE WITH INNERNATIONAL AFFAIRS IS WE USES UP SO MANY INITIALS FOR OUR DIFFER'NT BOARDS AND COMMITTEES.
ABLERT
NOT ONLY DOES WE NOT KNOW WHAT WE'S TALKIN' ABOUT, BUT WE GOT NO LETTERS LEFT TO TALK WITH.

SUPPOSE THE FOREIGN MINISTER OF A RIVAL POWER RUSHES IN AND HOLLERS "I'M THE V.I.P. OF THE P.D.Q. SO F.Y.I. THE S.N.A.F.U. AND R.S.V.P. SOONEST."
SO YOU GO TO WAR, 'CAUSE NOBODY KNOWS WHO HE WAS, WHAT HE WAS TALKIN' ABOUT OR..
BUT IF HE TOOK TIME TO EXPLAIN, YOU'D FORGET WHAT YOU WAS FIGHTIN' ABOUT.

JUS' WHY DOES YOU WANT TO DEFEND THE MOON WHEN THER'S SO MUCH TO BE DONE UNDER YOUR NOSE?
YOU TRYIN' TO SAY I DIN'T SHAVE UNDER MY NOSE?
NO...BUT IF YOU GONNA HELP THE WORLD, WHY START ON THE MOON?

SET DOWN AN' LEMME EXPLAIN... WE CAN'T HAVE PEOPLE CRAWLIN' ALL OVER OUR MOON.. IT DESTROYS OUR MOTHER TONGUE... IF SOMEBODY SAYS "I DON'T KNOW HIM FROM THE MAN IN THE MOON," YOU GOTTA ASK "WHICH MAN IN THE MOON?"
IF YOU DON'T KNOW NOBODY UP THERE, IT GETS CONFUSIN'.. PEOPLE ON THE MOON DON'T PAY .. 'SPECIALLY IF THEY'S STRANGERS.

JUS' HOW DOES YOU INTEND TO DEFEND THE MOON, ALBERT?
NOTHIN' TO IT.. I'LL PROTECK IT FROM INVADERS.
Y'MEAN YOU'S GONNA THROW EVERYBODY OFF WHAT LANDS ON THE MOON?
EV'RY-BODY

THEM RUSSIANS IS FIGGERIN' ON POPULATIN' THE MOON WITH DOGS 'CORDIN' TO THE WAY THEY GOIN' AT IT.. WHO WANTS TO LOOK UP AN' SEE A MESS OF OL' STRANGERS ALL OVER THE MOON?
BUT HOW ABOUT IF OUR OWN GUMMINT SENDS FOLKS UP THERE?
OH, WELL, THAT'S OKAY.. STRANGERS WHAT WE KNOWS MIGHT BE DIFFER'NT.

HOORAY! YOU TWO IS JUST IN TIME! OL' FLEA IS DECIDED TO COMMIT SUICIDE UNDER OUR AUSPICES BY GOIN' TO THE MOON... ..HE'S UNFORTUNATE IN LOVE.
HE GONE BE WORSE THAN THAT! I IS HEAD OF A NEW GROUP CALLED "THE DEFENDERS OF THE MOON!"

YOU HAVE THAT BOY COMMIT SUICIDE THAT WAY AND YOU SENDS HIM TO HIS DOOM... NOBODY GONNA MESS ROUND WITH THE MOON WITHOUT WE SAY SO.
NO FAIR! IT AIN'T GONNA BE SAFE TO COMMIT SUICIDE NOW.
HOW'S IT GOIN'?
WELL, SUNDAY COMIN' UP, THANK GOODNESS.

SO... THIS BEIN' SATURDAY, HOW ABOUT A BATH?
GOOD IDEA... IT MIGHT WET OUR APPETITES.

Chapter 13

OVER OUR HEADS

In which the shallow thinker finds himself in rather deep~~~

IS IT COLD?

NO...
NOT HARDLY COLD AT ALL.
WHAT YOU WAITIN' FOR THEN?!

LAST ONE IN IS A ROTTEN....
--GUG!

IT JUST AIN'T VERY DEEP.. THAT'S ALL.

IT'S DEEPER OVER THIS WAY.. ..WE CAN SWIM AROUND HERE.
CRACKLE CRACKLE
SOMEBODY'S COMIN'.
IT MIGHT BE MIZ BEAVER OR MISS MAM'SELLE... GRAB YOUR CLOTHES AN' GIT DRESSED..
CRACKLE
CRACKLE
NO TIME!

HELLO!? HELLO!?
THANK GOODNESS I'M DRESSED.
CRACKLE
HELLO?
IT'S OL' MOUSE!
HOW COME YOU CRACKLE SO LOUD? YOU SKEERED ME INTO PUTTIN' MY CLOTHES BACK ON.

I READ THAT MARRIAGE LICENSE YOU HAD AND IT WASN'T YOURS.. IT WAS FOR YOUR GRAN'FATHER.
WHO'S ARGUIN'?
BUT YOU LED THE FLEA TO BELIEVE YOU WAS MARRIED SINCE LAST CENTURY.
A DEFENSIVE MOVE.

THE FLEA (WHAT I DON'T EVEN KNOW IT'S NAME) IS MADLY IN LOVE OF ME, WHICH I CAN UNDERSTAND.. BUT MARRIAGE! IT'S LIKE YOU WANTED TO MARRY A ELEPHANT.. HOW RIDICULOUS!
WHAT'S RIDICULOUS ABOUT THAT?
THINK WHERE EITHER ONE OF US WOULD BE IF ALL OUR BROTHER-IN-LAWS COME HOME AN' STARTED LIVIN' ON US.

JUST EGG-ZACKLY WHAT IS ALL THE CURRENT FUSS ABOUT?
THEY STILL IS ARGUIN' ABOUT GOIN' TO THE MOON.
OL' ALBERT GOT ALL CHARGED UP ABOUT DEFENDIN' THE MOON FROM FOLKS WANTIN' TO SPOIL IT BY TRACKIN' UP THERE.
ADMIRABLE.

OWL WANTS TO SEND THE FLEA UP..WELL, I JUST THINK MORE FOLKS IS WORRIED ABOUT THE MOON THAN THEY IS ABOUT POOR OLD EARTH.
WE COULD DO WITHOUT THE FLEA.
MEBBE... BUT WHY NOT GET EXCITED ABOUT WHAT'S UNDER YOUR NOSE..'STEAD OF WHAT'S OVER YOUR HEAD?
WELL, MAYBE WE CAN COMPREHEND BETTER THE THINGS WE DON'T UNDERSTAND.

Chapter 14

THE PLOTTERS THICKEN

Here the ordinary intellect is staggered with a blow to the lunar plexus~~~

NOW THIS IS THE WAXIN' GIBBOUS PHASE OF THE MOON, NAMED AFTER SAM GIBBOUS, A EARLY EXPLORER.
IT IS NOT! IT'S FROM LATIN! ..AN' IS TOOK FROM "HUMP" LIKE ON A CAMEL AN' MEANS SHE'S SWOLE!
DOWN IN FRONT!

THERE WASN'T NO SAM GIBBOUS AN' WASN'T NO EARLY EXPLORERS... THE MOON IS A TOTAL UNEXPLORED OR-BITIN' PLANET AN' IS CONSTANT ROUND AND..

SO MUCH FER THEM HERETICAL HYSTERICAL PROGRESSIVE MODERN EDUCATORS... NOW WHERE WAS WE?
WE WAS WAXIN' SAM.

NOW, LIKE I SAY, THE WAXIN' GIBBOUS PHASE OF THE MOON IS NAMED AFTER SAM GIBBOUS, THE FAMOUS COW JUMPER, OF WEST WYCOMB.

NEXT TIME YOU STOP INTO YOUR FRIENDLY NEIGHBORHOOD GAS STATION GET A ROAD MAP OF THE MOON --- YOU'LL SEE A COUPLE SPOTS NAMED MARE IMBRIUM AND MARE NUBIUM ETC ETC.

THAT'S 'CAUSE EARLY HISTORICAL BRAINS THUNK SAM JUMPED OVER THE MOON ON A FEMALE HORSE, WHEREAS IT WAS ACTUAL A LADY COW... PEOPLE COULD OF UNDERSTOOD A HORSE JUMPIN' OVER THE MOON BUT NOT A COW...
...THEY WAS ASHAMED TO NAME THESE SPOTS AFTER A COW SO THEY CALL 'EM MARES...Y'SEE, ALBERT, THERE'S MORE TO THE MOON THAN MEETS THE EYE.
BOY! YOU GOTTA BE THINKIN' ALL THE TIME.
BROTHER!

NOW MY PLAN IS TO PUT THE FLEA ON THE MOON -- HE'LL PREPARE THE WAY FOR YOU..
GOOD FOR HIM.

THEN, SO'S YOU CAN DEFEND THE MOON FROM ALL USURPERS, YOU WAIT 'TIL THE MOON SQUISHES DOWN TO A CRESCENT, RIGHT?
GOTCHA.

THEN YOU LURES THE TRESPASSERS DOWN TO THE POINT AND SHOVES 'EM OFF! GOT IT?
GOT IT!

OF COURSE, WE GOTTA MAKE THE PLAN FOOLPROOF.
IT'S ALREADY FOOLPROOF! WHAT COULD GO WRONG?

WE'LL SHAKE THE FLEA OUT OF THE BOX AND SEE WHAT HE THINKS OF OUR PLAN FOR DEFENDIN' THE MOON.
WE'LL DEFEND THE TAR OUTEN IT.
DO YOU SEE ANYTHING WRONG WITH OUR PLAN?
NO! OF COURSE NOT!
YOU MEAN YOU LIKE IT?

NO! I WAS IN THE BOX AN' DIN'T HEAR.. HOW COULD I LIKE IT?
YOU MEAN YOU DON'T LIKE IT? AN' YOU NEVER HEARD IT!?
BOY! WHAT A BIGOT! MIND ALL MADE UP! GOOD THING YOU DIN'T HEAR IT.. YOU'RE THE TYPE WHAT'D PROB'LY BLAB IT TO SOME FOR'N POWER.. GWAN, GIT!
A CLOSE CALL!
THANKS.

WE GOTTA PUT EVERY FOOT POUND OF HEAD POWER INTO THIS, ALBERT.
WE GOT TO DEFEND THE MOON! IT'S A NATIONAL TRUST.
ANYBODY NEAR US?
JUST YOU AND ME...

I BEEN STUDYIN' THE PLANS OF THAT OTHER FOR'N POWER, AND DO YOU KNOW WHAT THEY'RE GONNA PEOPLE THE MOON WITH IF THEY GETS A CHANCE?
UM -- UH - WELL -
DOGS! THEY'RE GONNA PEOPLE IT WITH DOGS!
GONNA PEOPLE THE MOON WITH DOGS! ... UMM....

.. YOU'RE GONNA LURE THE TRESPASSERS TO THE POINT OF THE MOON AN' PUSH 'EM OFF?
ANYTHING FOR MY COUNTRY, YES!

AN' THE FOR'N POWER'S GONNA PEOPLE THE MOON WITH DOGS... YOU ARE GONNA HAFTA LEARN HOW TO LURE DOGS, RIGHT?
RIGHT.

HEH HEE HO HOO! IF THEY'S GAL DOGS, WE GOT NO PROBLEM.
TROUBLE IS YOU'LL BE LURIN' BOY DOGS! YOU'LL HAFTA DISGUISE AS A BEAUTIFUL SPY QUEEN.
WE'LL TRY IT OUT WITH OLD HOUN' DOG ... YOU'LL DISGUISE AS HIS HEROINE ... HIS DREAM GIRL IS LULU ARFIN' NANNY ... A FORTY-NINE YEAR OLD DOLL WHAT HE'S IN LOVE OF ..
MY COUNTRY, RIGHT OR WRONG

Chapter 15

"Blunk" Go the Strings of My Heart

In which the lost labor of love is unfounded~~~

HEIGHDY, MIZ BEAVER, AND HEIGHDY, MISS MA'M'SELLE HEPZIBAH.
US COME OVER TO PAY OUR RESPECKS.
JUS' IN TIME FOR TEA, AS YOU KNOWS.

WE WAS JUST DISCUSSIN' A QUESTION OF MARRIAGE... MEBBE YOU COULD SETTLE IT.

WAIT'LL I PERTIES UP!
WAIT! WAIT! THE QUESTION IS.. SHOULD A FLEA MARRY ME ?
WHAT? THAT'D BE LIKE A CANNIBAL MARRYIN' A HUMAN.

I SURE THINK IT'S NICE YOU COME OVER TO GIT MY ADVICE ON MARRIAGE, BEAUREGARD, HONEY.
YOUR ELDER-BERRY FRAPPY IS DELICIOUS, MIZ BEAVER.
MY FIRST HUSBAND, GASLIGHT, SAID THE WAY TO A MAN'S HEART IS THROUGH HIS STOMACH... HAVE A SCONE?

POOR GASLIGHT, HE WAS TOOK SUDDEN.. AN' HOW HE LOVED THEM THERE SCONES!
KRUNK!
OOG.. WHAT DID HE PASS ON OF, MIZ BEAVER?

THE DEAR MAN ET A BUNDLE OF THEM SCONES AN' WENT IN FER A SWIM... A COUPLE DAYS LATER WE WAS STILL LOOKIN' FOR HIM... BUT...

IS IT NOT NICE AN' BEAUTIFULS TODAY WITH MIZ BEAVER AN' BEAUREGARD, YES?
YEH

YES... SO NICE! THEY ARE INSIDE DISCUSSING MARRIAGE.

I SAY THEY ARE IN THE SIDE DISCUSS MARRIAGE.

Y'KNOW THIS BANJO IS MAKIN' SUCH A UPROAR I DON'T HARDLY CAN HEAR YOU ATALL.

QUOI? WHAT IS?
A INVISIBLE CATERPIGGLE MOTH... A RARITY!

WHOOP! WOWF! YAHOO! HOO HA! YOICKS!

YOU SAY YOU'RE BEIN' PURSUED BY SOME GAL TYPE OF INSECK--? WANTS TO MARRY YOU?
YEH-- A FLEA, MIZ BEAVER.

A FLEA? NO SELF RESPECTIN' ANIMAL WOULD LET HISSELF BE CAUGHT BY NO FLEA.

RATHER'N MARRY A FLEA WHO WOULD YOU RATHER?
I ALWAYS CARRIES HER PHOTO NEXT TO MY HEART.

PERTY NICE, HUH?

WHAT HAPPENED TO HER? BAD ACCIDENT?
NOTHIN'.. IT'S LULU ARFIN' NANNY, STAR OF THE SILENT SCREEN.

OH, A OL' COWBOY STAR.. HUH?
NO.. AND IT'S NOT HIS HORSE, NEITHER!

YOU RECALL HOW LULU ARFIN NANNY, WITH HER EYES BLUNKED OUT, DEFIED THE VILLAIN IN "SANDS OF ICE."
SHE'S OLD ENUFF TO BE YOUR PA.

""SIR CHILBLAIN," SHE CRIED. "GET THEE HENCE!" SHE SAID. SHE HOLLERS, "GET THEE HENCE, SIR CHILBLAIN!""
HENS?

SHE CRIED, "LEAVE, SIR CHILBLAIN!" SHE SCREAMS, "GET THEE HENCE," THAT'S WHAT SHE HOLLERS, "GET THEE HENCE!" SHE SAYS...
HENS?!
WHAT'D SHE WANT WITH HENS? WAS SHE A CHICKEN-LIVER LOVER?
HOW DO I KNOW? HELP ME GET MY EYES UNBLUNKED. THEY'S STUCK.

I'VE SEEN YOU DO A LOT OF JOSTLE-WIGGED TWITCHES IN MY TIME BUT NEVER ONE LIKE THIS.
CAN I HELP IT IF MY OLD LOVE FOR MISS LULU ARFIN' NANNY IS SO GREAT?
BUT DO YOU HAVE TO BLUNK OUT YOUR EYES LIKE THAT... --AN' THEN NOT BE ABLE TO UNBLUNK THEM?
IT AIN'T EASY TO DO AND..

NOTHIN' TO IT, IMITATIN' LULU, THE SILENT SCREAM STAR... "GEE WHINEGARS, DOODY, DO YOU OWN EVERY BLINKIN' STAR IN THE FIRMAMINK?" HOW'S THAT?
AND IT AIN'T EASY TO UNDO.

WHAT'D YOU SAY? --AN'--WHERE'D YOU GO?
ARF

HERE WE SITS... OUR EYES BLUNKED OUT-- HOW'D WE GIT LIKE THIS?!
BY IMITATIN' THAT GLASS-BRAINED SILENT SCREAM STAR, LULU ARFIN' NANNY.
MADAME, YOU IS TALKIN' ABOUT THE WOMAN I LOVE.
I THOUGHT YOU WAS MOSTLY PLEDGED TO THIS HERE FLEA.

Chapter 16

QUEEN OF THE DOGS

Here we see that the dog's best friend is another~~~

HERE'S A PICTURE OF THE SILENT SCREAM STAR, LULU ARFIN' NANNY.
HOUN'DOG SECRETLY ADMIRES HER?
HOW CAN I MAKE HIM THINK I IS HER? SHE'S A DOG... A REAL DOG.
OH, YOU'LL DO.

NEXT YOU GOTTA LEARN TO ACT LIKE A DOG... NOW SPEAK... SPEAK! SHOW YOU'RE GLAD TO SEE YOUR MASTER.. SPEAK!
SPEAK?

RONALD!

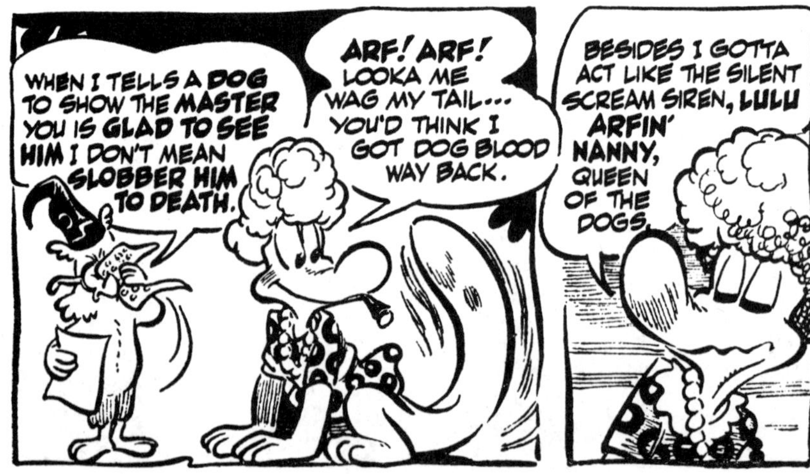
WHEN I TELLS A DOG TO SHOW THE MASTER YOU IS GLAD TO SEE HIM I DON'T MEAN SLOBBER HIM TO DEATH.
ARF! ARF! LOOKA ME WAG MY TAIL... YOU'D THINK I GOT DOG BLOOD WAY BACK.
BESIDES I GOTTA ACT LIKE THE SILENT SCREAM SIREN, LULU ARFIN' NANNY, QUEEN OF THE DOGS.

KEEZ ME, MY FOOL.
LULU ARFIN' NANNY WAS A HOMEBODY.
A HOMEBODY! DADDYKINS! DOES POPSY LOVE HIS WITTOO WUVVY BOO?

PUT ME DOWN! PUT ME DOWN!
SNAP
SNIP
A LITTLE HOME-BODY AN' A LI'L' HOME BREW.
IN A LITTLE POSY ROSY COVERED BUNG-ALOO! BUILT FOR BABY MINE AND YOUR SHEIK MAKES TWO...
DA DA! DA DA! DA DA DUM!

WITH PUDDLES OF SUNSHINE, AND MILLIONS OF BLISS, HUG ME, HONEY BUNNY, WITH A GOOD-NIGHT KISS... 'CAUSE I'M A GOOD-BYE, GOOD-BYE, GOOD-BYE, MISS!
DA DA! DA DA! DA DA! DA LUM!
WHAT EARLY MOVIE QUEEN DOES I REMIND YOU OF?
THE LATE GERTIE, THE DINOSAUR.

NOW YOU GOTTA PRACTICE LURIN' THE DOG, LULU ARFIN' NANNY.
YEP.

A LITTLE HOMEBODY AN' A LITTLE HOMEBREW, CRAZIN' TO AMAZIN' DIXIE LINE OR TWO, SHOVEL AN' SHUFFLE IN YOUR SHIFTY SHOE, DA DA! DA DA! DA DA! DA DUM!

MY LITTLE HOME BIDDY'S BITTY EYE OF BLUE WITH A DINKY, PINKY, WINKY QUICKIE BLUE BOO HOO, SNIFFLE AN' SNUFFLE BUT IT'S TOODLE-OO.. TIBBY-TUBBY-TABBY....

TA-BOO!

NOW, AS LULU ARFIN NANNY, YOU SNEAK UP ON THE DOG.. OL' BEAUREGARD'S MAD IN LOVE WITH YOU--HE THINKS YOU'RE THE OLD SILENT SCREAM STAR!
RIGHT, CHIEF.
LULU ARFIN NANNY, QUEEN OF THE DOGS! BOY! I'D OF MADE A GOOD DOG... NONE WOULD OF BEEN LOYALLER NOR ME...NONE TRUER, NONE BLUER.

IF I'D OF BEEN A DOG I WOULD OF BEEN LEAD HUSKIE--BRINGIN' THE SERUM FROM GHENT TO NOME --STOUT HEARTED...BRAVE... DRAGGIN' ALL OTHERS WITH ME, THE LAZY BUMS.

THEN I WOULD OF COLLAPSED.. MY MASTER, CRYIN' HIS EYES OUT, WOULD HOLLER, "DON'T DIE, OLD PAINT! DON'T DIE!" BUT REMORSELESS I WOULD GROAN AN ROLL OVER, HAVIN' GIVE UP MY EARTHLY SPAN FOR A LOVED ONE--BUT AS A ALLIGATOR DO I GET ANY LUCKY BREAKS LIKE THAT? NO! AN' WHAT A PITY! WHAT A WASTE--

THE MORE I THINK OF IT, THE LESS I THINK OF IT...DOGS DON'T MAKE THE BEST DOGS.

GIVE ALLIGATORS A EVEN START WITH DOGS AN' THEY'D BE GETTIN' THE LEFT-OVERS, A PLACE BY THE HEARTH, PEDICURES, FRONT SEATS AT THE DOG SHOWS--

ALONE AT NIGHT! GUARDING THE SMALL CHILDREN FROM FIRE, FROM PTOMAINE, FROM DEATH BY NIGHTMARE... GROWLING A LOYAL GROWL GRRRR! GRRR!

WHY DO PEOPLE LOVE DOGS? WHY DO DOGS GET ALL THE GOOD PARTS? ALLIGATORS CAN OUT-DOG DOGS THE WORST DAY THEY EVER CRAWLT.

BUT DO YOU THINK HUMAN BEANS APPRECIATES ALLIGATORS? NO! THEY PLAY FAVORITES-- --DO THEY EVER LOOK DEEP INTO MY SOFT BROWNED EYES?

FAUGH! ALLIGATORS CAN OUT-GULP, OUT-FAWN, OUT-ROMP, OUT-WAG, OUT-SIMPER AN' OUT-WHIMPER ANYBODY IN THE DOG BUSINESS.

STILL AN' YET, BEAUREGARD, THE HOUND, IS ALERT, AWARE AN' DEEVOTED TO THE BEST OF HIS MEAGRE ABILITY... ..FOR A DOG, HE'S A GOOD DOG.

HE'S GOT THE JOB OF BEIN' A DOG-- SO, HE GETS ALL THE GLORY---HE'S NICE TO ME-- PASSES THE TIME OF DAY, ALWAYS READY WITH A BIG "HA-HA!" IF I NEEDED ANY-THING, HE'D BE THERE.

ON THE OTHER HAND HE MIGHT SNEER! MIGHT SAY "THAT'S WHAT YOU GET FOR TAKIN' A POSITION AS A ALLIGATOR.." HE MIGHT BE PATRONIZIN' ...OFFER ME THE PAT ON THE BACK... THE EMPTY HANDSHAKE.

NO DOGGONE DOG IS GONNA TREAT ME LIKE A DOG!

Chapter 17

AWAY WE WOO

It is proven that the way to a girl's heart is thru your stomach~~~

THE MORE I THINKS OF IT, THE MORE I BELIEVE WE OUGHT TO FORM A ANIMAL SOCIETY TO PREVENT CRUELTY OF PEOPLE TO PEOPLE.
UNCLE WASHBOARD TRIED TO FORM A SOCIETY FOR PEACE ONE TIME.
THE HON. CARLOS P. ROMULO

HOW'D HE MAKE OUT?
WONDERFUL, WHILE HE HAD ONLY ONE MEMBER, HIM... BUT WHEN HE INVITED COUSIN SPLAT INTO IT THEY GOT INTO A ARGUMENT ABOUT WHOSE IDEA IT WAS IN THE FIRST PLACE... COUSIN SPLAT BIT UNCLE WASHBOARD ON THE EAR AN' UNCLE POURED CORN SYRUP INTO OL' SPLAT'S SHOES... THEY AIN'T SPOKE FOR TWENTY YEAR... WHICH IS SORTA PEACEABLE.
GEN'L. CARLOS P.

WE DIN'T DO BAD ON THE FISH... MY MOUTH KIND OF IS WATERIN'.
YEP, NOW TO TAKE 'EM OVER TO MISS MAM'SELLE.
OH... YOU GONNA GIVE 'EM ALL TO HER?
MOSTLY JES' FOR COOKIN' PURPOSES.. THEN WE ALL DIGS IN.

THEN WE OUGHT TO SCALE 'EM AN' ALL FIRST.
US SCALE 'EM?

SURE...YOU CAN'T WALK UP TO A GAL AND HAND HER A BOUQUET OF FISH TO CLEAN...SHE'LL THINK YOU DON'T LOVE HER.
I DON'T KNOW WHY ROMANCE GOTTA GIT IN THE WAY OF CLEANIN' A FEW FISH.

I'LL RUSH IN MY HOUSE AN' PICK OUT A MUSICAL INSTRUMENT TO SERENADE MISS MA'M'SELLE WITH.
VERY GOOD, SIR.

AN' I'LL POP THIS FISH BOUQUET FOR OL' HEPZIBAH INTO A NICE COOL BUCKET OF WATER LIKE THE GOOD FELLOW I IS, TO WIT, DUM DUM HO HO HA AND HOO!

ANOTHER WONDER OF THE G.O. FIZZICKLE YEAR! WHY IN THE WORLD IS YOU GONNA SERENADE MISS MA'M'SELLE HEPZIBAH WITH A DRUM?
OKEFENOKEE GLEE PERLOO & FIRE SOCIETY

WELL...IT HELPS PERVIDE A BACKGROUND FOR SUCH REMARKS ABOUT MARRIAGE AS SHE MAY LET SLIP...THE DRUM CLARIFIES 'EM A LI'L'... I CAN'T HEAR A THING...

Chapter 18

ARE WE DOWNHEARTED? YES!

Here the hangover of tomorrow is the braw brew of today~~~

OH, I STARTED THIS LIFE WITH A WILL... YEARNING FOR WINGS... A TRIP THRU THE WILD BLUE WONDER.. ...NOW IT'S ASHES... I'M A BURNED-OUT ROCKET... I'M GONNA WRITE A BOOK..
BUT..

....I'LL CALL IT "LOOK BACK FROM HUNGER" --A MOTORCYCLE RIDE THROUGH THE BLACK JACKET OF EXISTENCE.
BUT SOMEBODY ALREADY WROTE A BOOK.

IF WE ALL JOINS THE BEAT GENERATION WHAT'LL HAPPEN TO THE OTHER GENERATIONS? THE LOST... THE HIP... THE EGGHEADS... THE SQUARES... THE SACKED.. THE GASSED?
PHOO ON 'EM.

THEY'RE TRYING TO PULL A BRODIE AN' COMMIT SUICIDE BEFORE THE BEAT GENERATION BEATS THEM TO IT... THERE'S GLOOM ENOUGH FOR ALL...THESE OTHER GROUPS ARE JUST TRYING TO STEAL THE GLORY.

HAVIN' BEEN HEARTBROKE BY A DOG, I GOT A WEALTH OF MISERABLE EXPERIENCE BEHIND ME WHAT I WOULDN'T TRADE FOR LOVE OR MONEY.
NOT EVEN IN COLD CASH?

AS A PROFESSIONAL FLEA, I CAN TELL YOU THAT LOVE DON'T COME IN COLD CASH... LOVE COMES IN SMOOSHERY LUMPS... WHAT SOMETIMES GOTTA BE THAWED OUT...SOMETIMES GOTTA BE WARMED UP...
OR COOLED DOWN?

LOVE COMES IN INDIVIDUAL GOBS, IN FAMILY SIZES AND THE LARGE ECONOMY WEEKEND CONTAINER FOR ALL THE WORLD..(WORKS ONLY ON SUNDAYS) ---LISTEN AT THE LOVE POUNDIN' THRU MY HEART
BOOM BOOM! BOOM BOOM
WHAT SAY?
BOOM BOOM BOOM BOOM
I SAY LISTEN TO THE LOVE.
I WOULD IF YOUR DAGNAB HEART WOULD STOP MAKIN' SO MUCH NOISE.
BOOM BOOM

THE FLEA HERE GOT A BUG IN HIS EAR ABOUT THE BEAT GENERATION AN' THINKS HE OUGHT TO JOIN UP.
GOOD FER HIM! DO HE GET TO WEAR A UNIFORM?
UKEFENOKEE GUSE PERLOO & FIRE SOCIETY
NO..AH, BUT, NAY! AND NEIGH IN THE NIGHT NOSTRILS OF THE STAMPEDIC STALLION.. OUR CLOAK IS BUT A DAGGER OF NONEVITY --OH, OF ADORE AND NON-ADO TO SING!

I MAKE UP STUFF LIKE THAT AN' BAM! THEY THROWS ME INTO A COMIC STRIP ---FER LIFE!
AN' WHEN YOU'S THRU WITH THAT YOU CAN GET A JOB IN A SAN FRANCISCO CELLAR.
DID WHAT YOU SAID MEAN ANYTHING OR WERE YOU JUS' TALKING?
YOU CAN BE SURE I MEANT NOTHIN' PERSONAL WHATEVER IF AT ALL.

YOU CAN USE THAT POEM FOR WHAT IT'S WORTH, THANK YOU.
DON'T MENTION IT.
NOT IN A FAMILY NEWSPAPER.

WE COME OVER TO SERENADE YOU--ME BRINGIN' A DRUM, MISS MA'M'SELLE.
AN' ME BRINGIN' A PAIL OF FISH.
FRIENDS OF YOURS, NO DOUBTS, YES?
THEY COME OVER FOR SUPPER.... WE'D OF BEEN HERE EARLIER EXCEPT THE FLEA TOLD US A NEW POEM FROM THE DEAD BEAT GENERATION'S VAST FILES.

THE WINDOW IS UNWOUND, BUT WOUNDED. ITS SINGLE EYE STARES THRU THE BLIND TO HOPE UNWIND THE MYSTIC OF THE MIND THAT SPIRALS THRU THE SPARROW-HUNG DOORWAY.
EHEU!
THERE'S SOMETHIN' WRONG WITH THAT.
MAYBE THE DRUM SHOULD BE A LITTLE LOUDER.
THE FISHES ARE LEAVE.

Chapter 19

HICKORY DICKORY, DOC.

In which we learn the formula for remaining on two feet is to crawl---

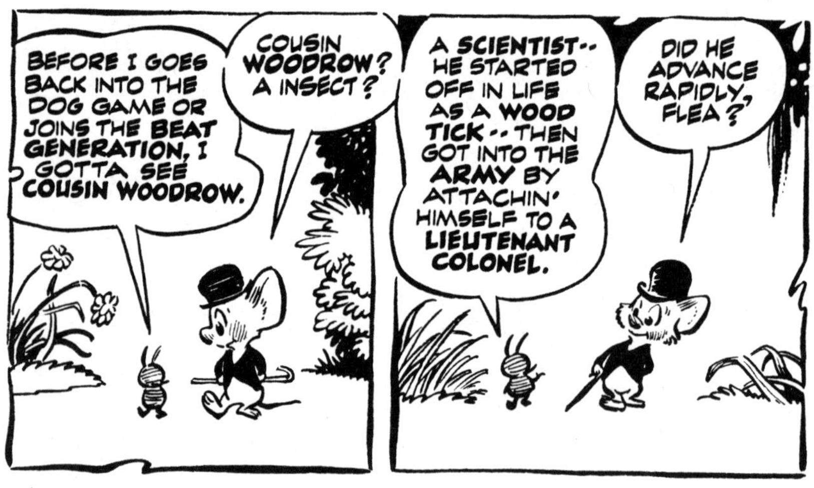

COUSIN WOODROW LIVES IN A PLACE THAT LOOKS LIKE THAT.
LIKE WHAT? THAT'S JUST A DUMP OF OL' LEAVES AND STICKS.

STIR IT UP IN THERE A LITTLE AN' HOLLER, "COUSIN WOODROW."
COUSIN WOODROW! COUSIN WOODROW!

CUT IT OUT! CUT IT OUT! YOU KNOW I'M TICKLISH.
SNAVELY!
WOT?

WE'RE LOOKIN' FOR MY COUSIN WOODROW-- HE'S A WOOD TICK.
A TICK? OH, HIM AN' A GROUP OF HIS ASSOCIATES IS DOIN' TIME IN A CLOCK FACTORY... CAN I HELP?

I WAS HOPIN' WOODROW, THE TICK, WOULD OF BEEN ABLE TO GIVE ME SOME ADVICE.
SEEM LIKE HE DID LEAVE A MESSAGE.

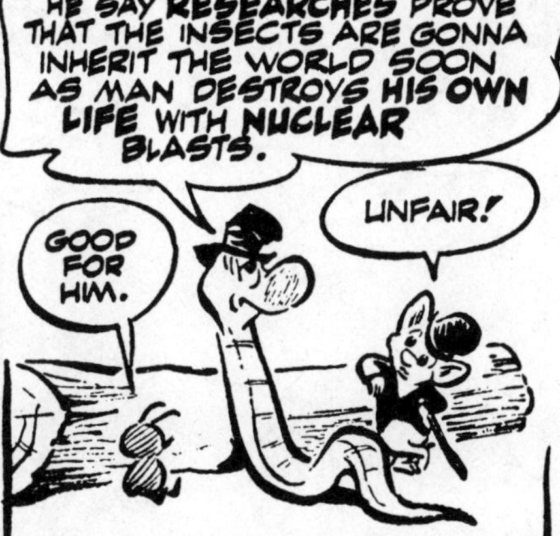
HE SAY RESEARCHES PROVE THAT THE INSECTS ARE GONNA INHERIT THE WORLD SOON AS MAN DESTROYS HIS OWN LIFE WITH NUCLEAR BLASTS.
GOOD FOR HIM.
UNFAIR!

HOW COME UNFAIR? US BUGS AIN'T NEVER HAD NO BREAKS.
ALL YOU GOTTA DO IS SURVIVE 60,000 ROENTGENS OF RADIATION... AN' YOU'LL BE EVEN WITH THE WOOD TICK.
MICE CAN DO IT ONE HAND.
THAT OUGHT TO SLOW A FEW PEOPLE DOWN.. IMAGINE THE ELECTIVE OFFICES BEIN' FILLED WITH WEEVILS, FLEAS, LADY-BUGS, SPIDERS.. WOULDN'T THAT BE A CHANGE?
WELL UH MM

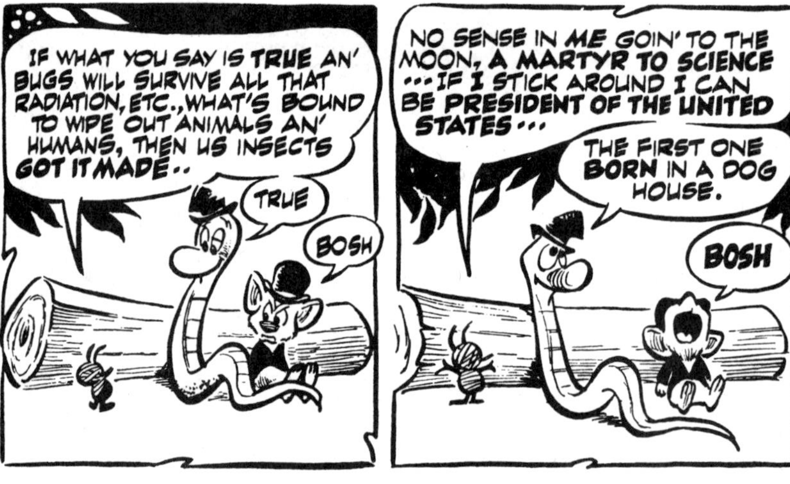
IF WHAT YOU SAY IS TRUE AN' BUGS WILL SURVIVE ALL THAT RADIATION, ETC., WHAT'S BOUND TO WIPE OUT ANIMALS AN' HUMANS, THEN US INSECTS GOT IT MADE..
TRUE
BOSH
NO SENSE IN ME GOIN' TO THE MOON, A MARTYR TO SCIENCE ...IF I STICK AROUND I CAN BE PRESIDENT OF THE UNITED STATES...
THE FIRST ONE BORN IN A DOG HOUSE.
BOSH

WHY DO YOU KEEP BOSHIN' THE FLEA? HE GOT A RIGHT TO BE PRESIDENT IF BUGS GOT THE VOTE.
IF NUCLEAR WARFARE KILLS OFF ALL HUMANS WHAT WILL HE EAT?
DOGS, BEIN' HUMANS, WILL BE GONE -- HE'LL HAFTA EAT OTHER BUGS.. AN' THIS COUNTRY WILL NEVER STAND FOR A CANNIBAL IN THE WHITE HOUSE.
FOR SHAME.

I WON'T DO IT.. I WON'T TAKE THE JOB..IF BEIN' PRESIDENT MEANS EATIN' UP MY FRIENDS, I'LL RESIGN.
YOU GOTTA EAT SOMETHIN' ..YOU WAS ALL BOASTY ABOUT INSECTS SURVIVIN' ATOMIC WARS WHICH WOULD KNOCK OFF ALL OTHER LIFE INCLUDIN' DOGS.
BY JING, YOU ANIMALS ALWAYS GETS THE BREAK.. THERE YOU'LL BE, ALL COMFORTABLY DEAD, WHILST US BUGS IS STARVIN' TO DEATH.. UNLESS WE WANNA..UGH!
LIFE IS TOUGH.

WELL, NOW'S THE TIME TO GO TELL OWL I AIN'T GOIN' TO THE MOON...WHY REACH FOR THE MOON WHEN US BUGS GOT THE EARTH IN THE HOLLER OF OUR HANDS?
YEH, YOU GOT ALL THE TROUBLE YOU CAN HANDLE AS IT IS.
HE AIN'T GONNA HAVE THE SNAP HE THINKS IF RADIOACTIVITY KNOCKS OFF ALL US OTHER HUMANS... ..ALL HE'LL HAVE TO TALK TO IS BUGS.

AND THEM UGLY AS SIN, TOO.
SURE....THE ATOMIC EXPLOSIONS WILL PROB'LY MAKE BUGS THAT IS LONG AN' SKINNY..WITHOUT ARMS NOR LEGS ...THINGS WHAT JES' CRAWLS.
PLEASE! NOT JUST BEFORE DINNER!

Chapter 20

E=MC, SQUARE?

Wherein nothing is proven to be the equal of anything~~~

NOW THEN, THIS ROCKET TO PUT THE FLEA ONTO THE MOON OUGHT TO BE A THREE STAGE JOB--- ONE: IMPULSATORICAL INITIATIVE STEP.

THAT'S THE PRIMARY BLAST WHICH PRECEDES THE NOMINATIVE SECONDARY--OR, FIGURED IN FOOT POUNDS, ABOUT EIGHT BUSHELS TO THE QUANDARY.

THE COUNT-DOWN WOULD PROGNOSTICATE THE EXPLOSIVE- -YOWP!
BAM

GRUNDOON, YOU STOP THAT!
BNXTQ?

NOW KEEP QUIET, GRUNDOON, BECAUSE I GOT TO FIGGER OUT THE COUNT-DOWN WHAT TRIGGERS THE ENTIRE CELESTIAL EXPERIMENT--- LESSEE, JUST AFORE THE BLAST OFF I STARTS WITH--UM-- SAY, TEN.

LESSEE--NOW--TEN--THEN GO DOWN TO--UH--LESSEE-- UM--NINE--RIGHT, THEN, LESSEE--THEN-- LESSEE---
MTPSNK? QXF?

YOU'RE A MENACE TO SCIENCE! KEEP OUT OF THIS -- HOW CAN I FIGGER 10 - 9 - ETC. IF YOU KEEP SAYIN' X AND Y AND QZ WHILE I IS SAYIN' EIGHT, YOU SAYS SMFT -- I SAY SEVEN -- YOU SAY---
WNPS?

SEE!? THAT DON'T MAKE SENSE --UH-- WHAT, RABBIT?
I SAYS IT SOUND LIKE YOU AN' GRUNDOON IS TALKIN' PURE ALGEBRA!

IF WHAT YOU SAY IS TRUE, BUN RAB, THEN GRUNDOON IS A SCIENTERRIFFIC GENIUS.
HE MUST BE -- HE TALKS AUTHENTIC ALGEBRA.
FNPT?

I'LL TRY THE COUNT-DOWN AGAIN -- SEE IF HE CHIMES IN -- TEN -- UH -- MM -- NINE ---
XY
UM
LESSEE -- UH-
EIGHT
BNS

LESSEE -- HUM-AH- SEVEN-
TCH
UH- EIGHT- UH- NO SIX -- SIX ---
DSG

WHAT DID WE SAY? WHAT DID WE SAY?
GRADE-A ALGEBRA! --TEN-UM-NINE XY OVER UM EIGHT BNS AFORE AH-SEVEN OVER TCH UH EIGHT NO SIX-SIX OVER DSG! AMAZING!

Chapter 21

HEARTS AND BEAUX AND NARROWS

Cupid is found unstrung, unbloodied, unbowed and outgrabed~~~

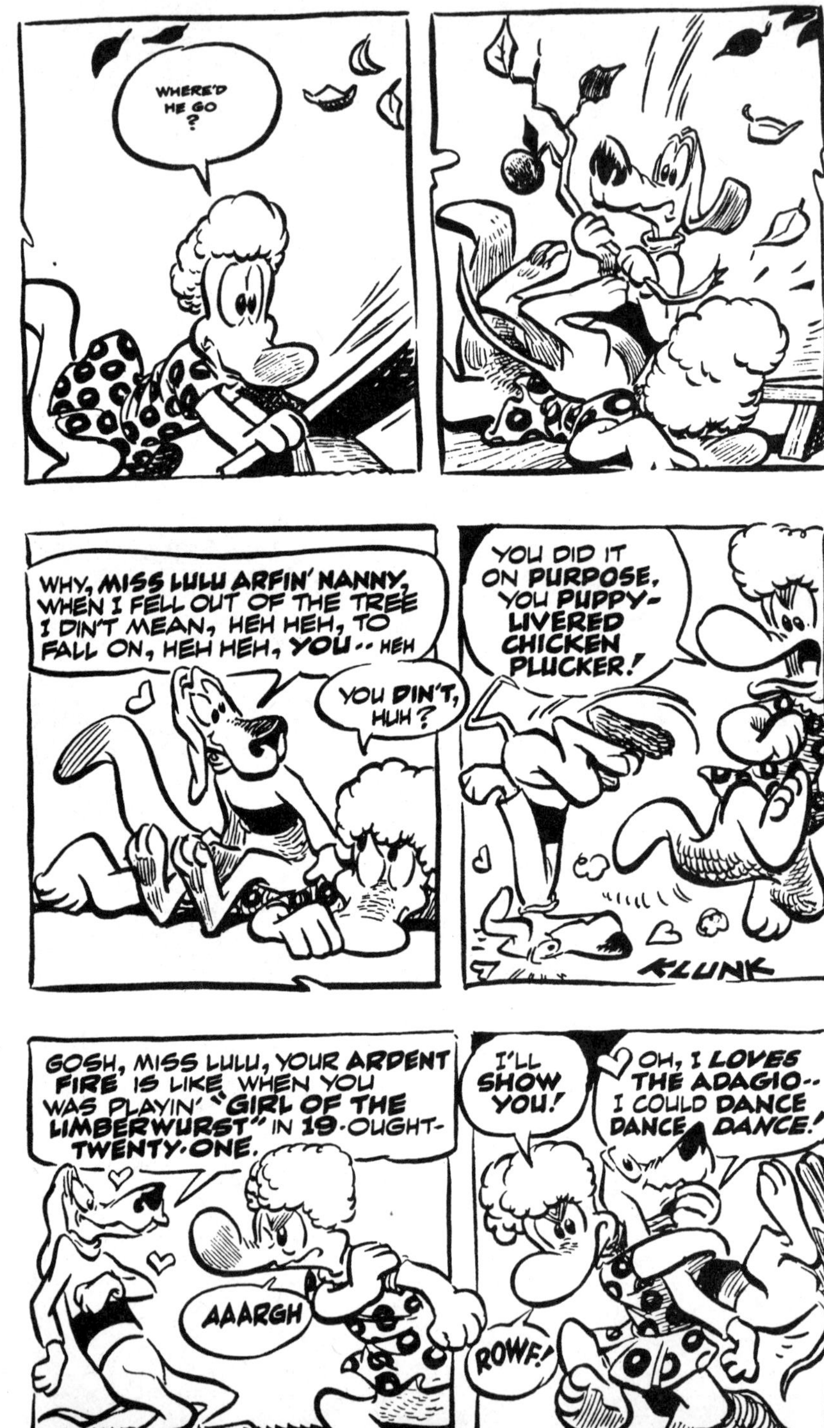
WHERE'D HE GO ?
WHY, MISS LULU ARFIN' NANNY, WHEN I FELL OUT OF THE TREE I DIN'T MEAN, HEH HEH, TO FALL ON, HEH HEH, YOU -- HEH
YOU DIN'T, HUH ?
YOU DID IT ON PURPOSE, YOU PUPPY-LIVERED CHICKEN PLUCKER!
KLUNK
GOSH, MISS LULU, YOUR ARDENT FIRE IS LIKE WHEN YOU WAS PLAYIN' "GIRL OF THE LIMBERWURST" IN 19-OUGHT-TWENTY-ONE.
AAARGH
I'LL SHOW YOU!
OH, I LOVES THE ADAGIO -- I COULD DANCE DANCE DANCE!
ROWF!

AAARGH! ROWF! GRRR!
HUM .. TUM TUMMITY HUM HUM

GOLLY WHIZ, MISS LULU, I COULD JUST WALTZ THE EVENIN' AWAY --- YOUR RHYTHM IS DEE-VINE.
WALTZ!?

DOGGONE IT, I AIN'T DANCIN' --- I'M FIGHTIN'.
YOU IS? WITH WHO?

WITH YOU, DAGNAB IT! Y-O-O-H-U!
MY WORD! WHO'S WINNIN'?

I GOT A GOOD MIND TO NOT GO TO THE MOON.
MOON? WHY, MISS LULU ARFIN' NANNY, I DIN'T KNOW YOU WAS ...

DOGGONE IT! I'M NOT LULU, LOOK!
YOU'RE BALD! URG! EVEN WORSE.. YOU'RE ALBERT!

TO THINK! I'VE BEEN LED ON! DEE-CEIVED --- BETRAYED BY A FICKLE FRIEND WHO PLAYED CAT AND MOUSE WITH MY HEART STRINGS ...
OH, BALD R. DASH!
IF ONLY I'D STOLEN ONE LITTLE KISS WHILE YOU WAS STILL LULU ARFIN' NANNY -- NOW IT'S TOO LATE.
IT WAS ALWAYS TOO LATE FOR THAT!

I'M GLAD THAT YOU AIN'T LULU ARFIN' NANNY -- I LIKE TO THINK OF HER AS A UNATTAINABLE DREAM.
YOU COULD THINK OF ME THE SAME WAY.
ALWAYS I'LL REMEMBER HER FACE IN THE SILVERY MOONLIGHT.

THAT REMINDS ME, I'M GONE TELL OWL I AIN'T GONNA GO TO THE MOON!
'COURSE NOT! ---THE MOON ONLY COMES OUT AT NIGHT----IT'D BE CONSTANT NIGHT WORK.
GO TO THE SUN --- IT'S OUT ALL DAY -- PLEASANT HOURS --- WARM WEATHER AT ALL TIMES.

Chapter 22

A MINE SHAFT TO THE MOON

Wherein the tunnel to our first-born satellite is filled with jam---

ALL RIGHT NOW, WE'LL START PLOTTIN' THE BALLISTICS OF THE CALIBRATION OF THE DIAGNOSTICS... WHAT WOULD YOU SAY IS THE FORMULA FOR OUR TRAJECTORY, GRUNDOON?
NXBCKRS

VERY GOOD... LET'S SEE, THAT WOULD BE EQUAL ROUGHLY TO ABOUT WHAT?
GZT MFL!
NXBCKRS EQUALS GZT MFL?

EXACTLY! IT'S A NEW AND IMPROVED FORMULA.. ..IT GOT NXBCKRS, THE MAGIC INGREDIENT WHAT IS EQUAL TO ANYTHING.
YOU PUT A NEW MAGIC INGREDIENT LIKE THAT INTO ALL FORMULAS AN' NOBODY'D HAVE TO THINK AT ALL.
HOO HA

YOU TWO IS JUS' IN TIME TO WITNESS THE WIZARD OF THE AGE.. GRUNDOON IS HEADIN' THE MATHEMATICAL DEPT. OF OUR MOON PROJECT.

JUST LISTEN TO THIS STUFF HE GOT OFF... NXBCKRS EQUALS GZT MFL AND NXBCKRS EQUALS PDQ.

NOW WHEN THE FLEA GITS TO THE MOON HE PULLS UP THE THREAD, THE THREAD PULLS UP THE ROPE, THEN ALBERT CLIMBS HAND OVER HAND AND!..
YEH, BUT I AIN'T GONNA DO IT.
QUITE SO ... THEN WHEN YOU GET THERE, ALBERT, YOU WILL HAUL UP THE THERMOS BOTTLE AND THE SAN'WICHES ...

I'M HERE TO TELL YOU I AIN'T GOIN' TO NO MOON.
NOW AS I WAS SAYIN', ALBERT WILL FOLLOW THE FLEA UP TO THE MOON HAND OVER HAND ON THE ROPE --HE'LL HAFTA CLIMB AT ABOUT 10,000 MILES PER HOUR.

I AIN'T GOIN' TO THE MOON ... THE DEAL'S OFF.
WHAT!?

SOON AS YOU HUMANS DESTROYS ALL ANIMAL LIFE ON EARTH US INSECTS TAKE OVER ... GOT MY EYE ON A TOP JOB IN THE STATE DEPARTMENT.
AFTER ALL OUR EFFORT?.. THE HONORS WE OFFER YOU? YOU AIN'T GOIN'? HOW ABOUT MY LIFE WORK? TO SAY NOTHIN' OF ALBERT'S DISAPPOINTMENT!
YEH.. LET'S SAY NOTHIN' 'BOUT THAT.
FIE ON THE MOON.

FOR SHAME! YOU, THE FLEA ON WHO WE DEPENDED FOR NATIONAL SOO-PREMACY IN THE RACE TO THE MOON... YOU BACKS OUT.
IT MAKES MY BLOOD BOIL.
BUT US INSECTS DON'T GOTTA GO TO THE MOON TO BE SOO-PREME.. WE'RE THE ONLY ONES WHAT WILL SURVIVE YOUR ATOMIC WARS.. WE'LL TAKE OVER.

SURE, YOU WON'T HAFTA GO TO THE MOON FOR THE JOY OF BEIN' IN BLEAK DESOLATE LANDSCAPES.. ..YOU'LL HAVE 'EM, HERE!
RIGHT, BROWN-EYES.
OH, YEAH?! WELL, SUPPOSE US INTELLIGENT HUMANS REFUSES TO CO-OPERATE.. S'POSE WE DON'T DESTROY EVERYTHING ON EARTH SO'S YOU'LL INHERIT IT?
THAT'D BE KINDA SNEAKY, WOULDN'T IT?

BY JING, IF THEM COWARDS IS ASCARED TO GO TO THE MOON, WE'LL SHOW 'EM.
SHOW 'EM?
YEH.. YOU'LL LOOK FOR A COUPLE OF OTHER TRUSTIN' SOULS.
WELL, DOLL, INASMUCH AS IT'S STILL JUNE, WE COULD STILL GET HITCHED.
NO.. I'M ALL BROKE UP ABOUT LULU ARFIN'NANNY ...I LOST HER HAND.

IF ONLY I COULD FORGET HER.
PRETEND YOU OWE HER A COUPLE HUNDRED.
YOU ALL NEED CHEERIN' UP.
I'LL TAKE YOU ALL OVER TO POGO'S HOUSE FOR COOKIES AN' MILK.
ALBERT, YOU IS A SPORT.

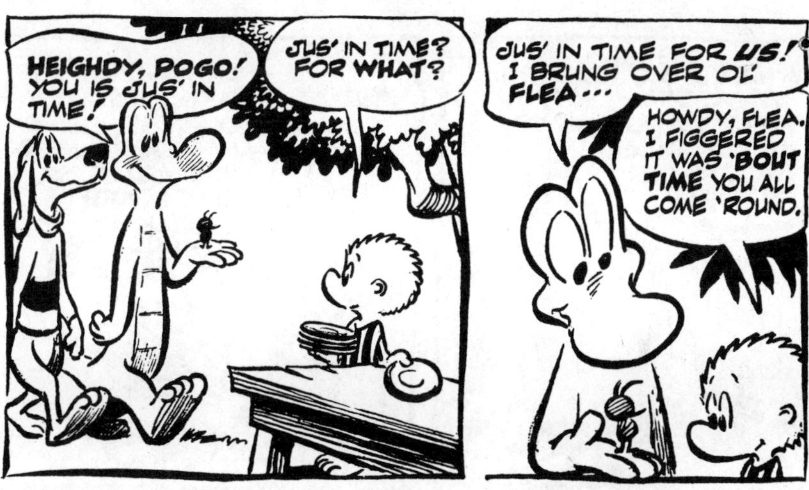
HEIGHDY, POGO! YOU IS JUS' IN TIME!
JUS' IN TIME? FOR WHAT?
JUS' IN TIME FOR US! I BRUNG OVER OL' FLEA...
HOWDY, FLEA. I FIGGERED IT WAS 'BOUT TIME YOU ALL COME 'ROUND.

THING WHAT GIVES ME A LAUGH IS HOW WE GIVE OWL THE SLIP...
OH, I DUNNO.
HE'S INSIDE WASHIN' UP.. SAYS HE TOOK THE SHORTCUT.
HOO HOO!
WHAT'S THAT?
DOG COLLAR.. CLOSEST THING WE COULD GET FOR YO' TASTE.

Chapter 23
Polls Apart

The mystery of February, the tooth, rolls again around ~~~

WHY NOT GO HOME EARLY TODAY, LIKE I SAY, SO'S I CAN CONDUCT MY HOUSE-TO-HOUSE SURVEY?
TED SCRIPPS

IF YOU WAS ANY KIND OF A POLL-TAKER YOU COULD ASK ME HOUSE-TO-HOUSE QUESTIONS OUT-DOORS.
OL' TED

WHAT!? YOU SUGGEST THAT I FALSIFY THE RECORD? --- HOW CAN I CONDUCT ANY HOUSE-TO-HOUSE WORK WHEN YOU IS LOLLIGAGGIN' AROUND IN A BOAT?
WELL, SHUCKS! YOU WOULDN'T WANT ME TO SHIRK MY DUTIES, EITHER, WOULD YOU?
SAN FRANCISCO
THE HON. TED

I HATE THIS SWAMP! HATE IT! HATE IT!
WOWF!

AWK
THERE.. 'S THAT BETTER?
OOG... YOU SHOULDN'T OF DID THAT..
OH, THAT'S ALL RIGHT... 'TAIN'T LIKE IT WAS MY BEST UMBRELLA..

NOW THAT YOU MENTIONS IT, HOW COME YOU HATES THE SWAMP SO?
ON ACCOUNT OF POGO! HE REE-FUSES TO GO HOME SO'S I CAN MAKE A HOUSE-TO-HOUSE SURVEY.. --TO BE FAIR, HE GOTTA BE HOME WHEN HE RESPOND.
HE IS A CAD.

YOU CAN'T ASK HOUSE-TO-HOUSE QUESTIONS OF A MAN OUTDOORS IN A BOAT.
HE CAN'T DO THIS TO YOU; I'LL GIVE YOU A HAND.
I INVITES YOU TO POGO'S HOUSE... I WILL ANSWER YOUR QUESTIONS FOR HIM. YOU GITS A FREE, UNBIASED OPINION WITH COOKIES AN' MILK ON THE SIDE.
YOU IS A SPORT.

TURTLE, IT'S NICE OF YOU TO INVITE ME OVER TO POGO'S.
IT'S MY PLEASURE, OWL; DON'T MENTION IT.
NOW, WHAT'S THIS HERE HOUSE-TO-HOUSE SURVEY YOU IS MAKIN'?
THIS IS THE G.O. FIZZICKLE GROUND-HOG DAY.

AN' MIZ GROUN'HOG'S NEW GIRL BABY AIN'T GOT NO NAME SHE KIN RUN TO.
WHAT'S WRONG WITH THE ONE SHE STARTED WITH? ... HONEY BUNNY DUCKY DOWNY SWEETIE CHICKEN PIE LI'L' EVERLOVIN' JELLYBEAN
?
IF YOU CALLS THE CHILE BY HER GIVEN NAME SHE BACKS OFF.
I BET SHE WON'T ----THERE SHE COME NOW----- WATCH!

H'LO, THERE, AN' COOCHIE COO TO YOU, HONEY BUNNY DUCKY DOWNY SWEETIE CHICKEN PIE LI'L' EVERLOVIN' JELLYBEAN ..
WELL ... SIX MORE WEEKS OF WINTER.
KRUNK!

YO' LI'L' DAUGHTER GIRL SLUMMED THE **BUGGY BONNET** DOWN ON **TURTLE'S** HEAD-BONE.
HE POKED IT ***INSIDE***... ALL ON HIS **OWN** ...***UN*** ASKED.
BUT, MIZ GROUN'CHUCK, CAN'T YOU ***PREE***-VAIL ON THE CHILD TO ***UNLEACH*** THE CRITTUR?
BUT SHE ALREADY SNUPPED BACK INSIDE AFTER MAKIN' A ***GROUN'HOG DAY*** APPEARANCE --- TO COME BACK ***NOW*** WOULD BREAK THE GROUN'HOG **CREED.**
YOU MEAN HE AIN'T GONE BE LET LOOSE 'TIL AFTER ***SIX MORE*** WEEKS OF **WINTER?**
OH, IT DON'T ***PAY*** TO INNERFERE WITH ***NATURE LAW***, FRIEN' OWL.
'LONG AS YOU INSISTS GROUN'HOGS ***RE***-HIBERNATES FOR NO LESS'N **SIX WEEKS** WE BETTER GET ANOTHER **BRAIN** ON THIS...
A FIZZICKLE **G.O. FACT.**
YOU GOTTA ***AD***MIT IT AIN'T NO CINCH TO BE SHUT IN WITH A ***BABY GROUN'HOG*** FOR SIX WEEKS.
FOOF

Chapter 24

THE TURN OF THE TURTLE

A good deed is repaid with slings and arrows and a dog's life is had by all---

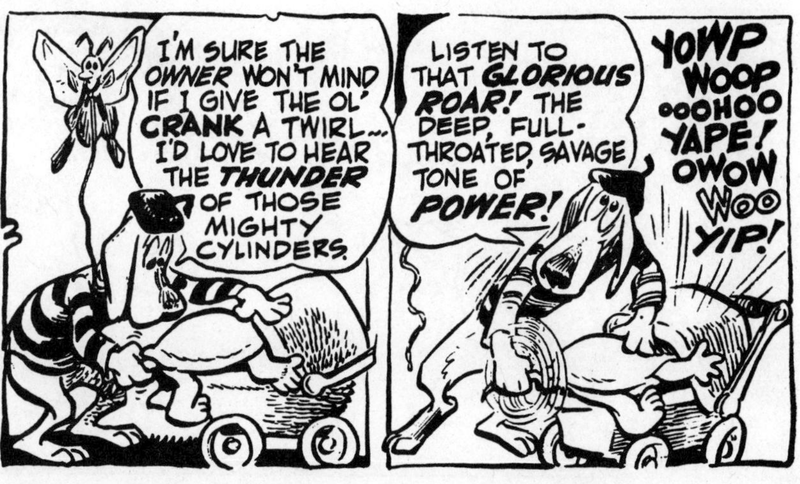

OH, I'D GIVE A PERTY TO OWN THIS GRISLEY-TORQUE! LISTEN TO ITS FOREIGN MOTOR PURR.
GRRRR GRRR GRRRR

WONDER IF THE OWNER WOULD MIND IF I LOOKED UNDER THE HOOD?
GRRRRR

WOWF!

MY! THIS ISN'T A GRISLEY-TORQUE, IS IT? WHAT IS IT?
IT'S A DAGNAB OUTRAGE! THAT'S WHAT IT IS!..NO GROWED MAN SHOULDN'T BE KIDNAPPED BY NO INFANT.

HOW'D YOU MANAGE TO GET YOUR HEAD CAUGHT IN THE BABY'S BUGGY BONNET?
NOTHIN' TO IT... I STUCK MY HEAD IN LIKE A IDIOT AN'...

SNAP!
THAT'S IT! SNAP! AN' THERE I WAS.

WOOF! LOOKY AT TURTLE!
HE'S CHANGED! FOR ONE THING HE IS GROWED A BUTTERFLY!

WHAT DO YOU S'POSE IS HAPPENED TO OL' TURTLE?
HOW COULD HE OF GROWED A BUTTERFLY?
ONLY ONE THING TO DO IS BREAK THE HONORABLE CODE OF THE GROUN'HOGS AN' OPEN UP THE BABY BUGGY.

GOSH! THANKS, FRIENDS!..THANKS FOR FREEIN' THE NOBLE DOG FROM A IGNOMINY WORSE'N DEATH OR TAXES.
WHY YOU AIN'T TURTLE..
A IMPOSTOR!
A FRAUD!.. THOUGHT WE'D THINK YOU WAS TURTLE! HAW!
?

WELL, SUCH IS THE FATE OF THE GOOD INTENTION... ALL I DID WAS SAVED MIZ GROUN'HOG'S CHILE FROM BEIN' DEVOURED... LEFT ALONE, AS IT WAS, WITH WILD BEASTS.
WILD BEASTS?
BUTTERFLIES IS S'POSE TO BE ORNAMENTS.. THEY AIN'T S'POSE TO HAVE NO SPEAKIN' PARTS... BUT INASMUCH AS YOU ASKS, I'LL TELL YOU... THE WILD BEASTS WAS YOU.
ME?!

YES, YOU! I SAVED THE CHILE FROM POSSIBLE BEIN' ET ALIVE BY A RAMPAGIN' BUTTERFLY... AN' WHAT THANKS DID I GET... NONE! N-U. DOUBLE N.. NONE!
HOW COULD I OF DID THAT?
I WOULDN'T EAT A WHOLE RAW CHILD! I'M A VEGIO-TARIAN.
I DON'T CARE WHAT CHURCH YOU GOES TO.

WHAT YOU DON'T SEEM TO UNDERSTAND IS THAT A VEGIO-TARIAN DON'T EAT MEAT... JES' FLOWERS, FRUITS, VEGETABLES AN' MEBBE CHOCOLATES.
WHY NOT? AIN'T YOU GOT NO SPUNK?

WELL... NO MOSTLY, (BEIN' A BUTTERFLY) I AIN'T GOT NO TEETH.
WHAT A PITY... THE GUMMINT SAY EVER'BODY GOT A RIGHT TO HAVE TEETH.

FREE HAIRCUTS··· FREE TEETH··· THAT'S WHAT OUR COUNTRY OUGHT TO PROVIDE FOR EVERY LAST MISERABLE SOUL IN-CLUDIN' WORMS, CATERPIGGLES AN' BUTTERFLIES.
POGO GOT A BUNCH OF TEETH LEFT OVER FROM A DO-IT-YOURSELF DENTAL KIT··· WHAT SIZE DOES YOU TAKE ?
'BOUT SIX AN'A HALF.. IS HE GOT ANYTHING IN SUEDE ?

THERE HE IS... HE MUST BE ASLEEP... OR DEAD.
HOME IS HOME

ARE YOU DEAD ?

ISN'T THAT A RELIEF? HE'S JES' ASLEEP.
YOU COULD OF FOOLED ME.

DON'T LET US DISTURB YOU, SIR.
YOU COULD STILL FOOL ME.

Chapter 25

OPEN WIDE, SESAME

Here it is seen that a muzzle for the missile would muscle out the fizzle---

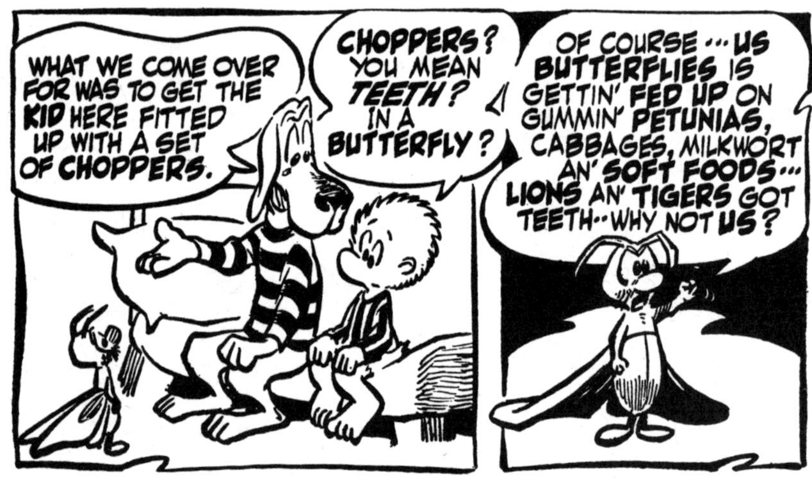

NOW, WHERE I WANTS THESE TEETHS IS IN MY MOUTH··· ONCE HAD TEETH ON MY TAIL BONE BUT THEY BELONGED TO A ENEMY...
I DON'T B'LEEVE MY OL' DO-IT-YERSELF DENTAL KIT IS GOT A SET OF TEETH IN IT SMALL ENOUGH FOR HIM.
OH, FANCY FUDGE!

LESSEE··· MAYBE WE COULD CUT THE TEETH DOWN A LI'L'··· WE MIGHT EVEN REDUCE THEM TO ONE UPPER FANG AND ONE LOWER··· YOU'D STILL HAVE MORE TEETH THAN ANY OTHER BUTTERFLY.
NOSSIR! I WANTS A FULL SET.
MEBBE WE COULD SORT OF BORE A BIGGER ORAL APERTURE... YOU GOT A DRILL?

NOSSIREEBOOB! I'M NOT DRILLIN' TO PUT TEETH IN NO BUTTERFLY··· WAIT'LL I GET OUT MY DO-IT-YERSELF DENTAL KIT.
POGO, YOU IS A SPORT.
I'LL BE MUCH OBLIGED.
POGO

FIRST I PUTS ON THE UNIFORM.
HOW IS YOU GONNA BE ABLE TO SEE?

NOW **YOU** GO SIT DOWN AN' WAIT··· ···HERE'S A OLD **MAGAZINE**···
BUT I CAN'T READ.

THAT'S **ALL** RIGHT. SOMEBODY TORE ALL THE PAGES OUT··· NOW, **WHERE'S** MY **DIPLOMA** WHICH I CAN HANG UP ALONG-SIDE THE VIEW OF **ALTOONA IN 1908** FOR YOU TO ADMIRE.
SEE, EVERYTHING IS STRICTLY PROFESSIONAL.
POGO

WHAT'S THE VIEW OF **ALTOONA** FOR? BESIDES IT DON'T **LOOK** LIKE **ALTOONA**.
IT'S TO UNSPIRE **CONFIDENCE**... AND IT GOT CAUGHT IN A FIRE ONCE.

HOW CAN A PICTURE LIKE **THAT**··· WET AN' ALL··· PROB'LY **UPSIDE-DOWN**··UNSPIRE **ANY** CONFIDENCE?
S'POSE YOU GOT A TOOTH-ACHE AND YOU'RE FROM PITTSBURGH.

WHILE WAITIN' FOR **ME**, THE BUSY DOCTOR, YOU PACES AROUND ADMIRIN' THE ***OBJETS D'ART***··YOUR EYE LIGHTS ON THIS PICTURE···"***WHAT***," YOU EXCLAIM, "**IS THAT**?" THE NURSE SAYS, "WHERE ***YOU*** FROM?" YOU SAY, "**PITTSBURGH**." SHE SAYS···"***THAT'S ALTOONA!***"
"WE'RE ***NEIGHBORS!***" YOU CRY WITH DELIGHT AN'···.
BUT **I'M** FROM **FORT MUDGE**.

THE OTHER THING I DON'T LIKE ABOUT YOUR DENTIST OFFICE IS THE DIPLOMA ···IT SAYS: "THIS CERTIFIES POGO IS A SURE FIRE DENNIS" ··DENNIS ?
I KNOW·· I KNOW.
I BOUGHT IT OFF AN ITINERATE LETTERING MAN AN' COTTON PICKER NAME OF AL CAPPAGE WHO COULDN'T SPELL AS GOOD AS US WHO KNOWS DENNIS ONLY GOT ONE "N"..
POGO

HERE'S THE NURSE'S COSTUME··· ···HOUN' DOG, YOU GOTTA WEAR IT, WHILST I GITS OUT THE OTHER DENTAL 'QUIPMENTS, NAMELY, THE APPOINTMENT BOOK.
UM···I NOTICES MY FIRST APPOINTMENT HERE IS TO TAKE THE NURSE OUT TO LUNCH··· BUT··I ··UH- AFTER STUDYIN' YOU I· UM· WELL

COME ON! COME ON! ARE YOU GONNA KEEP FOOLING AROUND PLAYING OFFICE OR ARE YOU GONNA FIT ME WITH A SET OF CHOPPERS ?
BUT THERE'S NOTHING IN THE APPOINTMENT BOOK ABOUT YOU···YOU NEED A APPOINTMENT.
AN' BESIDES I AIN'T GOT NO TEETH TO INSTALL WHAT FITS YOU.

AIN'T YOU GOT NO MODELS FOR THE G.O. FIZZICKLE YEAR?
ALL'S I GOT IS THIS OL' 1928 SET WHAT WAS NEVER HARDLY USED EXCEPT BY A QUIET ELDERLY COUPLE.
HOW'S THEY LOOK, NURSIE?
YOU LOOKS LIKE A TEEVY PIANO PLAYER AND HIS PIANO.

TIE 'EM ON, POGO. I'LL TAKE 'EM OUT FOR A BITE AN' SEE HOW WE GETS ALONG.
PUTTIN' TEETH ON A BUTTERFLY IS KINDA MESSIN' UP THE BALANCE OF NATURE.

GIVIN' A HIGHPOWERED SET OF TEETH LIKE THAT TO AN' INEXPERIENCED DRIVER IS RISKY --WHERE'S HE TAKIN' 'EM?
OUT DOORS ..THEY IS OUTDOOR TYPE TEETH.
SNAP
SNAP

YOWP
I KNEW IT.

HE BIT THE MAILMAN.
RIGHT ON GUMMINT PROPERTY TOO... THAT'S TREASON!

Chapter 26

A THINK IN THE DEEP

From somewhere east of Suez comes a wurst that is not the best~~~

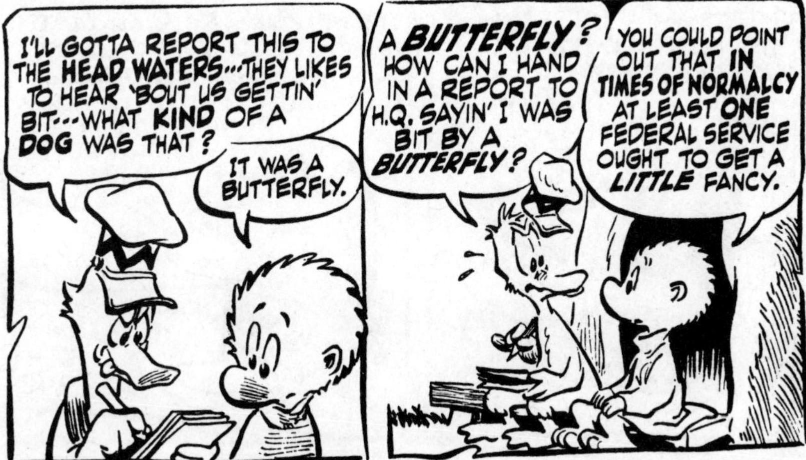

ONE THING WHAT I HATES IS TO GET BIT IN THE **MAIL POUCH** SO'S I CAN'T READ THE POST CARDS.

DON'T YOU KNOW THAT READIN' OTHER PEOPLE'S MAIL IS ***AB-SO-LOOT-LY DEE-SPICK-ABLE?!***

WOZZIT SAY?!

THAT **BUTTERFLY** BIT THE **NAME** OFF THIS POST CARD... SO I GUESS IT'S ALL RIGHT TO **READ IT.**

IT SAYS, "*Dear Mr. President: Well, I guess you've heard how they plugged up the Canal..*" THEN THE REST IS ALL ***TOOTH*** MARKS.

YOU KNOW WHAT THIS IS! IT'S A SECRET STATE DOCUMENT ··· I BETTER GET IT TO THE CAPITAL RIGHT AWAY··· THE PREXY OUGHT TO SEE THIS···
WHICH WAY TO RICHMOND?
THAT AIN'T THE PLACE NO MORE·· THEY MOVED IT SOMEWHERES.

HEY! YOU BIRDS ARE MISSIN' THE BIG SHOW··· A BUTTERFLY HAS GROWED HISSELF A SET OF STORE MOLARS AND IS RUNNIN' AROUND SNAPPIN' AN' GROWLIN'.
SHHH··· WE KNOW.
WODDYA MEAN "SHHHH!" IT'S THE BIGGEST THING SINCE SCARNE INVENTED TEEKO··AN' YOU SAY "SHHH!"

IT MAY INTEREST YOU TO KNOW WE'VE BEEN DOIN' SOME BIG INNERNATIONAL THINKIN'···WE'RE PRETTY BUSY, FRIEND, ME AND THE KID HERE··· AND WE'RE SOLVIN' PROBLEMS OF WORLD-WIDE IMPORT!

GOOD··MOVE OVER··· I'LL GIVE YOU A HAND·· I ALWAYS WANTED A JOB DOIN' SOMETHIN' IMPORTANT AN' LYIN' DOWN.

Chapter 27

A BASE CANAL

In and out of the big ditch with a few guttural remarks---

HOW'D YOU LIKE TO HEAR MY LATEST SONG?
ZZZ

THE NAME OF IT IS "YUM YUM." ♫ OH, MARCH COMES IN LIKE A LION AND A LION COMES IN LIKE A LAMB. BUT WHAT DO I SMELL FRYIN'? ♫ IT'S A FRIENDLY LITTLE PIECE OF HAM! ♫
Z

SNRPH?

I JUST HAD A WONDERFUL DREAM--- IN IT I COMPOSED A SONG CALLED "YUM YUM"... A REAL SOLID HIT--- WANNA HEAR HOW IT GOES--?

WELL, HE CAN HAVE THE SONG.. LET HIM MAKE A MILLION DOLLARS...

ALL GOLD AIN'T WHAT GLITTERS, FRIEND--- YOU MOUGHT OF STOLE MY SONG, BUT WHO STEALS MY NAME STEALS TRASH! THINK THAT OVER!
AHUM!

YOU CAN TELL ASCAP THAT YOU CAN KEEP THE MILLION DOLLARS WHAT THE SONG WILL MAKE ...
TELL 'EM THAT, TO ME, IT'S PEANUTS!
PEANUTS!?
LISTEN---KEEP THAT DOUGH. HOW WOULD YOU LIKE TO SINK IT INTO A CANAL?
WHAT FOR? WHO WANTS SOGGY MONEY?

MY IDEA IS TO OPEN A CANAL HERE IN THE OKEFENOKEE WHAT CAN BE USED BY THE MARIOTIME NATIONS OF THE WORLD--- WHY SHOULD WE GET HUNG UP IN THE SUEZ?

BUT--- THIS MAY SEEM LIKE A SILLY QUESTION.. BUT WHERE WOULD IT GO--? WHERE WOULD IT WIND UP?
WHERE DOES ANY CANAL WIND UP? WHO WOULD OF THOUGHT THE SUEZ WOULD--UH.. I MEAN--WHY PLAN?

NOW THIS SONG YOU WROTE YOU SAY WILL MAKE A COOL MILLION DOLLARS--EH? AND HOW MANY VERSES HAS IT GOT?
ONE
MISS NINA

THAT'S A MILLION PER STANZA, RIGHT?! NOW, HOW MANY MILLION WOULD YOU HAVE IF YOU WROTE TWO VERSES? ---IN OTHER WORDS ONE MORE VERSE---
UM ---WELL... LET'S SEE--- UH -- NOW--

Chapter 28

AN ADULT CATERPIGGLE ON THE LOOSE

Wherein we learn that one should never look a gift butterfly in the teeth---

IS YOU GONNA HELP ME HOUND DOWN THIS DOG OF A BUTTERFLY OR NOT?
NOW, MIZ BEAVER, LET'S TAKE THE CALM VIEW.

I AM CALM!
NOW THAT'S PRECISELY WHAT WE SHOULDN'T DO IN A CASE LIKE THIS ... WE SHOULD CALMLY TURN THE

OTHER CHEEK AND SAY - - - - -
GIMME THAT BLUNDERBUSS!
CRUNCH

COME BACK HERE, YOU BUTTERFLY, AN' FIGHT LIKE THE INSECK YOU IS!
MEBBE HE DON'T WANNA ANSWER WITH HIS MOUTH FULL.
ALL THAT RACKET IS HAVIN' A DISTURBIN' EFFECK ON MY THINKIN'.

WHERE WAS WE ?
WELL, I WAS SAYIN' LET'S DIG A NEW CANAL FOR WORLD SHIPPIN' THRU THE OKEFENOKEE... WE GOT THE WATER... THEN NOBODY'D HAFTA GO TO SUEZ TO USE THAT ONE AN' YOU WAS GONNA THROW IN A COUPLE MILLION DOLLARS IN CASE YOU GETS IT.
RIGHT! LET'S GO AN' MAKE 'EM QUIET DOWN THAT RACKET! IT'S DISTURBIN' A SERIOUS DISCUSSION.
YOU AIN'T FOOLIN'.

THE THING TO DO IS TO SNEAK UP ON THIS CRITTUR AN'..
HEY! WHAT'S GOIN' ON?
SHH.. I'M GONNA LET THIS LI'L' BANDIT HAVE A SHOT OF OL' BLUNDER-BUSS.

BUT YOU WOULDN'T SHOOT A SITTIN' BIRD!?
THIS ONE, YES!
BUT HE'S SITTIN' TOO CLOSE TO YOU.. YOU'RE IN THE LINE OF FIRE!
YOU'RE RIGHT... IT MIGHT AMOUNT TO PERSONAL SUICIDE... PEOPLE WOULD JUS' TALK.
THINK OF THE SCANDAL.

NO MATTER HOW HE GITS WAGGLED AN' SHOOK, THAT OL' BUTTERFLY HUNGS ON LIKE GRIM DEBT!
HE GOT JAWBONES LIKE UNTO A BULLDOG.
"Forsooth ~ Has it come to this pass? Abusing a child of Nature?

"Pray desist in this evil work, friend --- Beat not thy slave --
SLAVE? HE AIN'T NO SLAVE!
Then you have no right to beat him, be he not your slave.
BE HE BUTTERFLY! THAT'S WHAT HE BE HE!

A Butterfly? In all my years as Captain of the Bird Watchers I have never seen a butterfly with teeth.
MAYBE THAT'S 'CAUSE YOU BEEN WATCHIN' NOTHIN' BUT BIRDS.
AIN'T BUTTERFLIES BIRDS?
NO.. BUTTERFLIES IS MORE LIKE PAPER ...BIRDS IS MADE OF FUZZ AN' CHICKEN BONES.

That creature should be banded to see where he goes ~ to see how he nests -- to get data on his breeding.
SIR! YOU INSULTS MY BUTTERFLY -- HOW'D YOU LIKE TO HAVE SOMEBODY PRY INTO YOUR NESTIN' HABITS--? WHERE I GOES MY BUTTERFLY GOES -- HE'S STUCK ON ME --- AN' IF YOU BANDS ME I'LL POP YOU ONE.
SNEAK OUT WHILE NOBODY'S LOOKIN'.

This is always, at least fairly often once in a while, a sure-cure or nearly so--
PEPPER, HUH?
SNN--
SNN--
SNNNOO

KA CHOW!

Well, that's that --- the good will of a noble effort dulled on the blunted brain of a bone-head...

You may rest assured I will never help you get a butterfly off your tail again ---

DON'T COME BELLYACHIN' TO ME IF I LEARNS HOW TO DO IT IF YOU EVER GETS ONE ON YOURS 'CAUSE I WON'T NEVER TELL YOU SOONER'N YOU WON'T TELL ME AND LONGER TOO!

THAT'S TELLIN' HIM, CHIEF.

WELL, I'M GONNA LOOK UP A PAL WHAT FELL HEIR TO A EAR OF CORN.
G'BYE ... NOW MY TAIL WILL BE LONESOME.

Chapter 29

A SPADE IS TRUMPED

In which we see our heroes decide to shovel off to Buffalo, or possibly Sydney---

TELL YOU WHAT.. YOU SET THERE AN' WAIT FOR A FELLA WITH A SHOVEL.. I'M GONNA GET SOMETHIN' TO DRAW OUR PLANS ON.
THERE'S A OL' PAPER BAG AN' A PENCIL IN MY HOUSE.
WELL! HEIGHDY HOWLAND.
HEIGHDY, CHURCHY.

CONGRATULATIONS! YOU IS JUST IN TIME TO POSSIBLE GET A GOOD JOB.
JOB? DOIN' WHAT?
STAND THERE A MINUTE..
LESSEE.. MOUSE SAY HE
1. GOTTA HAVE A SHOVEL
2. GOTTA BE STRONG
3. GOTTA BE STUPID.
CHECK ONE: YOU GOT A SHOVEL.

NOW THEN, WE'RE READY TO START WORK ON OUR NEW CANAL TO REPLACE THE SUEZ ... ALL YOU GOTTA DO IS START DIGGIN'.
WHAT!?
HOW CAN I DO THAT WHEN I'M SITTIN' DOWN? BESIDES THIS A BRAN' NEW SHOVEL AN' I DON'T KNOW HOW THIS MODEL WORKS... I COULD RUIN IT BY USIN' IT WRONG.

GIMME THAT SHOVEL! DON'T YOU KNOW ALL SHOVELS WORK ALIKE? WATCH!
GOSH DO THEY?

LOOK! SEE! LIKE THIS! LIKE THAT! LIKE THIS! LIKE THAT! LIKE THIS! LIKE THAT! HOW CAN YOU BE SO STUPID?

IF YOU'S LOOKIN' FOR BAIT, I'SE GOT A-PLENTY... COME ON ALONG..
NO.. 'TAINT THAT, POGO... HE'S DIGGIN' A CANAL.

HE IS?
YUP.. WE WAS LOOKIN' FOR SOME-BODY WITH A SHOVEL WHO WAS STRONG AND STUPID.. AN' HE TOOK THE JOB.

DOES HE QUALIFY?
SURE.. HE GOT A SHOVEL... HE'S STRONG AND HE'S SO STUPID HE DON'T KNOW HOW TO USE IT.

SO I GOTTA SHOW HIM.

I GOT IT! THE SUPER PLAN WHAT WILL KNOCK THE SUEZ RIGHT OUT OF THE CANAL GAME.
I IS ALMOST KNOCKED OUT OF IT MYSELF.
HOW COME? DIDN'T NOBODY STUPID DO THE DIGGING?
NO! THAT'S THE TROUBLE.. I HAD TO DO IT MYSELF.

WELL... PROB'LY NOT AS GOOD AS IF IT WAS DONE RIGHT, BUT.. LOOK HERE! THE EXCITING NEW PLAN.
A CANAL FROM HERE IN GEORGIA STRAIGHT DOWN RIGHT THROUGH THE WHOLE FAT EARTH... 8000 MILES LONG... NEVER BEEN THOUGHT OF BEFORE.

Humph, what's going on here?
WE'RE DIGGIN' A CANAL... AN' CHURCHY IS DOWN THERE SHOWIN' US HOW TO USE A SHOVEL.
Canal? Why, it does' nothing but go straight down--
SURE.. RIGHT THRU THE EARTH.. IT'LL REPLACE THE SUEZ.

Verily? Perchance it comes out in the Ocean of the Indies--Ha-the sea will gush through, dooming whomever is digging..
?
GET ME OUT OF HERE!
PSSST

OH, IT WAS TERRIBLE! DEACON MUSHRAT SAID IF I CONTINUED DIGGIN' THE INDIAN OCEAN WOULD RUSH INTO THE CANAL AN' DROWND ME.
YOU WASN'T EVEN HALFWAY THRU THE EARTH!
I KNOW, BUT S'POSE SOMEBODY PLAYED A TRICK? AFTER ALL IT'S APRIL FIRST WHICH IS ALLUS APRIL FOOL'S DAY.

ONLY ONE THING COULD BE WORSE... THE MERE THOUGHT MAKES ME FAINT...
WHAT? WHAT!?
SUPPOSE APRIL FOOL'S DAY EVER HAPPENS TO COME ALONG ON FRIDAY THE THIRTEENTH, WOOF!
D'YOU WANT TO TAKE THE SHOVEL AN' COVER HIM UP OR SHALL I?

Chapter 30

WHAT IS AMOUNTING TO A MOLEHILL?

Wherein the blind leads the bland---

You hit me on the head, and all my life I've resented people who do that.
WE ALL HAVE OUR IDIOSYNCRASIES.
I mean to say that I can't feel enthusiastic about you.
WELL, I'VE ALWAYS BEEN ABLE TO CONTROL MY ENTHUSIASM FOR YOU.

In fact I've always had a sneaking distrust of your type...
MY FEELINGS EXACTLY ABOUT YOU! A CLUNCH-MINDED CLABBERLIP.
WHAT I DO LIKE ABOUT YOU IS YOU'RE NO HONEYMOUTH! A PAL KNOWS WHERE HE STANDS.
Precisely, Crony boy -- Our mutual dislike will never interfere with our true friendship...

THEY'RE DIGGING A CANAL RIGHT THROUGH THE EARTH.

Yea! And they shall be drowned ---- they come out in the Ocean of the Indies ~

SO MUCH THE BETTER -- A CANAL SHOULD CONNECT WITH SOMETHING WET.
"But the waters of DOOM will rush in! ~~~~ Inundating them as they break through...
YOU FORGET..FROM HERE THRU IT'S ALL DOWNHILL! THE WATERS WILL FLOW DOWN, CARRYING OUR SHIPPING ON MERE WATER CURRENT TO THE OTHER SIDE OF THE WORLD... A VALUABLE PROPERTY, DEACON.
By Ginger!

NOW SEE, DEACON... LET THEM BUILD THIS CANAL TO REPLACE THE SUEZ... IT WILL GO 7,926 MILES THROUGH THE EARTH ITSELF ... THEN COMES OUR CHANCE.
WE WILL SEIZE POSSESSION ... WE WILL CONTROL WORLD SHIPPING... WE WILL BE IN CHARGE.
No one must know too soon...

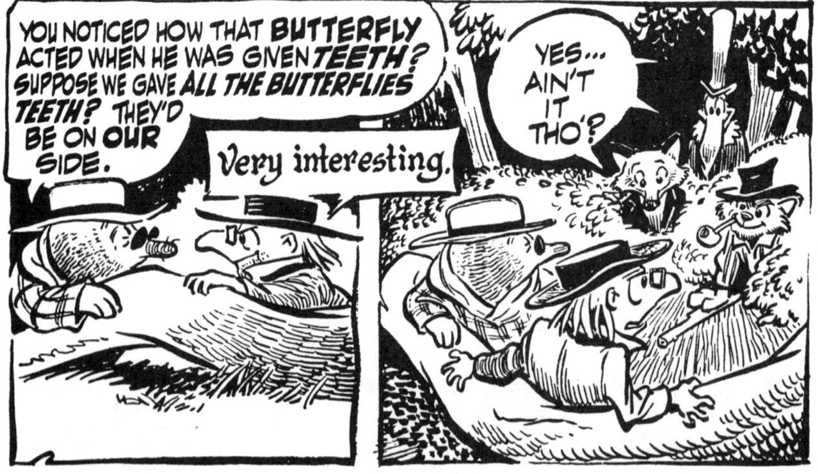
YOU NOTICED HOW THAT BUTTERFLY ACTED WHEN HE WAS GIVEN TEETH? SUPPOSE WE GAVE ALL THE BUTTERFLIES TEETH? THEY'D BE ON OUR SIDE.
Very interesting.
YES... AIN'T IT THO'?

Well--uh, Wiley Catt--Seminole Sam--Sarcoph-
AYE, DEACON OLD FRIEND ~ IT'S ME--~ SARCOPHAGUS MACABRE-- YOU AIN'T DANCIN' FOR JOY.

THAT'S BETTER! --THEY JES' NEEDED A LI'L MUSIC, SARC.

WE LIKED YOUR IDEA, MOLE, ABOUT PUTTING TEETH ON THE BUTTERFLIES.
THANK YOU.
AND SO WE'LL HELP YOU-- WHEN THE CANAL IS FINISHED--ALL THE WAY THRU THE EARTH--

-- AND YOU'VE GOTTEN THE CONTROL OF IT BY TURNIN' THE BUTTERFLIES LOOSE ON THEM AS **DIGS** THIS NOW ***TUNNEL***.

WE'LL TAKE IT OFF YOUR HANDS! WE'RE YOUR PALS.

IT'S GOING TO BE ***YOUR*** JOB, DEACON, TO ROUND UP THE **BUTTERFLIES!**
Me!? I don't know any butterflies.
WHILE **SARCOPHAGUS MACABRE** AND **WILEY CATT** GO GATHER SOME **TEETH**, ***YOU*** LINE UP A FEW BUTTERFLIES.

YES, OLD FRIEND, YOU'RE AN OLD **CAPTAIN OF BIRD-WATCHERS**.. BUTTERFLIES ARE THE SAME AS BIRDS! **GO TO IT! STOUT FELLOW!**

AND ***HURRY!*** OR YOU KNOW **WHOSE** TEETH WE'LL USE ...

Chapter 31

Butterflies and Butterfingers

Here we see that the flap of a wing is not in proportion to the flap of a lip~~~

Why are there no more butter-flies than there are?
WAIT'LL I GIT INTO A ISOLATION BOOTH--I'LL TELL YOU FOR 39¢
I've searched everywhere; --not a one in sight--
MEBBE THE CATER-PIGGLE CROP WAS POOR.
But they have a chance to wear teeth--- --to belong to a Cause--- a chance to live like Lions.
ELKS WEAR TEETH --THEY BELONGS TO CAUSES AN' THEY GITS THEIR HEADS MOUNTED OVER FIRE-PLACES.
But wouldn't you like to live like a Lion?
WHAT!? AN' HAFTA GOT A LADY LION FER A WIFE? AN' EAT RAW ZEBRA?
I DON'T SEE HOW HAVIN' TEETH CHANGES A BUTTERFLY FROM A AIRBORNE PETUNIA INTO A LION.
It's a matter of fire-power.
Suppose you're a Caterpiggle at first-- you'll crawl about like a lowly creepy wormified maggot---
I RECOGNIZES THE TYPE.. GOOD JOB!

Then the glory and power of your lovely wings bursts upon you -- you *leap* --- you glide -- you soar

YOU SORE ?

That teaches *me* a lesson; it's the last time I try to teach you a lesson; let that be a lesson to you...
YOU STILL DIN'T TELL ME WHY BUTTERFLIES **CHANGE** WHEN THEY WEARS TEETH.

As long as I'm on all fours, I'll proceed -- first the tiny caterpiggle learns to crawl --
WAIT...! YOU RAN OVERBOARD SHOWIN' ME THIS BEFORE.

Then, after he learns to fly, what would the next step be for the butterfly if he acquired teeth --?

A-WAY.
SPLASH

Help!

THAT SOUNDED LIKE A CRY FOR HELP.
YES.. AND A LITTLE EARLY IN THE SEASON, TOO.
FIRST ONE I'VE HEARD THIS YEAR.

Help!
ANOTHER! WE SHOULD REPORT THIS TO OUR CAPTAIN OF BIRDWATCHERS.
TWO IN ONE DAY!

Help!
THREE! OH, THE DEACON WILL NEVER BELIEVE THIS!

"Might as well rescue myself -- a man could starve to death while he's drowning waiting for somebody to save him --
THE DEACON!
DEACON MUSHRAT! HONORED CAPTAIN OF BIRDWATCHERS! WE HEARD THREE CALLS FOR HELP AND IT'S ONLY APRIL.
OR IS IT MAY?
JUNE?

LET'S SEE.. THIRTY DAYS HATH MY UNCLE, APRIL, JUNE AND CARBUNCLE.
ALL THE REST HATH THIRTY TWO.
TWENTY NINE!
How would you three like regular jobs as insects?
NO MONTH HAS THIRTY-TWO DAYS.
I DIN'T SAY THIRTY-TWO DAYS.. IT COULD OF BEEN 32 ANYTHING.
ALASKA COMES AFORE JUNE.

I'm in a position to offer you bats steady work as Butterflies.
BUTTERFLIES? WE'D BE A SIGHT STEADIER IF WE WAS BATS.
ALASKA IS NOT A MONTH.
NEITHER IS HAWAII.
Think of it! You can visit foreign climes ~~~ arrayed in the dazzling finery of Velvet wings.
WE COULD BE THE FIRST BUTTERPEOPLE TO FLY THE ATLANTIC.

How well do you fly personally, Sir?
I AIN'T BEEN UP SINCE THEY GROUNDED THE PX CANTEEN.. BUT GIVE US A LI'L BOOST, I'LL SHOW YOU.
Pooph?! Do you call that flying?!
HE USED TO BE IN THE SMALL BEER BUSINESS.. "SHORT HOPS" THEY CALLED HIM.
INTO THE WILD BREW, YONDER?

If you take the job of being butterflies, you'll have to wear a more becoming type of wing...
WHAT'S WRONG WITH OUR WINGS?
They're not exactly the butterfly brand. They look more like the wings of an out-dated pterodactyl -- one which had been shot down.
WHAT!?

AT LEAST THEY LOOKS BETTER'N YOUR UM-BRELLA -- YOU DON'T HAVE TO INSULT US 'CAUSE WE NEED A LITTLE HONEST WORK --- WE QUIT!
Honest work? I didn't say the work was honest.
NOT HONEST...? YOU MEAN WE'D MAKE A LOT OF MONEY BY SOME KIND OF CROOKED, EASY LAZY MAN'S GAME?.. HOW DARE YOU?..HOW DARE YOU LET US QUIT!?!?
Let's go.

Dig up some gaudy paper or some Japanese fans -- make wings out of them -- and then report to me as butterflies ----
B. WITCHED
B. OTHERED
AND
B. MILDRED
AYE
AYE
SIR
AS BUTTERFLIES?
SO FLIES THE NATION.
BUT WHENCE?

IF WE'S GONNA REPORT TO HIM ··· WHAT WE GONNA REPORT?
MAYBE ABOUT THE WEATHER?
THE LATEST RUNDOWN ON RUNDOWNS ?
MAYBE HE WANTS A REPORT ON HOW IT FEELS TO BE A BUTTERFLY.
WE COULD SELL THAT REPORT TO SOME DIGEST MAG ·· "WE WAS BUTTERFLIES FOR THE F.B.I AND FOUND PEACE."
SURE FIRE.

YOU TWO WILL HAFTA BE BUTTERFLIES WITHOUT MY HELP ·· I'M WRITIN' OUR MEMOIRS OF THIS IMPERSONATION AND I'M GONNA SEND IT OFF TO A DIGEST MAGAZINE.
BUT WE GUARANTEED A TEAM OF THREE BUTTERFLIES.
ARS LONGA VITA BREVIS... GET YOURSELF ANOTHER BOY.
WHAT KIND OF TALK IS THAT FER A FRIEND ?

THAT'S LATIN OR FRENCH OR ONE OF THEM ·· IT MEANS YOU GOTTA DRAW FAST BEFORE YOU DROPS DEAD ·· IT'S A VERY HIGH-TONE REMARK ALL ABOUT ART AND LIFE AND WHICH IS THE TALLER ·· THERE! ONE PAGE DONE!
THAT'S A PAGE?
OF COURSE IT'S A PAGE ·· WHAT'S IT LOOK LIKE ·· A BATH TOWEL?
HOW KIN HE WRITE THE MEMOIRS OF OUR EXPERIENCE WHEN WE AIN'T HAD IT YET ··?
MEBBE THE TIME TO REMEMBER A LOT OF STUFF IS BEFORE YOU STARTS.

Chapter 32

ANOTHER G.O. FIZZ-OUT

We find that to keep apace with science requires a stride of strident tone~~~

FOR EXAMPLE, THE SLIDE CAPACITY OF THE BORE IS FORTY FOOT POUNDS OF STATIC INERTIA WHICH IS THE EQUAL OF SEVENTY TWO INCHES CENTIGRADE AT THE SURFACE OR IN OTHER WORDS: PLUMB BOB.

WHAT DOES MOUSE ***THINK ABOUT*** WHEN HE'S PACIN'?
WHY, ***MAN!*** DON'T TELL ME YOU DON'T REALIZE ALL THESE FIGURES **GOTTA** BE THUNK OF!
US WORLD PLANNERS GIVES **EVER'THING** A **LOT** OF THOUGHT. PLANNIN' A CANAL THROUGH THE EARTH AIN'T NO MERE BAG-OF-TELLE -- LOOK AT THAT FIGURE: ***1,762,309 1/2!*** IT, *ALONE*, REQUIRED TWELVE HOURS OF ***SOLID*** THOUGHT.
1931
Tuesday
and Xmas
1762-309½!

OOP! OL' MOUSE IS **COLLAPSED**... HE'S WORE OUT WITH PACIN'.
QUICK-- NOT A MINUTE TO LOSE --***YOU*** TAKE THE FIGURES --***I'LL*** TAKE OVER PACIN' --***TEAM WORK*** DOES IT!

YOU MIGHT WAIT 'TIL HE'S, AT LEAST, **REVIVED.**
OUR WORK GOES ON AT **ALL COSTS**-- I'LL PACE AN' THINK 'TIL **HE** KIN **RESUME.**

THERE-- HE'S FEELIN' BETTER.
QUICK! WHERE WAS YOU WITH YOUR THINKIN' WHEN YOU COLLAPSED?

I WAS THINKIN' OF A BIG NUMBER-- MEBBE **96** OR EVEN **99!**
NINETY-**SIX** -- MM -- NINETY-NINE -- WELL WELL **99 - 96 - 96 99** HMM.

YOU LI'L' ENGINEERS WHAT IS PLANNIN' THE CANAL DOES A LOT OF THINKIN', BUT ABOUT WHAT? NUMBERS?
99-96-97? MEBBE 1886-202 ..MM 91?
SURE, WE DON'T LEAVE NO STONE UNTURNT.

WE IS EXPERTS IN OUR FIELDS.. PACIN' AN' THINKIN' -- 'COURSE OWL AIN'T AS GOOD AT PACIN' AS ME, BUT HE THINKS GOOD --WITHOUT HARDLY USIN' HALF HIS BRAIN.

SEEM TO ME ANYBODY'D BE GOOD AT PACIN'.
NO..IT TAKE A KNACK --YOU GOTTA HAVE CONTROL ..OOP
KLUNK

SEE? YESTERDAY HE WALKED OVERBOARD TWICE --TODAY HE KLUNKED INTO A TREE ... IS YOU OKAY, COLLEAGUE OL' BOY?

SEEM TO BE YOU COULD THINK WITHOUT WALKIN' INTO TREES AN' FALLIN' OVERBOARD..
THINKIN' IS A DANGEROUS GAME, POGO.. IT GOT ITS HAZARDS AN' ITS HAS-BEENS.
THIS LEMONADE WOULD OF BEEN BETTER IF IT HAD SOME SUGAR IN IT TO MAKE UP FOR NOT HAVIN' ANY LEMONS.
NOW, OUR PLANS FOR THE CANAL SHOW WE IS SPENT A HUNDRED HOURS OF SOLID THOUGHT UP TO HERE.

PAST THAT POINT WE IS PUT IN ODD HOURS ON A PRORATED BASIS TO BALANCE THE MINIMIZED FUNDAMENTALS OF THE MAN-JOB DAY QUOTIENT WHICH PONDERITES THE EQUATION OF THE EQUITABLES --OR, IN OTHER WORDS, WE'RE CONTRACTUALLY BIRD-DOGGING THE PLUNDERABLE POTENTIAL OF THE LOOT.

AND THAT'S NOT HALF.
YOU MEAN THERE'S MORE?
IF THERE'S NOT, WE IS WASTED A LOT OF SUNNY DAYS.

YOUR PLANS IS A LI'L' CONFUSIN' --WHAT, FOR EXAMPLE, IS THAT CHART MEAN?
THAT, AS ANY-BODY KIN SEE, IS A DIAGRAM OF A FLY SWATTER.

A FLY SWATTER..!? WHAT'S YOU NEED A FLY SWATTER FOR?
TO SWAT FLIES WITH, NATURAL!

I THOUGHT YOU WAS PLANNIN' A CANAL.. NOT FIGHTIN' INSECKS.
IT'S THE LITTLE THINGS THAT COUNT IN THE BIG PLAN, POGO.

NOW WHAT ELSE SHOULD WE DRAFT INTO THE PLANS.. HOW ABOUT A CHART ON EGG SAN'WICHES?
AN' HAM.. DON'T FORGET HAM.

Chapter 33

"If Yer Knows a Better Role---"

A hole in the ground is worth two in the round---

I AGREES WITH YER ON EVERY BLINKIN' POINT, REGGIE... NO NEED TO GET YER STEAM UP, LAD.
YOU SAID IT WERE AN OL' ..AN OL' WHAT!?
IT'S JUST AN 'OLE, REGGIE.. A SIMPLE RUDDY EMPTY 'OLE!
A SIMPLE RUDDY EMPTY OL' WHAT?

DASH IT! I'VE LOST ME PATIENCE... I'VE LOST ALL ME PATIENCE!
NOW I KNOWS WHY 'E'S IN SUCH A ROARIN' SWEAT.
DARE I ASK WHY?
'E LOST HIS PATIENTS.. USED TO BE A PHYSICIAN YOU KNOW.. NO PRACTICE, TOO BAD.
HE DON'T NEED NO PRACTICE FER THIS KINDA STUFF.

I WAS JUS' IN CONVERSATION WITH THE TWO COCKNEY BUGS AN' THEY TOLE A VERY DROLL TALE HAVING TO DO WITH YOUR CANAL...
ADD THE THREE, SUBTRACT THE NORMAL AND SACRIFICE THE ANTHRACITE THEN..
YOU GOT THE DIVIDEND UNDER THE UGH!
UNDER THE UGH? WHAT'S AN UGH?
I DUNNO BUT IT LOOKS PERTY UGHY.

IT SEEMS THIS FELLOW SAYS I LOST MY PATIENCE AN' THE OTHER FELLOW SAYS HE'S A DOCTOR AN' HASN'T GOT NO PRACTICE ··· AND A THIRD FELLOW SAYS THAT'S WHY HE LOST HIS ..
THAT'S NOT A UGH ···
WHAT IS IT?
THEY'LL GET IT WHEN IT'S TOO LATE.
HARD TO SAY BUT IT'S PART OF OUR ENGINEERIN' FIGGERS HERE ··ADD IT ON ANYWAY.
NO NO! DON'T ADD IT ··· ·· IT'S A JAM SPECKLE·· FROM BREAKFAST.

WE'VE DUG ENOUGH ON OUR REPLACEMENT FOR THE SUEZ CANAL TODAY··
WE?

YES, WE·· I BEEN UP HERE TALLYIN' THE SHOVELFULS OF DIRT YOU BEEN THROWIN' OUT --I IS EXHAUSTED--I FIGGER THERE'S 1,236,619,724,503 SHOVELFULS FROM HERE THROUGH THE ENTIRE EARTH·· YOU IS DONE A GOOD PART OF THAT, 503 TO BE PREE-CISE.
WOO

LET'S COVER HER UP WHILST WE'S AWAY··· IN CASE IT RAINS.
WHAT'S WE CARE IF IT RAINS?

MAN, YOU DON'T WANT TO GET OUR CANAL FULLED OF WATER, DO YOU?
G.O. FIZZ FAZZ

Chapter 34

FIVE IN ONE

Here it is seen that the last shall be left and right at that~~~

STOP PLOTTING AGAINST YOUR BETTERS ... HERE'S SOME TEETH FOR YOUR BUTTERFLY GROUP.
Seminole Sam! What sort of teeth did you get?
LET'S SEE -- AN OLD ELK'S TOOTH -- A BEAR TRAP WITH ONE TOOTH MISSING AND BUN RABBIT GAVE ME AN OLD UNION CONTRACT.

An old Union contract?
YEP, SAID IT HAD A LOT OF TEETH WRAPPED UP IN THE MINOR CLAUSES.
HMMM -- NOTHING.
WELL, DON'T LOOK A GIFT HORSE IN THE EYE -- WE'RE OFF TO INSPECT THE CANAL.

If Seminole Sam, Wiley Catt and Sarcophagus intend to inspect the canal, it proves they plan stealing it from us..
We could thwart their crooked plans by fill-ing in the hole ~~~ ho ho - they'd be served right -- eh? ho ho?

LET'S LOOK FOR THE HOLE AS **SOON** AS WE GET OUT OF THIS **DENSE WOOD**.

That's not a dense wood -- It's just *one* tree -- you are a little near-sighted.

I'M A LITTLE NEARSIGHTED **WHAT?** A NEARSIGHTED **WHAT!?** FINISH IT LIKE A MAN.

I'll go look for the hole --

FINISH YOUR BASE CANARD, SIR-- ***AARGH!*** IF I FIND MY WAY OUT OF HERE.

Poof! Trouble is *you* can't see where --

You're going....

CAN YOU DIRECT ME TO THE **HOLE** THEY'RE DIGGING TO START A CANAL RIGHT THROUGH THE EARTH?
Over here! Over here!
OVER HERE, EH -- THANK YOU, SIR -- JUST SO -- HOLD MY HAND WHILE I GET MY BALANCE --- SO THAT'S THE HOLE -- THANK YOU -- WELL, WELL.

MY SAKES, **THAT'S** NOT YOUR HAND -- IT'S A SHOVEL --- HMMPH!
NOW --- WHO'S DOWN IN THE HOLE ? I CAN HEAR SOMEONE STIRRING AROUND -- -- IS THAT **YOU**, WILEY CATT OR SEMINOLE SAM OR SARCOPHAGUS ?
No! It's me, the Deacon!

HA! **YOU LIE!** THE DEACON IS TOO STUPID TO FIND THE HOLE -- **I'M COVERING YOU UP -- SARCOPHAGUS -- WILEY CATT -- SEMINOLE SAM -- GOOD RIDDANCE -- AND GOOD NIGHT!**
awk!
NIGHTY NIGHT, MOLE.

DON'T WANT YOU TO STRAIN YOURSELF WITH THE SHOVEL, MOLE... WHAT WAS YOU DOIN'?
UH-WELL.
AH--HE WAS ENGAGED IN A FASCINATING ENDEAVOR.
BURYIN' A PAL! HOW THOUGHTFUL!

DOESN'T HIS FRIEND LOOK FINE--? SO NATURAL--SO LIFELIKE?
WHAT MORE COULD A CHUM DO?
I am Lifelike-- get me out of here!
OH, I DIDN'T KNOW IT WAS MY ESTEEMED FRIEND DOWN THERE... I THOUGHT IT WAS YOU THREE.

I AND SIS BOOMBAH HERE IS TAKIN' A DAY OFF AND GO FISHIN'... WHERE'S THE BAIT SHOVEL I GIVE YOU THE BORRY OF?
OVER'T THE CANAL WE WAS DIGGIN'.
BUT WE GIVE IT UP.. IT WOULD OF TOOK TOO LONG TO DIG.

TOO LONG? JUST TO DIG A LITTLE BITTY CANAL THROUGH THE EARTH?
WE FIGGERED IT WOULD TAKE US 409 YEARS.
SIMPLY FIXED.. YOU COULD CUT THAT IN HALF BY USING TWICE AS MANY DIGGERS.
SHE'S RIGHT.. WHY DIDN'T WE THINK OF THAT?
WITH THE HIGH COST OF LABOR, IT WOULD BREAK US.

LOOK, LITTLE SPORT, GET IN WITH YOUR SIDE-KICK THERE AND WE'LL COVER UP THE PAIR OF YOU.
NOT WITH MY SHOVEL YOU WON'T!

WHO NEEDS YOUR ADVICE, YOU OL' WASHWOMAN?
TAKE OFF YOUR HAT WHEN YOU ADDRESS A LADY!
NOT WITH THE LUNCH, SIS...NOT WITH THE LUNCH.. IT'LL SPOIL MY PICCALILLI!

WAK
BAM
WOOF
HELP!
SOK
HEY
WOW

MIZ BEAVER AND SIS BOOMBAH CHUNKED US ALL IN THE HOLE--'CAUSE YOU INSULTED THEM.
THAT'S WOMEN FOR YOU--GIVE THEM A VOICE IN PUBLIC AFFAIRS AND THEY GET PERTY SHIRTY.

I think it's very unfortunate that we fight amongst our-selves --- Now, look, we can get out by one crawling up on another's shoulders and --

JUST SO! AND THEN ANOTHER AND THEN THE NEXT--

THAT DEACON'S GOT A HEAD ON HIM!
Hey!

Chapter 35

DEEP IN THE HEART OF ALBERT

Wherein a hero explores a bit of Inner Space with a G.O. Fizzickle result ~~~

IF YOU WAS BETTER AT FLYIN' WE'D HAVE YOU JOIN OUR BUTTERFLY TEAM ··· GOOD PAY ·· SHORT HOURS ·· BUT THE WAY YOU LANDED SHOWS YOU CAN'T FLY A LICK.
I LANDS RATHER ABRUPT, I ADMITS.

BUT LEND ME THE BORRY OF YOUR WINGS, BUTTERFLY FRIEND, AND I'LL SHOW YOU HOW TO SWOOP LIKE A GRACEFUL DIURNAL LEPIDOPTEROUS INSECT.

HERE I GO ··· FLAPPIN' AND FLYIN' ·· I'M THE WRIGHT BROS. ALL OVER AGAIN.
HEY ··· UH ·· HOOP ·· HOHA ··· EEH ··· HOOLYHOOLY ·· EE YAWP ··
I'M FLAPPIN' FASTER AN' FASTER BUT NIGHT IS FELL ·· I'M FLYIN' BLIND.
WELL ·· WE IS LOST ANOTHER MEMBER OF THE ESCADRILLE.

ALL OF A SUDDEN I IS ALL COME OVER QUEASY.
THAT'S 'CAUSE YOU GOT A BUTTERFLY IN YOUR STOMACH.
I KNOWS I GOT BUTTERFLIES IN MY STOMACH ·· WHOOIE! I MUSTA ET SOMETHIN'.
YOU SWALLIED A WHOLE, LIVE, LEAPIN' FROG!

SWALLOWED A FROG?!
HELLO OUT THERE --THINGS ARE PRETTY DARK DOWN HERE--AH-- HERE'S A MATCH--
THE VOICE OF THE BUTTERFROG!
EE--HEE! DON'T SCRATCH THEM ON MY BACKBONE NO MORE!
ALBERT DON'T QUITE PLAY THE GENEROUS HOST, DO HE?
HOW'D YOU LIKE YOUR INTERIOR WALLS ALL SCRATCHED UP?
SKRITCH

BY THE LIGHT OF THE MATCH I KIN SEE THIS IS A OLD PREHISTORIC CAVE--
ALBERT! YOU IS A ARCHEO-LOGICAL FIND!

BITS OF BROKEN POTTERY-- --OLD ARROW HEADS-- A FEW PITIFUL BONES-- AND THERE, ON THE WALL, A CAVE PAINTING!-- AND A MESSAGE!
WHAT'S IT SAY??

IT SAYS "KILROY WAS HERE".
ALBERT! IN AGES PAST YOU WAS INHABITED!

I'M LIGHTIN' ANOTHER MATCH, FRIENDS... THE STALACTITES AND STALAGMITES IN HERE IS A JOY TO THE EYE-- --RIGHT BESIDES "KILROY WAS HERE" I SEE SOMETHING CARVED IN PICTISH.
MAN! PICTISH.

THIS PLACE COULD BECOME A NATIONAL MONUMENT... ..MORE ARROWHEADS!.. AND..A NOTE ON BIRCH BARK.."TROOP 6, 1926 OVERNIGHT HIKE."
A MECCA OF THE LIMBERLOST!
THE REFLECTIONS ARE BEAUTIFUL ..AND THE QUIET! THE MAJESTIC QUIET.. AH!
SOUNDS LIKE THE KIND OF A PLACE I'D LIKE TO VISIT.
NOT ME.

THIS IS A FASCINATING PLACE IN HERE, FRIENDS.. I CAN SEE GUIDED TOURS THROUGH THE GROTTOES TURNING A PRETTY PENNY.

YAK! YOW WHAT'S THAT!?

RUN FOR YOUR LIVES!

Chapter 36

A DEMON STRATION

The probe of Inner Space continues and we watch which doctor is witch ~~~

HEIGHDY, SON..
ALBERT, YOU LOOK LIKE SOMEBODY IS CUT YO' BUDGET.
OOG
HOW'D YOU LIKE IT IF SOMEBODY CREPT INSIDE YOU AN' SAW A MONSTER.. ..AN' YOU NEVER KNEW 'BOUT IT BEIN' THERE?

SEEM FUNNY TO ME, ALBERT, YOU COULD HAVE A MONSTER LIVIN' IN YOU WITHOUT YOU KNOW IT.
THE FROG SAID IT WAS A BONAFIDE TERRIFYIN' MONSTER.
WHY DON'T YOU EXORCISE HIM, THEN?
WHAT'S I WANNA PAMPER THE CRITTUR FOR? LET HIM GIT HIS OWN EXERCISE.

NO..I MEAN DRIVE HIM OUT... IF YOU IS POSSESSED OF A DEMON HE KIN BE DRIV OUT BY WITCH DOCTOR DANCIN' AND MAGIC WORDS..HOOK A HOOKA
STOP! IF HE'S AS FIERCE AS OL' FROG SAY, I DON'T WANT HIM OUT HERE WHERE HE'LL ONLY SCARE ME!
HOOKA?

HOW CAN I GO THROUGH ALL MY LIFE POSSESSED BY SOME FIEND INSIDE ME ?

MAYBE PORKY IS RIGHT, YOU'LL HAFTA GET SOME WITCH DOCTOR TO CONJURE HIM OUT OF YOU.
UM

'COURSE IT MIGHT BE AGAINST THE LAW TO DIS-POSSESS HIM... HE PROB'LY GOT SQUATTER'S RIGHTS.
WHO'S THE MASTER IN MY STOMACH? ME, OR SOME FREE-LOADIN' DEMON?
THERE'S THE PATIENT -- THE ONE WHAT SEEMS TO HAVE A MONSTER INSIDE HISSELF.
OL' ALBERT? SOME FOLKS DON'T CARE WHOM THEY INHABITS.

IS YOU HEARD THAT THEY DISCOVERED A MONSTER LIVIN' IN MY INNERS ?
YEP.. PORKY IS TOLD ME YOU COULD MEBBE USE A WITCH DOCTOR.
IS YOU A BONAFIDE WITCH DOCTOR..? YOU GOT A DIPLOMA?
YEP, I IS THE HOTTEST WITCH DOCTOR IN THE GAME ... I GOT 109 DEGREES FROM FAHREN-HEIT U. ALONE.

YOU SKIPS AROUN' PERTY GOOD, OWL ··· G.O. FISTICUFF YEARS, CANALS ··· WHAT'S YOUR NEW PERFESSION GOT TO DO WITH ALL YOUR UNDONE BUSINESS?
EVERYTHING! WHAT'S MORE UP MY ALLEY THAN INNER SPACE ···? 'SPECIALLY WHEN IT'S INHABITED BY A DEMON ···I IS A EXPERT ON ALL THAT STUFF.

I KNOWS ALL THE SCIENTIFIC ASPECTS OF THE PERFESSION·· ··I LEAPS AN' HOLLERS, HOOTS, GROANS, SHAKES RATTLES, EXPLODES BALLOONS AN' SETS FIRE TO MY HAT ··· AN' THAT AIN'T ALL.

THAT'S GOOD ENOUGH FER ME! WHEN I HIRES A PHYSICIAN, I DON'T WANT NO PHONY FAKER WHAT DON'T KNOW HIS TRADE.
NOTHIN' BUT GENUINE WITCH-MENTS.

WE HAFTA GO GET SOME MASKS AND DRUMS AN' STUFF ··THEN THE TREATMENTS CAN BEGIN.
I'M IN YOUR HANDS, DOC.
IN·AND·AS·MUCH AS YOU GOT A DEMON IN YO' INNARDS WE GOTTA BE CAREFUL IT DON'T BE-COME A NATIONAL EPIDEMIC.
HOWLAND

BEIN' OCCUPIED BY A MONSTER IS AN OCCUPATIONAL DISEASE ---IT WOULDN'T PAY TO HAVE THE WHOLE UNINETY STATES SUFFERIN' FROM IT.
COURSE NOT-- THERE MIGHTN'T BE ENOUGH MONSTERS TO GO AROUND.
OH, I DUNNO, YOU FORGETS THE INGENUITY OF OUR POLITICAL PATRONAGE SYSTEM.

LONG AS I IS GONNA BE A PATIENT, I'LL GIT INTO BED AND WE KIN SEND OUT ANNOUNCEMENTS.
RIGHT.

THERE AIN'T NO SENSE BEIN' AT DEATH'S DOOR IF NOBODY AIN'T GONNA COME AROUND AN' WAVE GOOD-BYE WITH A BOX OF SEE-GARS OR OTHER HOSPITAL CONDIMENTS.
THERE'S A KNOCK AT THE DOOR.

HOWDY DO, MADAM, IS YOUR HUSBAND, HOWLAND, TO HOME ?
DON'T BE ADSURBED. --DID YOU HEAR A KNOCK AT THE DOOR ?
NO I DIDN'T, --NOT TODAY.. DON'T SEE NOBODY NEITHER.
THAT'S FUNNY... WONDER WHAT IT WAS ?

WELL, I GUESS WE'LL NEVER FIND OUT WHO WAS AT THE DOOR... BUT NOW I GOTTA GET BACK TO MY WITCH DOCTORIN'

HEY..
H. OWL

H. OWL

HELLO? THAT'S FUNNY.. NOBODY AGAIN.

WHAT'S YOU GOIN' AROUND ALL DOODADDED UP THIS WAY FOR, HOWLAND?..DID YOU BUY YOUR MIND IN A RUMMAGE SALE?

I IS WITCH DOCTORIN' A DEMON OUT OF ALBERT.... HEY! STEP OUTSIDE THE OFFICE!

YOU DON'T MIND IF I JUS' LOOK AROUND?

EE-NUFF!
UH-OOP?

GOSH.. I'M SORRY SIR.. IT'S PROB'LY IN THERE SOMEPLACE.
SOME-TIMES THE TURTLIN' TRADE IS A MODEST BLESSIN'.

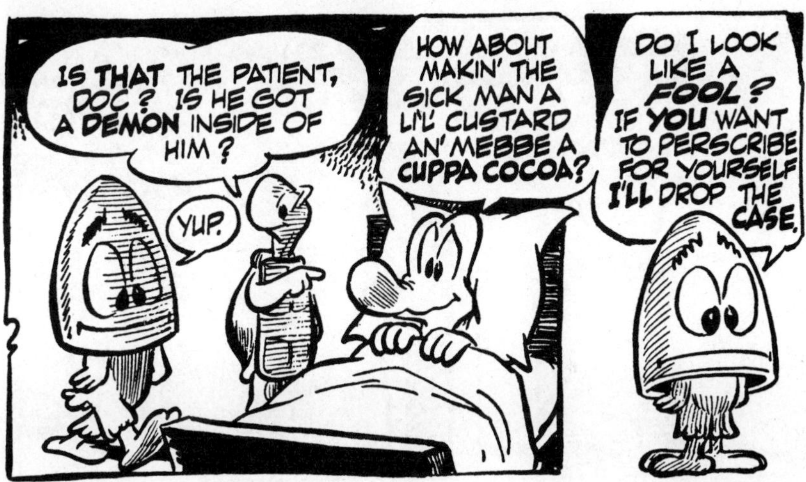
IS THAT THE PATIENT, DOC? IS HE GOT A DEMON INSIDE OF HIM?
YUP.
HOW ABOUT MAKIN' THE SICK MAN A LI'L' CUSTARD AN' MEBBE A CUPPA COCOA?
DO I LOOK LIKE A FOOL? IF YOU WANT TO PERSCRIBE FOR YOURSELF I'LL DROP THE CASE.

HOW'D YOU LIKE TO ASSIST IN THE OPERATION, CHURCHY...? YOU IS HAD MORE OR LESS A LOT OF SPERIENCE WITH DEMONS AN' SUCH?
SOME OF MY BEST FRIENDS.
GIT INTO YOUR NURSE DUDS THEN.. NOW SIR, HOW'S YOUR DEMON FEEL THIS MORNING?
HUNGRY

I DON'T WANT NO INEXPERIENCED QUACKS MUSSIN' INTO MY ILLNESS.
I ASSURE YOU, SIR, I'M ONE OF THE MOST EXPERIENCED QUACKS IN THE GAME.
I'VE HEARD OF WITCH DOCTORS BUT I NEVER HEARD OF WITCH NURSES.. WHERE'D HE GIT HIS TRAININ'?

FROM MY MOMMA WHAT WAS A SKULLERY MAID. SHE WORKED IN A SKULLERY AND BONED UP ON ALL SORTS OF SKULL SKILL.

GOOD TO HAVE YOU WITH US, NURSE LA FEMME.
I GOES INTO A TRANCE AN' LOCATES LOST LOCKETS AN' STUFF..

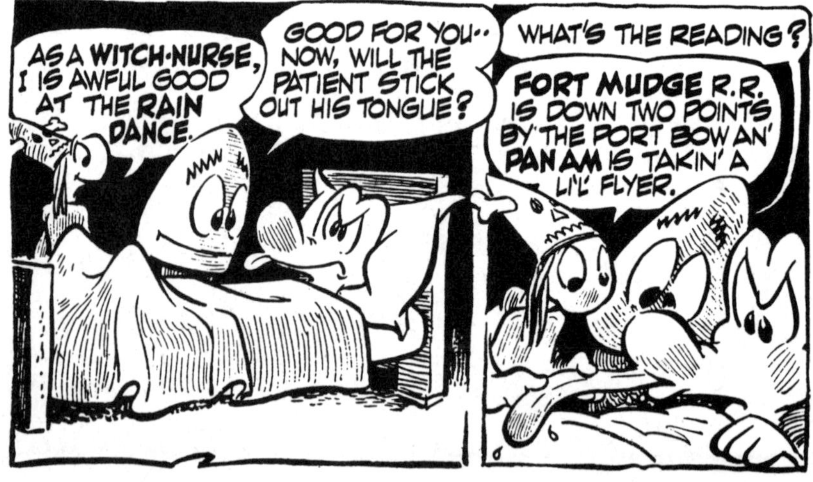
AS A WITCH-NURSE, I IS AWFUL GOOD AT THE RAIN DANCE.
GOOD FOR YOU.. NOW, WILL THE PATIENT STICK OUT HIS TONGUE?
WHAT'S THE READING?
FORT MUDGE R.R. IS DOWN TWO POINTS BY THE PORT BOW AN' PAN AM IS TAKIN' A LI'L FLYER.

KNOW WHAT THIS CASE LOOKS LIKE TO ME, DOC? I THINK THE PATIENT IS SWALLOWED A INNER-TUBE.
OH, LET GO OF THAT.
YOU'RE THE DOCTOR.
NOT HIS TONGUE! I DIN'T MEAN LET GO OF... I MEANT LET GO OF YO' THEORY.
SNAP
ZIP

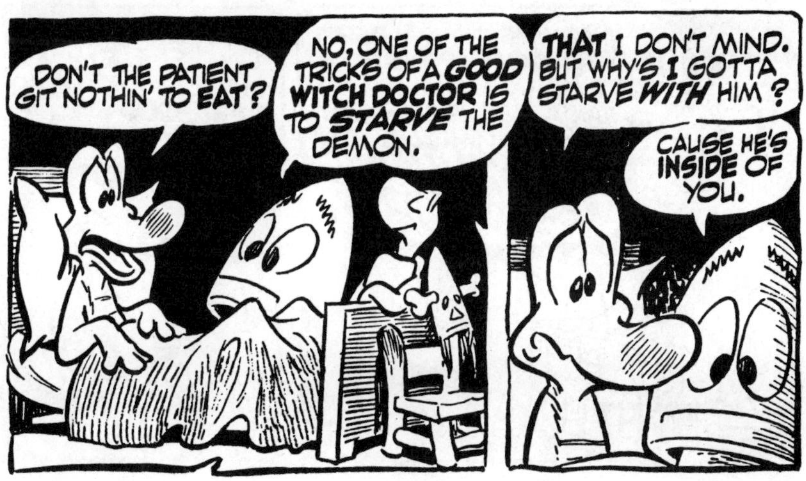
DON'T THE PATIENT GIT NOTHIN' TO EAT?
NO, ONE OF THE TRICKS OF A GOOD WITCH DOCTOR IS TO STARVE THE DEMON.
THAT I DON'T MIND. BUT WHY'S I GOTTA STARVE WITH HIM?
CAUSE HE'S INSIDE OF YOU.

IT'S LIKE LAYIN' SIEGE TO HIM... WE GOT HIM TRAPPED--LOOK AT IT THAT WAY.... IF HE WANTS TO EAT HE KIN COME OUT! RIGHT, NURSE?
RIGHT, DOC.
HEAR THAT, YOU DEMON?. NOTHIN' FIT TO EAT IS GONNA GET DOWN THERE UNLESS YOU COMES OUT.. EVEN IF WE HASTA OUTWAIT YOU ALL YEAR.

Chapter 37

OUTWITCHERY

A storm is brewed for a broody brood---

FROM THE MAGAZINE OF APARTNESS..LISTEN DEMON: TAKE TWO EGGS AN' A CUP OF LEMON JUICE, THEN TWO CHICKENS OR BUFFALOES, BASTE LIGHTLY AN'..
OOG.. MY MOUTH AN' TEETHS IS A-WATERIN'.
GOOD! MEBBE YOU'LL DROWND THE DEMON.
LADY FINGER
AN' THAT AIN'T ALL, DEMON! US WILL CONTINUE READIN' RECIPES FOR THE INNER MAN AN' EATIN' STUFF.. MEANWHILE STARVIN' YOU OUTEN ALBERT.

AS A MEMBER OF THE WITCH DOCTOR TEAM I WILL DO MY RAIN DANCE WHICH WILL DRIVE YOUR FIENDISH SELF OUT OF OUR PAL.

WUFF WUFF WUFF

STOP

I'LL BE RIGHT BACK WITH NEW EQUIPMENT.
MY COLLEAGUE WILL HAVE EVERYTHING UNDER CONTROL IN A JIFFY.

I'LL NOW DO THE RAINBOW DANCE.

BOOM
AND THAT OUGHT TO SORTA UNWIND THE SPELL.
NOW YOU IS DID IT -- YOU IS CAUSED A FLOOD.

A FINE HOWDYDO! YOUR RAIN DANCE IS CAUSED A FLOOD --- NOW WE'LL NEVER GET THE DEMON OUTEN ALBERT.
YEAH --- YOU DON'T SPECT HIM TO COME OUT IN ALL THIS WET, DO YOU ?

THERE'S ONLY ONE THING TO DO -- WE GOTTA SEND A ARMED POSSE IN AFTER THE CRITTUR.
A GOOD IDEA. THEN THEY KIN TRACK THE FIEND DOWN -- AND WHEN THEY GETS HIM IN THEIR SIGHT, BLAM!
BLAM, MY EYE! SUPPOSE THEY MISSES? ANYTHING ELSE THEY SHOOTS DOWN THERE WILL BE MINE -- I SURROUNDS THE RASCAL.

Chapter 38

INNER SPACE IS LEFT WITHOUT

Herein a few leaves are taken from the book of leavetakers~~~

--TOOK A LOOK AROUND AND HOLLERED: "MAN, THIS IS REALLY LIVIN'.." AT THAT, ALL EXCEPT ONE OF THE GROUP LEFT SUDDENLY.. AND..OOF!
COULDN'T YOU LEARN TO STOP DRAGGIN' YOUR FEET?

AH, THE DEEDS WE'VE DONE TOGETHER! THE FEATS OF DERRING-DO... ALWAYS TOGETHER! PALS TO THE END..
AH, YES.
JUST THE TWO MEN WHAT I AND MY ASSOCIATES IS LOOKIN' FOR.. YOU TWO CAN ROUSE OUT THE DEMON WHAT'S INSIDE ALBERT.
WHAT!?

WELL, SO LONG, SNAVELY.
I THOUGHT YOU TWO WAS ALWAYS TOGETHER, ...PALS TO THE END?
WE'RE WORKIN' A SHORT WEEK.. THE END COMES EARLY DURIN' THE SUMMER.

LISTEN! THERE'S MILLIONS IN THIS PROPOSITION... YOU MERELY GO DOWN INSIDE ALBERT'S DEPTHS AND SCARE OUT THE DEMON.
MILLIONS...? HOW COME?
THERE'S MILLIONS IN PUBLICITY VALUE ALONE ...YOU'LL BE THE ONLY DEMON EXTERMIN-ATORS IN THE GAME.
WHAT ELSE?

WELL.. YOU'LL GET TO MEET IMPORTANT PEOPLE ..UNUSUAL PEOPLE..
LIKE WHO?

SHUCKS, THE FIRST CRACK OUT OF THE BOX YOU'LL GET TO MEET THE DEMON HIS OWN SELF.

NOBODY KNOWS THE WORRY AND THE TORTURE, THE DEEP ROOTED ANXIETY AND NAMELESS FEAR OF HAVIN' A DEMON INSIDE OF HISSELF..
I DOES.
SSR

WODDYA MEAN, YOU DOES!? ONLY ME, WHAT GOT A GENUINE EVIL SPIRIT INSIDE, KNOWS THE NAMELESS FEAR..YOU DON'T KNOW NO NAMELESS FEAR!
I DO TOO!

THEY FOUND THE DEMON IN ME, DIN'T THEY? HOW COME YOU IS UMBRAGIN' IN ON THE ACT?.. I IS THE AFFLICTED ONE.. NOT YOU!

IT'S A FREE COUNTRY.

IT SO HAPPEN YOUR DEMON IS CONTAGIOUS.. I IS CAUGHT IT FROM YOU.. I KNOWS THE NAMELESS FEAR!

WHAT'S ITS NAME, THEN? YOU'RE SO SMART.

TROUBLE WITH PEOPLE LIKE YOU IS THEY'RE TOO PUSHY.. I'M THE ONLY ONE GOT REALLY A DEMON INSIDE SO I'M THE ONLY ONE KNOWS THE NAMELESS FEAR.

YOU WAS NEVER WRONGER.

HO HA! IT IS TO LAUGH! YOU SAYS YOU KNOWS THE NAMELESS FEAR AND YOU CAN'T EVEN TELL ITS NAME.

HOW CAN I?

WHO THUNK OF HAVIN' A DEMON INSIDE HISSELF FIRST?.. YOU IS A COPY CAT.
YOU IS A STINGY PIG HOG.

I AM NOT STINGY.. NEVER STUNG NOBODY IN MY LIFE..
THAT AIN'T WHAT I SAID!

IN ANY CASE, I IS LEAVIN' YOU.
YOU AIN'T LEAVIN' ME I'M LEAVIN' YOU.
OH NO YOU'RE NOT! I'M WALKIN' AWAY FROM YOU.
OH, NO YOU'RE NOT! I'M KISSIN' YOU GOODBYE!

I'LL SHOW YOU WHO'S KISSIN' WHO GOODBYE..
I'M TAKIN' LEAVE OF YOU.. WALKIN' OUT OF YOUR LIFE.
IT'S FAREWELL TO YOU, SHORTY... NO MORE "HI-YA CHOLLIE" FOR YOU, PAL.
PFAW
PARADE PARADE
HEY HEY

AND ANOTHER THING - AWK!
K'LOK
WOW

YOU LOST YOUR ELEFRONT, MISTER.
QUITTER.
TIN HORN! SUMMER SOLDIER!

WELL, WELL! HERE I IS, IS, IS! BRINGIN' A TEAM OF SPELUNKERS TO GO IN AFTER YO' DEMON AN' ROUSE HIM OUT.

NOTHIN' DOIN'! I IS SWALLOWED ENOUGH FOOFARAW .. BESIDES OL' CHURCHY CLAIM HE'S CAUGHT THE DEMON FROM ME.

AN' BESIDES, EVEN IF HE AIN'T I'D RUTHER HAVE A HOME GROWN DEMON INSIDE THAN MORE TRAFFIC IN LI'L' EXPERTS CRAWLIN' AROUND DOWN THERE WITH THEIR LI'L' COLD FEET.

MY STOMACH AIN'T NO PUBLIC INSTITUTION -- IT'S CLOSED TO ALL; PRIVATE PROPERTY. -- UNLESS, OF COURSE, ANY OF YOU GOT OFFICIAL BUSINESS DOWN THERE ?
NO NO NO--- NOTHING LIKE THAT.

Chapter 39

THE GRAND OLD PARTY LINE